METAPHYSICS
AND
THE NEW AGE

By

Dr. Peter Daley

ISBN: 1-4196-9868-0
ISBN-13: 9781419698682

Visit www.booksurge.com to order additional copies.

TABLE OF CONTENTS

PART TWO

PART THREE

PART FOUR

ABOUT THE AUTHOR

I was born and bred in Yorkshire in a working class family, but was fortunate in acquiring scholarships to finance my medical degree.

Following the completion of my army service in Egypt, there were eight years served in the British National Health Service, after which I emigrated to NZ. for a time before settling in Australia where I have lived for the last 40 years.

I retired from medical practice in 1989, and am now into my ninth decade, still in robust health which I attribute to my adherence to metaphysics and its spiritual practices.

This book is dedicated to my late wife, because of her gracious tolerance towards my interest in the weird and wonderful throughout our married life of fifty wonderful years.

I wish to acknowledge the help from my son Bernard without whose work establishing the book on the computer this book would never have reached the publisher.

I thank Ruth Richards for encouragement and help in compiling the manuscript, and Owen Waters for help in editing.

Dr Peter Daley

These are photographs of the principal sources of
the wisdom in this book.

George King (1919-1997)

Gurdjieff (1866-1949)

Helena P. Blavatsky (1831-1891)

Alice Bailey (1880-1949)

FOREWORD

The study of philosophy inevitably leads to metaphysics.

The intention in writing this book was to let the world know of the dangers the Earth has experienced. We would all be dead now, if it were not for outside help. This came from elevated beings millions of years in advance of our current state of evolution. They gained nothing from this, and suffered hell for us.

How the dangers faced in the latter half of the last century were overcome form the opening pages together with some pertinent details of my involvement.

I have borrowed freely from Theosophy, and describe metaphysical operations involving The Great White Brotherhood and Cosmic Masters.

The eternal questions, "What are we? Where are we from? Where are we going?" are answered. You may or may not like the answers, which religion has tried hard to suppress.

Man is fundamentally based on an energy structure, as a microcosm of The Macrocosm. We are all spiritual beings, here for experience which will lead us to becoming gods, though it may take a million years. I have expressed what is, to me, a reasonable account of things, and shows my personal bias as an exponent of The Aetherius Society. A degree of scepticism is to be expected, in view of the strangeness which is Truth as there are revelations about UFO's and life on other planets.

Enjoy the New Age trivia, which is included to lighten the heavy nature of some of the text, and some of the websites included. We are living in strange times. Great changes proceed in the hidden worlds and these directly affect this world. Everyone should be told.

The contention that we have been observed for thousands of years by cultures far in advanced in evolution, may cause some dismay. We were never alone.

INTRODUCTION

This book contains the most extraordinary information ever to be released to the public in one book.

The opening pages were originally left towards the end, so that after a suitable priming in metaphysical concepts, the reader was to be prepared for that which is most challenging. as you read, you will see why I thought this was advisable. In fact, dear reader, I am "dropping you in the deep end," so to speak, testing your tolerance and credulity to the limits. However, anyone led to picking this book will have the necessary imagination.

You will see how I changed my mind and have put the revelations of the New Age first. If you persist in reading I guarantee that you will be astonished at the happenings of the last half century. Because these events were on the hidden planes, most people didn't know what was happening.

The startling events in this book are there due to my privilege of being familiar with such material, and my encounter with that most extraordinary man who was most powerful occultist of the century. He was George King, and there will much to say as to his exploits and adventures on the inner planes, and more significantly, the way he was successful in creating an organisation specifically to co-operate with the Cosmic Masters in the metaphysical operations establishing the New Age, now well underway.

There is an anticipation of a dramatic change around 2012, in accord with the Mayan calendar and various prophecies. The reason why the dire significance of this is now held in doubt, is due to events having been brought forward 50 years. This is to be dealt with at some length in this work.

A mass of information speculates about the nature and origin of UFO's. These are truly space vessels, capable of appearing and disappearing as they switch between the different frequencies appertaining to the local levels of existence. Occasionally one of these has crashed, or was shot down. Intensive work is being done, in what is called "back engineering," which is the term for attempts to discover the source of the motive power they used.

Serious attempts are being made to find evidence of intelligent life in the galaxy in the pretence of hiding the contacts already made. All Major Governments have been in contact with the Space People since 1943. (Ref: www.ProjectCamelot.org).

I owe the new occult material to The Aetherius Society. The basic metaphysical material I owe to the writers Helena Blavatsky and Alice Bailey of The Theosophical Society. There are also some references to the work of Gurdjieff (1870-1949).

Read and you will be astonished, and you will see the old adage "Truth Is Stranger Than Fiction," repeatedly confirmed.

There is an great amount of deep philosophical thought interspersed throughout these pages, which I hope will be worthy of appreciation, or controversy.

PART ONE

Truth Is Stranger Than Fiction

The remote future beckons, we shall inevitably become transformations of a mystical kind, to become gods after many and varied experiences on this and other planets.

In this the opening chapters I am going straight into the most occult and startling of all the New Age Revelations. Many things were known in the ancient Mystery Schools, handed down over thousands of years, and survived in spite of the rigorous suppression by the Inquisition. But even the highest initiations of Ceremonial Magic did not touch on the recent revelations, which describe interplanetary action in the most important events in the long life of this planet. There are some things which happened when most of those reading this had yet to be born, but all within my lifetime.

On Earth there have been severe social upheavals as a reflection of disturbances on subtle levels below the threshold of human experience; relevant to what, in simple terms, has been a longstanding condition of spiritual crisis. Since the beginning of this the 21st Century, it is also becoming more obvious in climatic changes.

Following the world war of 1939–1945, the effects of the use of atom bombs began to filter through from the subtle realms.

On the physical level there was consternation in other parts of the galaxy, on perceiving the development of atomic power again by a race whose history was known to show every indication of using it for space travel and conquest.

In accordance with military expedience, therefore, plans were made to stifle this possibility. The threats eventually materialised and had to be dealt with by extraterrestrials, as we were completely helpless in the face of superior technology. In addition to this, there arose a more sinister situation involving the lower astral realms in which a new power was developing, and had the potential to invade this, the physical level and some of those even higher.

Many would not give it another thought as being too fantastic. Nevertheless, it is quite feasible if the principle of resonance which connects the different realms is understood, and is described as part of New Age Cosmology in its Metaphysical interpretation.

George King

In the first place, I should refer to George King, the man whose appearance on Earth was specially arranged for him to be available at this time, to establish and maintain contact with Cosmic Masters for urgent metaphysical operations, and to exercise those qualities, which made him unique for his ability to defuse global situations.

Born on January 23rd, 1919 (Wellington, Shropshire, England) with inherited psychic faculties, he became interested in Yoga, and ultimately achieved status as a Master of every form of Yoga. He was accustomed to devote 8 to 10 hours a day to this practice, besides putting in a full day's work.

There were some who sneered at his acceptance of lowly paid positions, such as taxi driver and hotel doorman. The press never missed an opportunity to mention this. At that time he had put aside personal wealth, which he viewed as a spiritual encumbrance. He had held an important position with an oil Company in the Middle East, and was once the Chief of Security for a large London office building. Being very keen on car and motorcycle racing, he was accustomed to funding a motorcycle and rider in the races in Europe. During the war, he refused to engage in military service and was employed in the London Fire Service during the Blitz, and became a section leader instrumental in saving many lives.

We are told that karmic manipulation was required to ensure the presence of his particular lifestream at this time. How can Karma be manipulated? By sacrifice of course! This means we are indebted to those who, being sufficiently high in the scale of spiritual evolution can endure sacrifice in order to loosen the karmic bonds of others.

A situation arose because of the atomic explosions, culminating in the use of atomic bombs to destroy human life. This caused a leap of 50 years in prophesied events which were not expected to manifest until 2012, the date from the Mayan calendar after which nothing could be foreseen. It all happened during the latter half of the 20th century, in association with the earlier anticipated release of the Earth Logos from the self-imposed limitation required for our continued existence.

The atomic explosions and their use in war had affected the karmic balance. Hostile elements were alerted, certain of which proved to be a threat to human life. This is where George King became an essential part in the defence of the Earth, and for his part in the introduction of the New Age conditions. He was chosen to be "The Primary Mental Terrestrial Channel" for communication with Cosmic Masters telepathically at all times, and to be a direct channel while in a positive Samadhic trance. This allowed his physical body to be taken over, and his voice used to deliver messages of encouragement, inspiration and new information of an occult nature.

Over 600 of such transmissions were received, some of which he performed on television and are preserved on durable tapes in a secure place for posterity. Let it be understood that this method of communicating with extraterrestrial intelligences is not the only one, and that there are other sources is not denied. However, George King was not called The Primary Mental Channel arbitrarily, but because he was the only direct channel for the purpose of Metaphysical Operations, in co-operation with Cosmic masters. He was born, and trained to be the only one used by The Cosmic Masters as a reliable agent, with the ability to manipulate power in metaphysics and to organise a body of people to support him and carry on his work after he departed.

In 1962, George King was advised by the Cosmic Masters to establish The Aetherius Society in the US, where he lived, apart from a number of important missions around the world, until he passed away on July 12th, 1997. There are more details of his life, tributes and accolades at the end of this book, which I have downloaded from the website of the Aetherius Society (www.Aetherius.org).

Mars and Venus Speak to Earth

How I came to be involved and acquainted with George King merits this anecdotal account of how I attended the public meeting in Caxton Hall April 1958, to hear him speak. The title of the address was "Mars and Venus Speak To Earth."

The decision to do this followed his receiving notification in a most dramatic fashion that he was chosen to be Earth's representative to the other planets. This was in May 1954, and is described in his book, "You Are Responsible."

He spoke of the dangers of radiation inherent in the use of atomic power and in the possible event of atomic warfare, and then described how the concern felt on other planets ensured the Earth's involvement in interplanetary affairs.

At the close of the meeting we were invited to attend a succession of transmissions from the planets, with the warning that the experience would change us forever. Nevertheless, I was one of 50 who volunteered to attend the 12 weekly transmissions of "The Twelve Blessings." The first was on Sunday July 27th, 1958, attendance of which was mandatory for admission to the rest. It was a mixed group of which more than half were women.

I had telephoned George King for information about the venue and hotels in the vicinity. He offered me accommodation for the night, and, because of a tight schedule and travelling 200 miles, I was glad to accept.

I cannot remember the full details of our discussion which lasted until midnight. We talked of many things relating to life and the fundamentals of existence. But I remember vividly the account of some of his out-of-body experiences. I was curious about the significance of the logo adopted by The Aetherius Society. In answer to this question he said, "When I was orbiting Sirius in the etheric body, I realised that because the first three symbols from the ancient language referred to The Supreme Being (an ancient Hindu symbol), by adding the triangle it was then symbolic of "God In Manifestation." Naturally I was a little astounded by this. He went on to tell me that "Love never dies and follows you forever, from life to life."

Later in the evening he related a strange experience he had in exploring the lower astral. In this very dark realm he encountered a dark Avatar. It presented itself to his mind as a giant bat. This was a very powerful being from a previous Sun* which was concerned solely with the evolution of matter, and had been residing in this part of the Earthly realms. On perceiving the presence of an intruder it immediately trapped his mind in a web of thought of material desires and strange vices. In desperation, he threw the image of its counterpart in the form of Jesus sacrificing himself on the cross. The creature disappeared in a flame of transmutation accompanied by a terrible mental shriek. George King was able to return to his body feeling somewhat shattered by the experience.

Note.* This Sun (2nd) is devoted to the evolution of Mind. The 3rd will be concerned with the development of Will.

I have mentioned "The Twelve Blessings" and how we were invited to attend them at the end of the public address in Caxton Hall. In the following chapter I describe what I can remember of this occasion which changed the lives of all who participated. The Twelve Blessings were given by Jesus. That He came from Venus will astonish most readers. If you know your Bible, it is written that he said, "I am not of this world." The planet Venus is the most advanced in the solar system next to Saturn. In one of the transmissions through George King, Jesus stated, "I came from Venus." Other Cosmic Masters referred to him as "The Master from Venus."

The Twelve Blessings

I am the last survivor of those who attended The Twelve Blessings, and so it is fitting that I should make some attempt to record these events, which did indeed effect a marked change in my life.

The Twelve Blessings consisted of The Venusian Master, Jesus, taking over the body of George King, who was able to enter a Samadhic Trance by raising the full power of the Kundalini up through the crown of the head into the state of Cosmic Consciousness. He accomplished this amazingly, in only two minutes! This allowed The Master Jesus to give the Twelve Blessings, using the voice of George King, and delivered at weekly intervals on successive Sundays.

Each session began with an Oriental Master, Goo Ling, giving an introductory address and encouraging remarks through George King. (Goo Ling is 2,000 years old and is The Keeper of The Seal for The Great White Brotherhood. It was he who instigated the formation of The Aetherius Society).

The twelve weekly transmissions by Jesus and were named "The Twelve Blessings," and are listed below in sequence commencing July 27th, 1958.

The Twelve Blessings are:

(1) Blessed Are The Peace Makers

(2) Blessed Are The Wise Ones

(3) Blessed Are They Who Love

(4) Blessed Are The Planetary Ones

(5) Blessed Are The Thanksgivers

(6) Blessed Are They Who Heal

(7) Blessed Is The Mother Earth

(8) Blessed Is The Mighty Sun

(9) Blessed Are The Supreme Lords Of Karma

(10) Blessed Is The Galaxy

(11) Blessed Are The Supreme Lords Of Creation

(12) Blessed Is The Absolute

During these transmissions great power was put into the Earth, and a relatively small fraction through those present. There is no satisfactory way to describe the atmosphere in that room, or the feeling of transmuting energy.

Note the ascending order of the titles, from the lowest to the highest. Emphasis was made on the debt we owe to the Logos of The Earth, and that "The Logos of the Sun is an Aspect of Brahma and the nearest thing to God in your concept of manifestation," (from The 8th Blessing).

The Galaxy is an extremely ancient Great Lord of Creation, and The Supreme Lords of Creation spring from the First Cause produced by The Absolute.

Reading the text aloud or reciting from memory, in the manner prescribed in the book amounts to a powerful form of magic. This causes spiritual energy to be liberated through the operator into the world. In reading, you should note that the current theme of The Twelve Blessings is sacrifice, and by sacrificing some time in the regular use you will gain benefit.

A personal note on the recitation of The Twelve Blessings: There are only 63 pages in this book. The actual text of the Blessings is short, and each varies from a half to one and a half pages, and so the task of memorising them is quite easy. Alternatively, propping up the book to free the hands and reading aloud from it is sufficient. The regular performance of this along the lines advocated by George King constitutes a powerful magical exercise. I recommend this for spreading light into the world, as was the intent behind its introduction, but also for health and spiritual upliftment. Such is my daily exercise, supplemented by an hour of yoga during the night.

Reading the Twelve Blessings is an education in occult metaphysics, but sounding the words is magical. For all who are troubled by nocturnal interferences or insomnia, this is a way of protection and natural sleep.

At the end of the Twelfth Blessing, all were presented with a small wooden cross which was blessed by Jesus through George King, with instructions to allow no one other than the recipient to touch it. It is a spiritual battery which cannot lose its power, and was intended for use during these difficult times, and the more it is used the more powerful it becomes. Some psychics who have seen it remark on its radiating white light, but one insisted it is mauve. Another felt faint and had to leave the room. So far I have been denied this faculty of actually seeing its light, but I can feel the energy. Some photographs show a white line spiraling above it.

In the closing speech after The Twelfth Blessing, The Cosmic Master Jesus had things to say about the significance of The Cross, some of which I quote:

"This, my children, is not a symbol of death. It is the Symbol of Resurrection. It is not the symbol the terrible death depicted by your foolish priests! It is the lasting Symbol of the Spirit of Man, up to the Mighty Godhead – through Karmic Experience. That is what it is!—. These Symbols are Blessed as the Symbols of Resurrection. They will hold that Power as long as this World does last. For even if you destroy them now, the Power will not leave them."

The impression resulting from the Twelve Blessings was everlasting, and although there was a long lapse in my active interest in matters metaphysical, due the pressures of work and rearing a family and particularly my isolation from the centre of activities, the feeling of initiation persisted.

I was later told that all but one of those who came to The Twelve Blessings had walked the Earth at the same time as Jesus.

A Preamble

In the following pages, I intend to relate how the Aetherius Society became an instrument for ongoing Metaphysical Operations in co-operation with Interplanetary Intelligences, interspersed with tales of the occult and space sagas which will seem fantastic to the uninitiated, but are true nevertheless.

The continued existence of terrestrial humanity has depended on the success of these ventures during events and conditions unprecedented in the long life of the planet, all in the space of 40 years. What is to follow in these pages will astound, and may arouse ridicule and disbelief in some readers. Keep an open mind and let it titillate your imagination, because it is a strange story.

The 20th century saw severe social upheavals on an unprecedented scale. All this is a reflection of disturbance on subtle levels below the threshold of normal experience, relevant to what in simple terms has been a long-standing condition of a spiritual crisis, and an increasing tempo of terrestrial vibrations.

The Planet Earth In Crisis

There have been a number of attempts to take over this planet during the period 1954–1984 in which the whole population could have been exterminated. In one case, worse would have been the fate of any survivors in a form of mental slavery too horrible to contemplate. Two onslaughts came from outside the solar system, and two from the lower astral realms. To begin, I will relate how a planetoid was sent to destroy the Earth.

This earliest attack came in 1957, when a planetoid originating from a system in the direction of the constellation of Orion was aimed at the Earth, and concerns the personal achievements of George King. To begin with, it appeared to be a wandering planetoid approaching the solar system, and being of an unusually high radioactive content* was detected, harnessed for research, and investigated with robotic mining machinery by the Martians.

Attempts to recover the products were disastrous. A manned freighter was destroyed by a power beam from the planetoid, as was the fate of the scout ship sent to investigate. A deadly projectile was then aimed at Mars. The only way to stop it from landing was for a scout ship to ram it, the crew sacrificing their lives in an atomic blast many times that of our own devices. This caused a magnetic storm of vast proportions drifting through space in an erratic manner. It was then neutralised to protect communications.

It was later discovered that the planetoid was intended for the Earth, until it was captured by the Martians. This was the only serious assault attempt made on the Earth on the physical level, the others were stifled before they reached the material realm.

Prior to this, George King had landed on the intruder due to an error in navigation when he projected himself in the etheric body in an attempt to land on Mars. Because of this he narrowly escaped with his life. He was thereafter commissioned to deal with this new enemy when it regained control of its motion and directed itself in a collision course towards Mars. (The details of this conflict are in his book, "You Are Responsible")

This planetoid was an irregular mass, about the size of the UK. The intelligence incorporated in the planetoid had modified the robotic mining machinery installed by the Martians to produce weapons, and, when discovered, initiated control of hidden motors to travel towards the planet Mars. It was eventually neutralised by a Martian device which deposited a large flood of material which immediately solidified, but in order to do this there were more Martian casualties (147 in all). Two ships were deployed for this. One had to be a decoy for the other and was destroyed.

In case you wonder at this strange method, the radioactivity was so high as to make it so unstable that any other way would cause it to explode in a very large atomic explosion, destroying the Martian satellites and endangering the planet. How George King managed to deal with this entity is beyond our comprehension. He had to land on it, and by being able to access that power which is "Pure Impersonal Love," the mind in the planetoid was unable to resist without total annihilation, and was transmuted. The body of the planetoid was split into two by the conflict, and subsequently towed away to a place of safety by vessels from Jupiter.

By its original destination it was the intention of its masters was to assume control of the Earth after our elimination, and to genetically alter certain marine life into suitable slaves. I have been informed that its planet of origin is in the grip of four Beings from another galaxy who are millions of years old. They are unable to reproduce themselves, and in the true tradition of all evil entities aim to live forever. Their planet is a watery planet with an intelligent race of amphibious water-dwellers who are kept in a condition of complete mental slavery.

The Earth, with its surface three-quarters covered by oceans obviously suits their requirements, and also coincides with a strategic position in the galaxy. Apparently, watery planets like ours are not very common. An attempt to help the enslaved race on the planet (code name "Garouche") was made by a Martian Adept, at the cost of considerable personal suffering, and is related elsewhere (see ch. "Mars Sector Six").

*Note. The very high radiation level damaged the etheric body of George King irreparably. People who have had radiation treatment in high doses may require special attention in the afterworld.

UFO's and Radiation

These interplanetary vessels have an important role in the protection of the Earth from the more dangerous incursions from outside, and to press the point a bit further, from below as well.

Without the help from these vessels the radiation from the atomic bombs and the leakage from nuclear facilities would have been much more deadly. UFO's were seen over the site of Chernobyl and were instrumental in preventing an atomic explosion.

This was not the first of such a disaster, there was another in 1957 which was cleverly kept from the rest of the world by Soviet authority. The Aetherius Society, however, had known about it.

The Enemies in The Lower Astral

The greatest menaces to our existence came from the hidden worlds of frequencies below the level of this, the material.

The first was an Android, which was an artificial intelligence endowed with mental powers vying with those of our most advanced Adepts. This creature was capable of destroying all human life. It had been asleep in the lower astral realm over a million years. The second case was also from the lower astral and held the prospect of literally Hell on Earth. It concerned the powers of the Lower Astral attempting to concentrate all factions into one force, under the control of one leader.

I have left this for later in the book. I do not wish to alarm readers before there has been more familiarity with the metaphysical measures undertaken for our protection.

The next chapter is about a regrettable incident in the remote history of this humanity, which has bearing on all which followed.

This humanity is very ancient, way beyond the brief periods in anthropology. Before the civilisations of Lemuria and Atlantis there was Maldek.

Maldek

Terrestrial man derives from a humanoid race which destroyed its home, the planet Maldek, by investing in atomic power for access to total conversion of the atom into available energy for use in war. Only a thousandth of 1% of the total power in the atom is normally available from the atom, and had been used safely for many years. In spite of the advice from the more advanced planets, the research continued. Their success caused a chain reaction destroying all life, and reduced the planetary body to rubble of various sizes, now wandering the orbit of the asteroid belt.

It was all so unnecessary, as they had an adequate source of energy in the way we are trying get from atomic power, but they had more success in terms of safety and efficiency. The population in general enjoyed an easy life of leisure, and were little concerned with political matters and the possibility of war. All physical work was carried out by robots and machines, to the extent that there was nothing to do other than enjoy life. But there were two contending factions busy seeking new weapons with the help of atomic scientists.

The destruction of this planet has resulted in a huge karmic debt and is being felt to this day. The Logos of the Earth kindly consented to accommodate the population of Maldek, to be reborn on her surface. The other planets were totally incompatible because of their higher rates of vibration. There was already an advanced civilisation on Earth preparing for a next phase in their evolution, which entailed leaving for parts unknown. That culture has been referred to as Pre-Adamic Man. It was decided to postpone their plans and remain to foster the new arrivals until they had established a stable community. Once there was a civilisation established to their satisfaction, they left and were never heard of again. Whether it was to raise their consciousness to a higher dimension or to leave the solar system has not been revealed.

The date given for this is 18+ million years ago. The number of preceding civilisations, from an unspecified higher source, is said to have been 15, and were not all humanoid.

The Story of Gaia, The Earth Goddess

If you are concerned about the integrity of the environment, keep in mind the Entity which is Mother Earth and her sacrifice. The Logos of the Earth has had to restrict her own evolution in order dampen down the vibratory level in Her substance, to be compatible with human life. Taking on a lower level of existence for the sake of another is called "Sacrificing Salvation."

This type of sacrifice is greater than the sacrifice of one's Life!

This self-imposed limitation of Mother Earth reached its conclusion by an edict from The Lords of Karma, with effect from July 8th, 1964, after the duration of more than 18 million years.

The Sacrificing of Salvation occurs so frequently in the spiritual parts of the text, and is so prominent in The Twelve Blessings, that some explanation is indicated. This expression, Salvation, is taken from Christian theology, as meaning saving from damnation. It means much more than that in metaphysical terms. Salvation can also refer to the condition of spiritual achievement and release from the cycle of rebirth.

For a Cosmic Master, the Sacrifice of Salvation entails the abandonment of an elevated state of consciousness and bliss established over millions of years. The experience of descent from a high spiritual plane into the limitation of the primitive coarseness and savagery of terrestrial embodiment cannot be imagined. The mind is continually bombarded by a storm of mental activity of the worst kind. All connection with the previous existence is extinguished, producing an isolation of a kind which is impossible for us to appreciate. This is only part of the Sacrifice of Salvation. In addition there is often the suffering of Karma, taken on out of Love for the spiritually impoverished and recidivist elements. It seems to be built into cosmic evolution and is an aspect in all The Twelve Blessings.

This Sacrifice of Salvation is limited by the Law of Karma, which will not allow it to persist beyond a certain time. In this way Jesus was not permitted to continue suffering on the cross. Mars Sector Six was not allowed to linger suffering in the sophisticated electronic prison on Garouche, beyond a specified time. In the same way the Logos of this Earth has had to be liberated from her sacrifice of salvation, hitherto made necessary for this humanity to continue its successive failures. It is impossible for us to imagine the magnitude of this sacrifice by the planetary Logos lasting millions of years. [1]

The enforced lifting of the limitation experienced by the Earth Logos constituted the Primary Initiation of the Earth, which is now producing changes in the planet and all life upon it. We are now facing the drastic changes in our environment as a result of the energy now being released, as foreseen by the seers and prophets of long ago.

One of the main purposes of The Aetherius Society is to ameliorate these events, thereby canceling or moderating the prophecies through metaphysical operations in co-operation with Adepts from the other planets. Many thousands of lives have been saved by Operation Sunbeam.

At the risk of repeating this elsewhere it can be said here, that events anticipated around 2012 have been brought forward 50 years by metaphysical means. The catalyst was The Primary Initiation of The Earth promoted earlier by Karmic decree.

The Logos of The Earth is the subject of the 7th Blessing.

The Earth Crisis

Therewith hangs a concatenation of events, from both Above and Below, necessitating Metaphysical Operations on a vast scale, the description of which makes this book unique.

First, more of our ancient history:

The failure of the ancient civilisations of Lemuria and Atlantis to survive, and progress at a normal rate to achieve something approaching parity with other planets exacerbated things greatly. Many thousands of years of degeneracy and barbarism elapsed in between the collapse of those ancient civilisations.

There is no doubt that some sort of atomic weapons were used in the wars of these ancient civilisations. There are records of flying machines, and descriptions closely indicative of radiation casualties. References to these are to be found in the ancient traditions and records of India. There are vitrified areas around the world, which could not have been made naturally, some of which have been found in Scotland.

Two weapons are described in the Hindu myths. One was the Brahma Weapon which was an atomic bomb, another was Indra's Dart which was a form of death ray. It is considered that this account relates to the Atlantean period, following which the Atlantic archipelago sank beneath the sea. One island remained until 10,000 BC and is mentioned in the writings of the Greek historian Herodotus, who received this from Egyptian priests who claimed to hold written records of 100,000 years.

There is a tradition in the Shamans of Hawaii of an influx of souls during the Lemurian epoch from a destroyed planet, and who brought with them elements which promoted disorder and conflict. The islands of Hawaii are the tips of submerged mountains of Lemuria.

The cyclic pattern of the rise and fall of civilisations tends to repeat itself, which is an interesting maxim found in the recent research into the Principle of Chaos. History is often spoken of as repeating itself.

The Global Holocaust which nearly happened

There was a world crisis in 1962, threatening to destroy everything in another atomic war in a repetition of Lemuria and Atlantis. The start of this crisis coincided with a planetary configuration on February 4th and 5th 1962 when all planets were in alignment, and is considered to have been astrologically significant.

This time, however, we are told that it was not allowed to happen. In those days, the two great world powers the US and Russia were poised ready to unleash a swarm of nuclear missiles onto each other as the Cuban crisis developed. This explains why the relations between the US and Cuba remain strained for many decades afterward.

Underground Refuges

Generals on both sides discussed the prospects of many millions of civilian deaths. Underground cities had been constructed, which were to be proof against nuclear bombs. Food, water and air were stored in readiness to await the time when the radiation level might be reduced enough for them to emerge.

These underground cities were to be occupied by an elite of military and government officials, scientists and others on "the list." Some of these establishments now house secret research into more effective weapons, and the back-engineering of downed UFO's. Strangely enough, there is reason to consider reports that new ones are still being built as refuges in steadily increasing numbers; some of these are in northern Europe.

Alien Involvement

Incidentally, there have been visits by extraterrestrials since 1943. The Germans had alien contacts using mediums from Tibet in 1937, and may have developed UFO type planes which they were not allowed to use in war. These are said to have been sent to secret places in Argentina and Antarctica.

There is increasing evidence that groups of Germans scientists were very advanced in technology, but were not coordinated due to their secret isolation, even from Hitler. This included the "Bell" which was an antigravity prototype, hurriedly transported to South America towards the end of the war.

Offers of technological assistance were made by certain aliens on condition that all nuclear missiles be deactivated and dismantled. President Eisenhower and Mr. Truman rejected this on the grounds of national security. This also occurred in Russia during the Cold War period, and has been repeated since then. Eventually, assistance was obtained from other aliens, but at a price.

Eisenhower and Truman were the only US presidents permitted access to their secret underground research centres. Australians can check theirs on the website about Pine Gap.

Reports of such encounters are to be found on the Internet, but like so many events have been withheld from the public. Individuals privy to such classified information were silenced under the threat of severe penalties, and some of these died under mysterious circumstances.

There is a wealth of information on the relations between aliens and the US government in their underground military bases. Recently released documents of the CIA, show how there was more concern about the possibility of an invasion from outside the Earth than from the USSR.

For more information, search for 'nazi ufo connection' on the Internet.

Metaphysical Operations

Just where should I begin trying to describe the events, and the complex web of metaphysical force put around the earth? I suppose the best way is to deal first with the most important, the one that has had the most far-reaching effect on the planet and our lives.

I refer to the event unprecedented in the long life of the Logos of The Earth, under the name of "The Primary Initiation of The Earth," which came about because of the time limit set on the self-imposed limitation of the Earth Logos by Karmic decree. It coincided with a nexus of events provoked and triggered by the abuse of the planet in atomic explosions, and ultimately the use of atomic bombs in war.

This scenario was not scheduled to manifest for another fifty years, about the time of 2012. The significance of the dire prophecies became completely changed. It is a strange fact that, paradoxically, prophesies tend to be reliable only at the time of seeing. The random effect of our freewill cannot always be foreseen in an accurate time frame, and neither can the effect of any support from outside the Earth.

An interesting prophesy is that of Mitar Tarabich (1829–1899), whose predictions were surprisingly accurate up to the present time. These relate specifically to the political and military events in Europe with emphasis on Serbia. But he also said "The whole world will be plagued by a strange disease for which no cure could be found." AIDS?

He predicted a Third World War of 2050–2100, in which missiles containing mind altering material subdue all aggression, and the only country to escape this is apparently Australia ("A country as big as Europe and surrounded by sea which manages to live in peace."). Time will tell!

The Primary Initiation of The Earth

This occurred on the 8th July, 1964, the most significant date of the century, and indeed in the long life of the planet.

The object was to provide the Earth with energy of a very high frequency, to make up for the self-imposed limitation taken by the Logos of the Earth over thousands of years. (The figure we are given in "The Treatise on Cosmic Fire" is 18,618,840 years). An end to this sacrifice was decreed by Karmic Law, precipitated by human actions and brought forward 50 years. The numerous atomic tests and finally the use of atomic bombs to destroy human life were responsible.

The magnitude of the power and the complexity of this operation required the combined efforts of seven vessels of the type of Satellite Number Three placed equidistant from the Earth, and the rare appearance of a Lord of The Sun through whom the power of the Sun was to be transmitted. The precision and calculations were to be of the utmost accuracy lest the power did not conform exactly to expectations, or all Life would be extinguished in an instant with a conflagration which could disintegrate the planet and also the moon.

Certain preparations were needed to prepare the way for this operation to be completely successful, unimpeded by the magnetic conditions produced by radiation contamination. (This required Operation Bluewater, and will be described separately).

This jolt of power lasted 54 minutes (10:00 pm to 10:54 pm Pacific Daylight Saving Time), and was calculated to cause a disturbance in the Earth's orbit and a declination of the polar axis. To prevent this from happening a host of smaller ships were positioned to englobe the planet in a certain pattern, and was accomplished with only a very minor discrepancy that involved a short hesitation of the Earth's motion in its orbit. A dramatic description of this cosmic event is held in the limited edition of the book "The Day The Gods Came" by George King, published by The Aetherius Society.

This metaphysical operation was directed by the Cosmic Master, Mars Sector Six, and increased for a time the Spiritual Index (which is a measure of the absorption of spiritual energy by the world population), and yet although the energy is being released gradually by the planetary Logos in order for us to adapt more readily, the number of people taking advantage of it is not great.

In addition to this, the ionosphere, which was put in place in Lemurian times to form a barrier to certain cosmic influences and was intensified further after the Atlantean disaster, will now be gradually taken down. The result will benefit the planet, but will expose us to the effects of cosmic and solar radiation more profoundly.

Regardless of the current disorder and strife throughout the world, the foundation for world peace and enlightenment has now been established and the way made clear for the next Christ-like Master to come to Earth, when conditions are right. When that will be is not known, even in The Great White Brotherhood (the "White," by the way, in this context refers to the opposite of black in the magical sense, and is mentioned only to eliminate any aspersions possibly arising in regard to racial colour.) The Great White Brotherhood consists of men and women from all the different racial groups. In fact, Caucasians are in the minority!

There was also an Initiation of The Solar System.

News of this did not each us until December 28th, 1969 in a transmission from Aetherius. The details were withheld, but we are since informed that all the planets and their inhabitants received a great input of energy, which permitted an even greater range of freedom and movement between the spheres or realms. Previously, it required much more effort and the expenditure of energy. This privilege was denied life on Earth, at least for the time being because of our karmic debt. But the ban on physical man's access to the other planets was lifted. In addition, the gates have been opened to facilitate easier communication with the unseen worlds.

There is a downside to The Primary Initiation of The Earth, as in all things in accordance with the maxim "As Above, So Below." This produced a dramatic reaction in the Lower Astral regions, allowing a surge of power eagerly exercised and resulted in two particular incidents, one of which was unforeseen and was countered by a metaphysical operation called The Alien Mission.

The Alien Mission

This started on 30th May, 1965 and involved the discovery of an Android creature which had been dormant in the Lower Astral for a million years. It was during a foray by a group of Adepts into the hells on a routine rescue mission that the presence of something wrong was sensed in a psychic way leading to the source.

Even the Cosmic Adepts were astonished at the power imbued in this entity. It was fortunate in that it was discovered before it was sufficiently awake to assume its full power. It had been created and put there in exact anticipation of The Primary Initiation of The Earth, which had now caused it to become active. It had been programmed to eliminate all human life, reserving any survivors for a ghastly enslavement.

Its mental power was capable of doing all that, and more. It could create a thought form, or artificial environment, indistinguishable from the natural environment 48 square miles in size. This great mental power and invulnerability made things very difficult. It resisted all attempts to destroy or transmute it, and it was only after a prolonged conflict that it was driven out of the solar system by the Six Adepts, requiring 24 sorties into the underworld over a period of 8 months. For the first nine Phases, the Three Adepts battled alone but later were joined by other Adepts and certain Members of the Great White Brotherhood.

We were spared extermination and the use of Earth as a strategic base by an ancient and formidable culture from another galaxy. Let us not forget that the threat may still remain!

I consider this to be the most startling of all the revelations of The New Age. The Alien Android was not destroyed, and seems likely to have been a problem for any galactic police to trace, and deal with effectively.

Footnote. The Three Adepts are Cosmic Beings who have saved us from extinction in times past during the chequered history of this humanity. Again they came to save us from the worst of threats. They suffered because of this, for which we are ever in their debt. In certain myths and legends they occur under different names. One Adept has appeared in history twice before, as both Samson and Hercules.

An Aftermath of The Alien Mission

The Alien had left five powerful interplanetary battleships hidden in a lower astral realm, each capable of destroying a large part of the Earth. Neutralising these was another chore remaining for the Six Adepts in response to instructions from the Interplanetary Authority on Saturn. Their ship had to be modified and strengthened on The Third Satellite for this task. The final battle in this Mission took place on January 22nd, 1966, three months after the alien was evicted.

The second case was a proposed invasion from the underworld, and held the prospect of literally Hell on Earth.

Again, our protection depended on certain Cosmic Masters, who although alien to us, were prepared to suffer in a terrible conflict on our behalf. It is difficult to convey how serious this threat really was.

It was countered by Operation Karmalight.

Operation Karmalight

This operation concerned the power of the Lower Astral Realms concentrating all factions into One Force under the control of one leader (codenamed Satan). This had never been a serious threat before, but there was now as a result of The Primary Initiation of The Earth, reflecting the Law "As Above, So Below."

The scientific developments in the Hells make it theoretically possible to access other planes of existence including the physical, etheric, astral and the lower mental realms by utilising the resonance in the octaves connecting the different levels of the cosmos (described in chapters on the Cosmos). This allows sophisticated technology to use the principle of resonance to transfer from one level of existence to another. This needs enormous amounts of power in a special type of energy. This became available by access to the great influx of energy from the events above, and was now a reality as all the combined forces and the ingenuity of Hell could be focused under one commander.

To abort this calamity, Operation Karmalight was put into action on 26th October, 1967. The Three Adepts were commissioned for this task acting on Karmic authority, but were only allowed a limited time for its completion. Everything hinged on neutralising the leader Satan, on whom the invasion by the combined forces of Hell depended. The Three Adepts were soon reinforced by three other Adepts, including the Lord Babaji.

Satan had protected himself by splitting his consciousness into many different parts, each in its own body, some in secret from his own forces. All these Satanic aspects had to be winkled out and transmuted, the final one requiring the personal attention of Babaji, the leader of The Great White Brotherhood. This great and mighty being has devoted himself to the evolution of man ever since his appearance on Earth. He has many names. More on Babaji can be read in "The Autobiography of A Yogi" by Paramahansa Yogananda, which is a book that should be read by all students of metaphysics.

The whole operation took 16 months in 24 phases. The longest phase, Number 15, lasted 1 hour 33 minutes and 39 seconds of Earth time. Time on the astral realms is on a different scale, and could be either longer or shorter in such places. This was within the period allowed by the Supreme Lords of Karma, who were represented by a Master from Saturn. We were saved by the efforts of those who have dedicated themselves for the time being, to protecting us until we can evolve sufficiently to have some sort of defensive capability.

How this conflict between the combined armies of hell and a few Adepts was waged is beyond our comprehension. They were limited by the basic ethics imposed by Divine Law, in comparison with the free use of anything which the opposition would use having no restrictions. The Three Adepts were also hampered by having taken physical bodies which they had to vacate during these astral sorties into the underworld. They received a dreadful battering which had to reflect in some degree on their physical bodies, so that one was killed. He insisted on being resuscitated and carried on.

It is interesting to speculate how the war was won. We are told that the ability to use the Divine Power of Love was the reason for this, and the superior experience of battle strategies held by the Adepts. Behind all that I perceive, the Angelic Forces may have been incorporated in these efforts. We will never know.

Shamballa is an etheric city which is the headquarters of The Great White Brotherhood. It is situated above the Gobi Desert, and is sometimes referred to as the 2nd Satellite, the moon being the 1st. To stress the instability of those times during Operation Karmalight, it is worthy of note that on the 8th July, 1968, Shamballa itself was under attack from the lower astral region. It was the first time it had been attacked by human agencies.

After Operation Karmalight, the situation below remains unstable. Efforts are still needed to monitor the situation and to prevent any likelihood of the threat repeating itself. The forces of Hell were in turmoil after the removal of the leader. There was jockeying for supremacy, and no doubt another attempt could be made to rise into the realms above.

The two main factions consist of the combined armies of the Military, in competition with those of the Priesthood of Black Magic. The balance has to be kept, lest another leader of the same calibre should be successful in uniting the opposing factions. Because of this, the Six Adepts were once again called upon make sure the balance was maintained. This crisis was called The Aftermath of Operation Karmalight and lasted from May 28th, 1969 to September, 1982. The situation may still need to be monitored for an indefinite period.

Two different threats to the Planet Earth

Having mentioned different assaults aimed at this planet in the latter part of the 20th Century, apart from those already mentioned there were two more either of which would have put an end to human life.

To outline two other specific events endangering the Earth:

(1) A very interesting thing happened in 1972 when we were beset by a strange race from outside the solar system. Their aim was to siphon off our vital energy from that particular etheric level on which life depends, for the benefit of their own species. They proceeded to begin just that, and finally had to be gently subdued and literally towed out of the solar system, as all attempts to communicate had failed. It took over a month to accomplish. This was just another little job for the Six Interplanetary Adepts, who have made it their business to protect us against raids coming from outer space.

If ever there was an example of the extreme variation of intelligent alien life this was one. These creatures were quite small, only a few inches in length and something like a large ant. They were of a metalloid constitution and very heavy, their movements were as fast as lightning in spite of this. They had come a long way, from the very rim of the galaxy. The size of their ships or their number was not mentioned. I was later informed that this very alien culture had been successfully contacted, and they were shown an ethical mode of access to the life energies they need for survival. They had been facing extinction, as only one in 100,000 remained fertile.

(2) During one of his privileged trips (by projection in the etheric body) to the Third Satellite, George King was shown a screen on which an alien space fleet appeared on its way to the earth. While being detected and viewed in this way it responded by taking a defensive formation in the form of a circle, vertical to the line of passage, which is rather reminiscent of the old wagon trains of the American Indian wars. This particular trace was being applied often enough to cause the fleet to repeat their defensive posture sufficiently to cause their power to be used up in this way. Eventually this made them abandon the invasion attempt, while they still had enough fuel to return home.

He was told that such invasion forces do not have to rely on ordinary soldiery, but use androids which are capable of fighting in the vacuum of space, do not need food, air or water, and do not need to sleep. Their only programming is to kill and destroy. One could assume that their fleet control was similarly under automatic control, in the way it responded to detection, which did not seem very smart.

The picture on the screen from many light years away it was so clear as cause George King to comment on its 3-dimensional appearance, and was informed that it was actually in 7 dimensions, producing the view of the distant place and conditions exactly, without the normal time lag caused by the vast distances.

Contacts and Abductions

I cannot say anything with confidence about the numerous reports of extraterrestrial contacts and the abduction sagas, although they are too many and too consistent to be dismissed lightly. How they fit in the overall picture is a mystery. It would appear, that there has been sufficient interest in earthly events to have attracted a variety of space-travelling species.

Some of them have been monitors of human evolution over thousands of years. There are records of these in all ancient civilisations, and in Europe during the Middle Ages. In modern times there seems to be a number of different space-travelling species, some of whom are perhaps students of anthropology, or tourists out of sheer curiosity. I can say, however, that they are not permitted to interfere with metaphysical operations, or their results.

Nevertheless, there is evidence of many individuals who have been subjected to the insertion of small devices which allow monitoring of all their activities. These are usually located in the nasal cavity and when located are removed because of distress, such as headaches or bleeding from the nose. When these have been discovered and removed they have the habit of disintegrating before they can be analysed. I know a family in which each member had experienced this.

There is a mass of material on the Internet, from many different sources which indicate there have been abductions for the sake of genetic material, by a race which is desperate to renew their genome in the face of imminent extinction. Apart from a recalcitrant group this culture has since left the Earth.

How to regard the assertion that the US government acceded to this activity in return for technological information is for the individual to decide by reading articles in magazines (e.g. Nexus and New Dawn), and from reports on the Internet of secret underground military bases.

The next section consists of the metaphysical operations leading up to The Primary Initiation of The Earth. Others were carried out to stabilise conditions on the surface of the Earth.

Operation Bluewater

This operation Bluewater was necessary to correct a disturbance in the Earth's magnetic field, resulting from atomic explosions, before The Primary Initiation of The Earth could take place. Energy had to be supplied to a psychic centre of the planet by discharging spiritual energy stored in radionic batteries into a designated area. The one chosen is below the surface of the sea off the coast of California.

Without this Operation there would have been a terrible disaster. The San Andreas complex of faults was due to give way and submerge that part of the coast of California. A ramification of magnetic and seismic disturbances throughout the earth of devastating proportions would have occurred. Control has been maintained, apart from minor fluctuations, and will continue within the foreseeable future, until there is some way of being warned of that effect which so far has been withheld.

Carrying out Operation Bluewater was difficult, because the power units had to be towed behind a boat steered in a precise pattern by George King, at the same time keeping in telepathic contact with Higher Intelligence relaying the navigational pattern.

This took place between July 11, 1963 and November 29, 1964 on four separate occasions at precisely predetermined times.

Operation Prayer Power

This is the secret of the power in the radionic batteries. Prayer is the transfer of spiritual energy, and this is accessed by teams reciting a mantra and taking the power from the Universal and Infinite Source into themselves. Then they send it out again from the outstretched hands and the heart centre towards the leader of the group standing in front facing the same direction, who passes it through himself and his right hand into a radionic battery. The trained teams are of varying numbers, working in relays. The leader has to be particularly qualified to fulfil this role, with a knowledge of the proper mudra (hand gesture).

The energy from operation Prayer Power is an essential part for the continued balance of Earthly conditions. The continued use is essential for the ushering in of a New Age in the best possible way. This is where The Aetherius Society is significant, and was described by the Master Aetherius as, "an important Cog in the Cosmic Plan on Earth."

Operation Prayer Power was devised by George King and given to the world on his birthday on January 23rd, 1973. In 1975, Operation Prayer Power was accepted as part of The Cosmic Plan. By 1978, it was also being used in the Spiritual Realms by 30 million, in the last reported estimate.

Anyone can contribute to Prayer Power by using The Practice Of The Presence*, and then demand the energy from the Universal Source and send it out. Act as receiver and transmitter of the special solar energies, and by this you can help the Earth in the most practical way. You need not be a member of The Aetherius Society to do this, but if you do it, you will be recognised by the Karmic gods. You can be a better person, and feel better by this. You can burn up negative karma in this way. We are all potential receivers and transmitters of this energy, as we are basically an energy matrix. It is so easy.

There is a record in the Old Testament describing how this power was used on one occasion. It was at the battle of Amalek. The Israelites were being hard pressed, so that Moses was seated on a rock and held out his arms to radiate power through his hands. When he tired and dropped his hands the battle went badly, so that his companions, Aaron and Hur, stood beside him and held up his hands so that he could continue sending power to his troops, who became victorious (Exodus 17:12). I am not sure as to the ethics of using power in this way, perhaps there were special Karmic considerations in those days.

I may say some unkind things about the indoctrination I received at a Catholic school, but I certainly ended with a good knowledge of the Bible.

Endnote. *The Practice of The Presence is appended to the chapter on Healing, although you can perform without, it is more effective this way.

Operation Starlight

The objective of this operation was to put into effect spiritual power sources around the Earth by charging certain mountains. In order to do this, it was necessary for George King to ascend the peaks, sometimes in very difficult and dangerous climatic conditions.

Power was sent through him by Jesus on Holdstone Down, and on each of the other mountains by certain Cosmic Masters (except Kilimanjaro, which was charged for him).

Each charged mountain has its individual type of power and will last forever. We are urged to go to these mountains, and send out power and love to our suffering world by practising The Twelve Blessings on the summits. This is the best of all spiritual practises.

Some of the peaks are very easy to climb, such as Holdstone Down. Kilimanjaro presents serious problems because of the danger of altitude sickness and the steep climb to the summit. This was the only one that was not charged through George King. The political situation in Kenya in those days was very dangerous because of the Mau-Mau uprising, and so it was left to the Master Goo-Ling to organise and charge this one.

I have climbed some of the charged mountains in the UK. Since being in Australia, I have visited Mt. Kosciusko and Mt. Ramshead. It was heavy going, and I do not propose to do it again, being in my ninth decade there is some excuse for that.

There was another older chap who has been doing just that every year, in spite of his arthritic knees. It was fortunate that he was with us on this occasion, as we would have been totally lost trying to locate the peaks. There was limited time for this, because the chairlifts closed at 4 pm.

The purpose of these pilgrimages is always to practice The Twelve Blessings on the mountain for the healing of the planet.

There are nineteen of the charged mountains around the world, their names and locations are;

UK

Holdstone Down (Devon)
Brown Willy (Cornwall)
Pen-y-Fan (Powys, Wales)
Cardnedd Llewellyn (Gwynedd, Wales)
Kinderscout (Derbyshire)
Yes Tor (Devon)
Ben Hope (Scotland)
Creag-An-Leth-Chain (Scotland)
Coniston Old Man (Cumbria)

USA

Mount Baldy (California)
Mount Tallac (California)
Mount Adams (New Hampshire)
Castle Peak (Colorado)

AUSTRALIA

Mount Kosciusko (New South Wales)
Mount Ramshead (New South Wales)

NEW ZEALAND

Mount Wakefield (South Island)

AFRICA

Mount Kilimanjaro (Tanzania).
This one was charged by Goo Ling. This mountain is a retreat of The Great White Brotherhood, likewise is Castle Peak in Colorado and Ben Macdui in Scotland (3 miles north of the Creag-an-leth-Chain).

EUROPE

Mount Madrigerfluh (Switzerland)
Le Nid d'Aigle (France)

Operation Starlight was performed by George King between July 23, 1958 and August 23, 1961, with very meagre resources and largely at his own expense. It was not easy going, there was facial sunburn and altitude sickness. On one occasion he suffered a hip injury from a falling rock but in spite of severe pain insisted on reaching the summit.

On another climb death threatened from exposure when trapped in a blizzard. His companion said what "What would happen if we were to die here." The answer was "Immediate rebirth!" For a full account, read "The Holy Mountains of The World" by George King.

It was later announced that power from all the charged mountains was henceforth to be released, whenever only one of them was activated by a pilgrimage to one of the peaks for the purpose of practising The Twelve Blessings.

Because there are nine of the nineteen charged mountains in Britain, it suggests that it has an important role to play in the future. The choice of Britain for the appearance of George King is also worthy of note, and also the English language being chosen for the transmissions from Cosmic Masters.

Operation Sunbeam

The main purpose is to return some energy, on the psycho-spiritual level, to the Logos of The Earth in recognition of the limitation* She has endured on our behalf.

This operation was entirely George King's idea, which led to his inventing radionic batteries capable of storing spiritual energy to be discharged over the psychic centres on the surface of the Earth, all of which are all beneath many fathoms of water.

Four Spiritual Energy Radiators have been established over the years in the following order: These are London (UK), Los Angeles (US), Auckland (NZ), and since 2008 in Barnsley, which is my home town in Northern UK.

These devices have been greatly improved to increase their capacity. The radionic batteries have to be laboriously handmade by members of The Aetherius Society to the precise specifications of George King. When The Third Satellite is in orbit, this allows some power to be held in reserve, to be released during calamities which occur on the Earth, and has resulted in saving thousands of lives.

The first phase of Operation Sunbeam occurred September 24–30, 1966 into the Psychic Centre 18 miles off Santa Barbara. So far-reaching was the significance of Operation Sunbeam that, 15 months later, this was hailed throughout the known parts of the galaxy and established on many other planets.

Since the advent of the three Adepts from Gotha**, they are able to remotely take energy from the charged mountains to supplement Operation Sunbeam, making unnecessary the hazardous towing of the batteries over water.

Endnotes.
*Lasted 18+ million years.
**Ref. The Gotha Mission.

The Saga of Gotha

This is taken from the tape transmitted through George King by a Master of a planet 36,000 light years distant, while his ship was in orbit around the moon.

"Thousands of years ago the people of the twin planets (code-named Gotha) roamed the galaxy seeking new planets and different cultures. Until one day, when they happened on a race which was hospitable and charming, but cleverly hid their belligerent nature. After cultural and scientific exchanges during which they received advanced information, this race attacked the visiting Gotha party. Some managed to escape and fled into space. However, they were traced and followed. They only managed to escape by raising the their ship into a higher octave of existence.

On return to the home planets it was decided to shut down all space adventures. In the isolation which followed the population concentrated on spiritual development, to the degree that they became a race of monks highly advanced in the occult sciences.

This continued for 25,000 years until one day spaceships were detected approaching their worlds, and soon established themselves in orbit around the two planets. Their hostility soon became apparent, but armed resistance was not possible because the population was conditioned into complete pacifism. They were able to establish a barrier of a force screen around the planets, which prevented any ship landing.

This screen was subjected to a prolonged bombardment and began to weaken and in danger of collapsing. They then raised the planets into a higher vibratory phase causing them to disappear. This could not be held indefinitely and when they came down the invaders had not given up and left as it was hoped, but were still there waiting in orbit around their worlds.

Inevitably, the enemy force landed and proceeded to build fortifications. As the situation became serious their earnest prayers and signals of distress were heard, and assistance appeared from an unexpected source. It was a very large spaceship carrying a culture accustomed to wandering the galaxy for thousands of years. They landed with a small powerful force and attacked the invaders who retreated to their ship. This was not the end, as a larger well-equipped force returned which was also repelled. After this the besieging fleet withdrew. At this stage, having done what they could, the "space gypsies" unceremoniously left.

This was not the end, as some time later the enemy returned and resumed the siege. The Patriarchs ruling the planets had decided that these invaders had the same right to the planets if they returned anyway, and counselled calm and preparation to surrender in their blithely distracted spirituality.

One man had other ideas and together with a few sympathisers began to prepare a spacecraft. This man was a psychic with keen farseeing abilities, and had witnessed the conflict which was The Alien Mission, and decided to make an appeal to the Six Adepts. He landed on Earth and actually visited George

King at the Aetherius Centre in Los Angeles, who referred the appeal as requested.

This was recorded as a "Visit from the Galaxy" and happened on February 13, 1966. Two months later saw the beginning of The Gotha Mission, which took eight months for its completion.

The Six Adepts returned with the visitors and immediately installed an impenetrable barrier, and set about conferring with the leading Tribunal, who only agreed to consider accepting help. While they were arguing, the invaders made a diplomatic gesture consisting of a message requesting permission to land for a peaceful settlement. It was agreed to accept them in good faith and allow them to land.

The Adepts addressed the planets' tribunal showing them how, were they to allow the invaders to base themselves there, they were endangering other peoples in the galaxy, many who were not able to defend themselves. The responsibility was emphasised in such a way that it seemed impossible that it would not be recognised as a moral necessity to resist, and allow the them to take over their defence, but they were adamant in wanting to talk to the invaders.

When the visiting ship from the enemy fleet approached the barrier, it was scanned and found to contain a strange virus. It consisted of spores which had the capacity of rendering every living thing drained of life, including the very substance of the planet. It was so highly radioactive that one molecule encountered would be enough for a rapid and painful death. Without more ado, the Three Adepts exploded the "mission of peace," destroying it completely, and its deadly cargo, before it could enter the protected space.

This demonstration of treachery was effective in reversing the extreme pacifism overnight, uniting the whole population in an enthusiastic defensive posture. They had been shown that complete devotion to self for thousands of years even as a highly spiritual ethic was wrong in the face of others being endangered by inaction. The long phase of isolation was finally over.

Two Masters from the Gotha System returned to remain on Earth, and devoted themselves to increasing the efficiency of Operation Sunbeam and other metaphysical operations, in recognition of the debt to the Earth, George King and the Six Adepts. In 1976, the two were joined by a third Master from Gotha. The Action of Three is a Universal Law which greatly increases the Power, in recognition of the Law of Three which typifies The Divine Trinity. There is a recording of this complete transmission on tape and probably on a disc by now, and is available from The Aetherius Society.

There was an Aftermath resulting from the Siege of Gotha.

The three alien battle ships of the invasion force were located at the rim of the galaxy. A mighty Cosmic Being took down their protective force screens and transferred all the alien life-forms into one of their ships and activated all the weapons of the other two on Itself as a show of omnipotent power. Having absorbed these energies it took them so far out of existence they could never be traced, even by Cosmic Masters.

The communication devices on the third ship were manipulated so that a complete record was imposed in such a way that it could not be interfered with or shut down and would be broadcast throughout that Galaxy. The disabled battleship and collective crews was sent back so that the information would be preserved as a warning against any further intrusion.

Operation Space Magic

I will now describe briefly this operation and the more recent arrangements for some spiritual energies to be suitably modified and enhanced, for the benefit of terrestrial man. These energies have always arrived from the other planets but only in a subtle manner.

Now, due to the generosity and efforts of The Six Interplanetary Adepts, modules have been planted on certain planets for the purpose of making this influence more effective. As popularly known, the physical conditions on the planets are extremely inhospitable, and required special spacesuits allowing only limited time on each planet's surface. In spite of these difficulties these mechanisms were securely installed.

This occurred between 5th and 9th of March, 1980 and the planets were: Saturn, Jupiter, Venus, and Neptune in that order.

On January 23rd, 1981, a special satellite was put around the Earth to receive such energies from the combined planets. It is undetectable and will remain so by any equipment that is likely to be developed on Earth in the next 1,000 years. A log of the phases of this operation, and the equipment used for the hostile conditions on the planets, is detailed in the book Operation Space Magic. This was next to the last of the metaphysical operations set up to allow increased spiritualisation of the planet and the hearts and minds of humanity.

Operation Earth Magic

The purpose of this operation was primarily to stabilise conditions on Earth, but also to raise human life to become more compatible with the New Age, as envisaged by prophets and seers. It was George King, who during the last years of his life conceived of this plan to enhance and stabilise conditions further. It involved creating a device constructed of earth materials with an antenna to broadcast radiations of the right quality into the subtle realms, on which this one, the material depends.

Aetherius enthusiastically approved, and forthwith produced a prototype by the exercise of his mental powers, but which was only allowed to exist for a limited time (18 days). It remained for selected members of The Great White Brotherhood to make three more of these prototypes, until certain Cosmic Masters undertook to supervise the completed construction, which was first activated on November 11th, 1990. Over the next 12 months the devices were perfected and put into action. Seven of them were created and installed in strategic places. These are now all operating satisfactorily and undisturbed in secret locations.

A few details of the nature of these "mechanisms" (as there are no moving parts): They are approximately 20 feet in height, have pure gold antennae and have many different coloured lights. I always imagine them to be conical or pyramidal shaped, but very little is known, as it is classified information.

A Visit To The Centre Of The Earth

Before the metaphysical Operation Earth Magic could proceed, George King was invited to visit the centre of the Earth and meet the Earth Logos. This was deemed necessary by a protocol which had been established for millions of years. This happened twice, and how it proceeded is written in his book, "Visit to The Logos of Earth." Normally, even if anyone could invent a suitable vehicle for such a visit, they would not survive the experience without a special invitation. Special suiting was required, and certain Adepts provided transport in a spacecraft. Entry was via secret places; one of these in is a desolate area of south England. Another is over the North Pole.

His visit to The Earth Logos was on November 29th, 1979. He was able to do this by freeing himself from the physical body and using his etheric body. He did this in spite of poor health and suffering from influenza, which caused considerable strain and necessitated special healing methods on his return to the physical. The description of this extraordinary experience is to be found in his book, "Visit To The Logos of Earth." He could not have accomplished it without assistance from the space people, who provided a special protective suit and transport facilities.

There are four known entrances to the interior of the Earth. The one used in this instance is in a deserted area of moorland in the south of England, and is well hidden. There was an invitation for a second visit to The Earth Logos on January 20th. 1980, and took place on January 23rd. On this occasion, he was to go through the North Pole entrance, requiring some changes in the methods and equipment used.

The purpose for these expeditions was to seek permission for Operation Earth Magic. The account of these visits to the centre of the Earth is truly astonishing, and constitutes a most profound metaphysical document.

Permission had to be sought from The Ancient Lords of The Flame even for the story of this to be written and released. The Flame is the Manifestation of the Life Force of the Goddess, and George King is the only physical Earth human ever allowed the privilege of seeing it. Without the assistance of the Cosmic Adepts, and the protection of the Lords of the Flame it would not have been possible.

An artistic representation of The Flame by George King, as he saw it, is included in his book. From the content of the book it appears that regarding the Lords of The Flame, there are only Three of them and they create as many duplicates of themselves as required.

The Saturn Mission

This operation is also designed to provide psychic energy to the Logos of the Planet, and to help the Devic Forces in maintaining the balance by reducing earthquakes and volcanic eruptions. The batteries are charged by Higher Intelligences under directions from Saturn and later discharged over underwater psychic energy centres of the Earth by towing the discharge equipment behind a boat. Certain of the Staff at the headquarters of The Aetherius Society have been trained to do this, and need to be proficient in the maintenance and handling of boats.

This operation has become a regular feature in the activities of the Aetherius Society and it releases great amounts of energy to the Devic Forces. It began in September 1981 over Loch Ness. The psychic centres of the Earth used are at present confined to the US and the UK. These had to be discovered before they could be so used. They are in Loch Ness (Scotland), Lake Powell (Utah in the US), and another is in the Bristol Channel in the UK. It is interesting to note that other psychic centres of the Earth which have been located, are always under many fathoms of water including one in the Arctic and one in Lake Tanganyika.

The Masters of Saturn take an active part in the Saturn Mission, but, for karmic balance, the involvement of physical Earth humans is necessary. This is achieved through the physical chore of towing the discharge equipment over water. There have been over 60 phases of this operation, benefiting all life on the planet.

It was thought that it would have ended when George King was no longer with us, but it has been able to continue, as suggested by The Lords of Saturn. The training given to the team by George King anticipated this.

The Cosmic Masters

The Cosmic Masters are elevated beings, some millions of years ahead in evolution in comparison with this humanity.

Mars Sector Six

The name adopted by this Martian Adept, is Mars Sector Six. He controls the huge special purpose space vessel, Satellite Number Three, and was responsible for organising and supervising the Primary Initiation of Earth, which took place on July 8th, 1964, effecting the onset of the New Age. This vessel is only one of a fleet for which he is commander.

Mars Sector Six is also the source of the material in the book, "The Nine Freedoms," given through George King who was in a full samadhic trance for the purpose, in the same way as that used for The Twelve Blessings. After the transmission of "The Nine Freedoms" by the Martian Adept, Mars Sector Six, the gift of a Charged Wooden Cross was also presented to those who attended.

Just as "The Twelve Blessings" are intended for practice, "The Nine Freedoms" constitute an advanced metaphysical text for study and contemplation. This book outlines our distant but inevitable evolution through life in different planetary environments. After the enlightenment of soul consciousness, there follows a train of lives in unselfish service, then there is the final initiation of Ascension and freedom from rebirth. This becomes the threshold of Interplanetary existence.

The discovery of the planet Garouche impelled Mars Sector Six to visit them in an attempt to alleviate the condition of their populace in whatever way he could. His spacecraft crashed on landing, whether accidental or due to a hostile reception I know not. He was then captured, and held in an electronic prison from which he could not escape. After being subjected to very painful treatment for a time, Karmic law prevented this from continuing. He was rescued by a Saturnian Master. The method employed is curious. It was by the projection of a ray of thought that he was able to access, and then be whisked away home on this beam.

Mars Sector Six is also a Lord of Karma.

Aetherius

This is the name adopted by the Venusian Cosmic Master under whose auspices The Aetherius Society was formed by George King, with the view to establishing a metaphysical organisation independent of all other occult societies.

Aetherius is based on Venus, but his activities range further than this particular solar system. He once said that he was 3,864 Earth years old, and that is young on Venus. In answer to the question, "Why is he bothering to help Earth in this way?" He said, "Because of my great love and regard for you in your limitations and suffering on Earth, and in all my millions of years of experience my main concern would be to help more directly, if not bound by the restrictions of Karmic Law."

The Master Aetherius gave us the ritual of "The Practice of the Presence."

The voice of Aetherius displays a very individual character, which is both melodious and pedantic in speaking. The voice of Mars Sector Six is forceful and somewhat intense, almost military in emphasis and authority. The voice of Jesus is very gentle and soft, for the most part, but occasionally very authorative and intense.

The Truth About Jesus

Jesus is a Venusian Master, millions of years along the evolutionary path, bearing in mind that the planet Venus is nearing the end of its 7th round of experience (refer to Rounds and races). The decision to be born on Earth at a certain time, and to sacrifice himself in the way he did, was his own. He did this in order to manipulate Karma in such a way as to prevent the catastrophe that was threatening the Earth.

When he was due to be born, certain measures were taken to obstruct any attempts to interfere by those evil agencies, who are always out to prevent anything likely to benefit mankind. And so, the "Star of Bethlehem" appeared, which of course was not a star or anything like such a massive body. The gravitational effects would have dragged the Earth out of its orbit. It was a sphere of golden light, which was the equivalent of a spacecraft occupied by a Master from Saturn. After hovering for a time it disappeared when the birth had been successful.

There has been much ado about the virgin birth, but the power of those involved in bringing it about was quite capable of arranging it. In these days of artificial insemination we are close to imitating it ourselves.

His mission was to die at a certain predetermined astrological time, and He managed to manipulate events accordingly. His teaching during the three years ministry were given leading up to the crucifixion, which was a brutal murder for which the human race on Earth is ever responsible.

The information regarding the period covering the remainder of His life is said to be apocryphal. The truth of the matter is, that He spent considerable time in receiving training in Egyptian and Himalayan retreats, and also on other planets. Limited as He was in a physical body, His education had to proceed in the usual way, which is the hard way through experience. (On other planets, the Earth is referred to as "The Planet of Hard Endeavour").

His main consciousness remained on Venus. The earthly incarnation part of Him is termed a "4th Aspect." Let me dismiss the uncertainty of the disappearance of the body. This was reverted to its basic atomic structure by His Will and Mental Power. Subsequent appearances were in the etheric body for those capable of seeing it. Imagine what would have happened if the body had been preserved. You have only to consider the medieval trade in relics and in the bits of dead saints, most of which were fakes. It could not be allowed to happen to this body.

On at least one occasion, Jesus materialised and ate some fish to reassure his disciples, as recorded in the New Testament. The "Ascension" described therein, however, was His mode of departure for the benefit of those present. The Ascension proper is an advanced Initiation Ritual endowing immortality of the body, and is described as witnessed by George King in his book, "The Nine Freedoms." Jesus had experienced this millions of years ago before man even appeared on this Earth in its present form.

There are many people who have been led to believe that the sacrifice of Jesus delivers them from sin. The phrase is, "washed pure by the blood of Christ." Nothing could be further from the truth. We are all answerable for our actions by Karmic Law, and will be judged in a most precise and fair way by none other than our own Higher Selves.

To expect eternal heavenly bliss after a single life is a delusion fostered by the Christian churches and they are not alone in this, as it is part of another world religion. Suppression of the principle of rebirths has been a terrible mistake. The Resurrection of the physical body as preached for nearly two thousand years is both ridiculous and macabre.

The Transubstantiation which the Catholics are still required to believe takes place during Holy Communion, led to cannibalistic connotations wherever the Catholic missionaries went, which is not surprising.

Actually, the ritual of the Bread and Wine was practiced long before in the so-called Pagan world, and The Last Supper was symbolic in the same way, the Bread being a symbol of Earth and the Wine of Spirit. Sometimes, water was used instead, representing the Water of Life which is the same thing.

Emphasis has also been laid on The Divinity of Jesus and caused Him to be worshipped as God. This is also an error, He never claimed to be God and referred to Himself as The Son of Man, and, although He is so much nearer to The One Divine Source as an elevated Cosmic Master, it is quite wrong to conceive Him as God.

The rationalist has erred in the opposite extreme, and states that Jesus was only a man, and some recent publications have tried to prove that he never died on the cross, was revived or had a substitute on the cross and lived to a ripe old age in Damascus! Do not be misled by the erudite treatment such works display.

Whether he married and fathered children is not known, but it seems possible considering the customs of the Jewish people of the time. It is recorded that Buddha was a family man before he went into seclusion. He also came from Venus, and Krishna was from Saturn.

The Cosmic Masters seldom leave their home planet in their Full Aspect to descend on another planet. The next and final visit will not be in the 4th aspect, as in the case of Jesus, Buddha, Krishna, etc, but will be in the full and awesome majesty of The Full Aspect, but this will not be Jesus.

When that will be has not been revealed, whatever you may hear to the contrary. I think it will not be until we have achieved some sort of world order and peace, which at the present rate is not likely to be for some time.

To confirm how Jesus is still very active on our behalf, we have had "The Twelve Blessings," which I had the honour of witnessing in 1958, during which great power was invoked and radiated into the Earth. In a later transmission Jesus revealed the secret of the successive protections, which we have had over the thousands of years. This is also available for purchase, in the book by George King "The Three Saviours Are Here," but a word of warning to those merely curious, such occult information carries some obligation of a spiritual nature.

The Rehabilitation of Judas

How Judas was involved in the precise scenario of the capture and imprisonment of Jesus has now been established as co-operation rather than betrayal. This has been apparent in the translation of ancient Coptic texts bearing the title, "The Gospel of Judas." The death which Jesus had planned to occur at a particular time required such a performance and precision. I had always suspected that this was the case.

This discovery made public and being the subject of a TV programme has caused consternation and confusion in the ecclesiastical world, on a parallel with raising of the status of Mary Magdelene as the possible spouse of Jesus!

The mother of George King was a reincarnation of Mary Magdelene! Her ancient association with Jesus was confirmed by His request for her to deliver a copy of The Twelve Blessings, which was done by a meeting between 2.30 a.m. and 3.30 a.m. on January 19th, 1959. She was met by a spacecraft at a predetermined rendezvous and transferred to a mother ship. The meeting is described in the opening chapter of subsequent editions of The Twelve Blessings.

Satellite Number Three

This is vessel is ovoid in shape and 2,000+ metres long, and is crewed by a variety of interplanetary beings, male and female, and commanded by Mars Sector Six. It belongs to a class of Special Purpose Vessels.

It orbits the Earth 1,550 miles above, at certain times of the year in a predictable sequence. Such times are given below and have been in effect since 1955. Its purpose is to raise the frequency of vibration in earthly substance, and to raise the consciousness of terrestrial man. All unselfish spiritual activities are enhanced 3,000 times when it is in orbit. It was responsible in this way for the aborting of an atomic holocaust in 1962, when the US and USSR were poised ready to exchange atomic missiles!

It is not detectable, because all photons and energy particles that approach it are subjected to reversal of 360 degrees, so it is invisible to radar and this also prevents interference affecting its operation. Inside, there are three crystal prisms 7 feet tall, revolving in an anti-gravitational field. Radiation, from energies of the Sun taken through the roof, is filtered and modified by passing through the three prisms, and then transmitted directly into an ovoid crystalline structure 30 feet high, which is also floating in an anti-gravitational field. From thence, the energy is transmitted to the Earth, via a matrix in the lower surface of the satellite.

This operation is guaranteed to continue for not less than 1,000 years. The dates and intervals appertaining are as follows, with all dates referring to midnight GMT on the day.

For example, "April 18th – May 23rd" means at the very end of the day on April 18th through the end of May 23rd, GMT.

Spiritual Push Dates every year

April 18th	to	May 23rd
July 5th	to	August 5th
September 3rd	to	October 9th
November 4th	to	December 10th

You are invited take advantage of this information and thereby help the Earth and suffering humanity, and, when you do this, you are also helping yourself spiritually.

Metaphysical Philosophy

The whole aim of metaphysical study is to be aware of the true nature of human existence and its purpose.

The foundation of Metaphysics is to be found in Gnosticism. It is not a belief system or a religion and was originally the core of Christian Doctrine, before the Romans adopted it as the State Religion.

Metaphysical Philosophy is based on some a priori assumptions, which are distinguished by the affirmations of those who have preceded us on the evolutionary path.

Many things were only allowed the High Priests of Egypt and Babylon, and later to the High Initiates in the Mystery Schools of Hermetism. This was changed dramatically in the latter part of the 19th Century by the Theosophists, and by The Aetherius Society in the 20th Century.

There was one more source of information yet to be mentioned, and that is the work of Gurdjieff and his 4th Way*. His detailed description and the significance of the Enneagram and its correlation with the Kabala was entirely new. It was known from ancient times among the high initiates of Gnosticism, but this was the first time it was to be exposed and written down.

Philosophy starts with a basic premise as an A Priori Truth, and builds on that. Descartes said "I think, therefore I am." In Metaphysics it is, "I AM and I think," and it questions, "What am I? Where am I from? Where am I going?"

This leads to the fundamental of all metaphysical thought being based on the I, and provides an inescapable conclusion that The I is ALL. But this I is much more than the person, but is the foundation of ALL THINGS. The sensorial world is an illusion. Part of this is the illusion of solidity. Being part of it makes you believe that it is real because you are made up of the same.

The one thing which is certain in this appearance of reality is CHANGE, which on this stage is governed by Time. In the analysis of this experience it is posited by some, that there is a smallest unit of time which is of the order of so many trillions of zeros after the decimal place. It is further suggested that the universe exists by renewing itself with the passage of each of these ultra-small intervals. If the mind is able to slow down in meditation into a certain resonance with this, then could some glimmering of appreciation of the NOW moment be achieved?

It is suggested that there may be different Timelines which cross at a certain nexus of events which determine the development of the future. For example, it can all be summed up in the phrase, "What if?," just as we could visualize the state of the world, where Napoleon did not venture East, or if Hitler was victorious in some alternate universe. These are subjects of fiction as you know, but What IF?

There is an element of logic in these fantasies if we regard their origin in The Ideal World of Kant, and that of Plato, as being an Abstraction of ALL Possible Ideas. According to this precept, there is no such thing as an original idea, because all ideas have to come from the Source.

Note. *The 4th Way is so-called because of the other three ways to Enlightenment. These are of the Fakir, the Monk, and the Yogi.

The Metaphysical Cosmos is held together by the Principle of Resonance. Each level of existence vibrates at a different frequency, the lowest being the gross material. The highest is thought to involve a level of Abstraction relating to the Three Supernals of the Kabala.

The principle of resonance permits energy of different frequencies to descend from the higher to the lower. It is the path of evolutionary power, or if you like, the Will of God, and allows communication between those of the same number and frequency in the relevant octaves. For example, the fourth level of each octave of the three main octaves, are in resonance.

By sophisticated metaphysical science, it is possible to exploit this feature by raising material vibration to resonate with that of higher realms, and so in certain conditions intrusion and invasion from the lower astral realms can be a threat. We narrowly escaped this in the 20th Century. Most of the UFO's are vessels which can transit between the realms.

In these days, there is resonance between Groups of Minds, thinking and meditating about the same things. On a higher level this occurs between Group Souls. The Will and Intent producing Action resulting from this will help save the world, and is an effective way minds can contribute.

Truth and Law

A feature of the metaphysical is the concept of TRUTH. Sometimes it is asked what is Truth? It's a very old question. As regards Existence, the answer is very simple. "Truth just IS." It is trite, but it has to suffice. A valid corollary is, "If it is not True, it cannot exist." This is too simplistic for quibbling pragmatists, but will have to do here.

There is only ONE TRUTH. It is an essential part of The Metaphysical which is LAW. It is perceived that all runs according to ONE LAW. The framework is so founded within certain limitations for Creation to proceed with Evolution, and to inexorably drive all life back to the One Source as conscious gods. Life goes through phases requiring repeated Grand Cycles of Creation/Dissolution.

All human life has had to pass through the Three Lower Kingdoms, and now we, as units of this Humanity are on the royal road to higher levels of being, towards group combinations of increasing size and complexity, having then abandoned freewill. This, the human phase, is very short compared to the previous phases, and the future seems an endless progression into realms which even the gods do not visualize.

Eventually, All become drawn back into the ORIGIN of ALL THINGS, and it is only then that there is full realization of TRUTH in its Fullness and Abstraction; and then of course, the whole thing starts all over again, as it has no beginning and no end. Everything restarts at the stage where it had reached in the ladder of evolution, in the last cycle. The description of the Metaphysical Cosmos starts with this, and is described by the

Circle of Plotinus, but in effect is a multidimensional SPIRAL spreading outwards and at the same time drawing inwards.

It is perceived in meditation how there is no difference between ideas of The Infinitely Small and The Infinitely Big, in the Inconceivable Abstraction of BEING. We have already tried to show that there is nothing which does not have some semblance of Life, according to the definition and nature of things arising from a common origin. There is a centre of consciousness implied even in the atomic particles, destined for passage through the three kingdoms on the way to the human phase.

Monads and Devas

At Creation there is a twin diaspora of monads, in the human they are divine sparks from the Centre of All Things. There was another issue co-incident with the human monads. These belong to The Devic Kingdom. They are the Intelligences behind the Creation and its maintenance. They are not human, but the embodiment of energy itself on all the different frequencies of the known energy spectrum, and way beyond what is known. I say embodied, but that is not quite correct, because for the most part they do not have bodies. They are the Angels. Nevertheless, they are capable at certain levels of this separate hierarchy, of creating a body of the type most suited for the rare materialization, either as a necessity or by the forces evoked in ritual.

The Devic Kingdom is more commonly expressed as the Angels. Nothing functions without some aspect of this kingdom being part of it – the lighting of a match, turning on an electric current and, indeed in every possible movement and function. These agencies are also monads but they are different, they are the essence of all energies and the controllers of energy. They are concerned with the balance of the Cosmos, and the balance in the developing microcosm that is the human unit, which is much more complex than we realise.

These beings evolve, but gradually and much more slowly than that of humanity. They are part of the WILL of God and so do not have freewill. The Angelic Hierarchy extends from the lowly entities of the Three Kingdoms, as described in folklore, to the highest beings of great beauty and power. They are written into our sacred texts as appearing in some crisis situations. Some are closely involved in human welfare as guardians, important in both birth and death.

Healing is always attended by a certain division of the Devas. The weather, in particular, is the office of the Devic kingdom, and they rely on the quality of thoughts and emotions of humanity for balance. Because of the wretched quality of our offerings over the millennia, our weather has been so reflected.

There is much more to this topic. For instance, the subject of their having wings whenever seen, and strangely enough their concern with birds, being so chosen by some as their planned entry into material evolution. (In some remote part of the galaxy are there some who have attained humanoid features, with feathered limbs and residual or even functional wings?)

For more information on The Devic Kingdom, the best book is that formidable tome, "The Treatise on Cosmic Fire" by Alice Bailey.

Abstract Reality

All that we regard as Real is a manifestation of Abstraction, which precedes Everything. In this way the reverse is true. It is The Abstract which is Real and what we perceive is Unreal!

The Human Race is a Unit in The Mind of God, and as a part of The Life which is the Logos of The Planet Earth. We all share the substance and the life of the planet. As a Body, the Human Race is the Totality of its combined deeds, which is again reflected in a Karmic Debt.

This gestalt contains a recidivistic element which is our most negative. It has been said by one of the Masters that "You are fortunate in that your Dark Ones are part of your Humanity!" I am not clear as to the significance of this, does it suggests that elsewhere humanoid races exist without such karmic encumbrance? Anyway, I throw that in to provoke some reflection in the minds of the readers.

The fact that the Great Ones are unable to assist us more effectively in our world of suffering and ignorance is not due to any reluctance on their part, as they have professed their distress of not being able to do more. This is because of The Law of Karma, which underlies the Totality of Manifestation and, in a mysterious way, they are, in their elevated state part of The Law Itself. Meanwhile, some of them sacrifice their bliss by incarnating here and take on Karma on our behalf!

The Human Unit is a Cell in the Body of the Whole which is Humanity, in spite of the separation in space and time of individual members. From the very beginning of the race, the various early components are included in the "matrix," and in the final sublimation becomes an Evolved Unit on a Higher Level of Being. Moreover, the Totality of Terrestrial Humanity from beginning to end is also related and part of a Perfect Whole, which is comprised of other human races elsewhere, of whatever kind exist in the galaxy.

On the principle of ALL arising from THE ONE SOURCE, All Life is connected by definition, being drawn back together inexorably over eons and repeated cycles of creation to its common origin. This idea of Human Life being One is difficult to grasp in the limitation of individual existence.

The Human Racial Unit is composed of a Hierarchy of Subsidiary Groups according to the Level of Evolution. At the highest level is a Being who represents the Whole and is a guiding influence over millions of years.

In this way you might say that IT is the Oversoul of the millions of other souls and is Itself a Unit in that which is The Anima Mundi. All Human Life is part of that which we sometimes refer to as Nature, or more clearly Manifest Life and Consciousness, and is in turn Part of The One which is The Source of All.

Below is a diagrammatic representation of a Cycle of Manifestation/Dissolution, which was described by Plotinus, who was a Gnostic and one of earliest founders of the Christian Church. The Circle of Plotinus is descriptive of Life descending in material involution and returning at the lowest point represented by Earth into the reverse process of spiritual evolution back to The Source, in which we are just passed the turning point.

Below, there is the '1' dividing into the multiple infinities and returning, followed by the sign used by The Aetherius Society for God in Creation. Without the triangle it is an old symbol for the God behind Creation.

At the foot is the symbol chosen for the Cosmos by Dr John Dee, which is the modern symbol for the planet Mercury.

The Circle of Plotinus (204–270 AD)

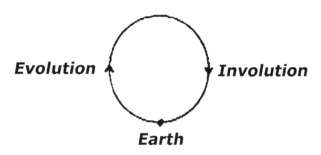

The Absolute

Evolution — Involution

Earth

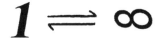

Dr Dee's Symbol

PART TWO

The Nature and Destiny of Humanity
The Human Unit

Each one of us is an essential part of a Cosmic Plan at the crossroads of Evolution. The Human Phase is a pivot on which the higher stages depend.

This particular dissertation could be aptly headed Esoteric Anatomy, as it describes that which cannot be found in medical textbooks.

Firstly, let us consider the illusion of solidity. All matter is made up of positive and negative subatomic particles, an atom being on the same scale as the solar system. This lattice formation has been described as, "a very loose type of three-dimensional chicken wire." As our physical bodies are made up of the same material, we have the illusion of solidity. The physical body is composed of millions of cells working in concert in a most wonderful way. Each cell is an individual life, a complex chemical factory, the processes of which are only very slowly being worked out.

We know much about the physical body, but its duplicate the etheric body, is entirely different. It is an energy body co-existent with the physical. The physical body is essentially an extremely sophisticated organic robot, self-maintaining and self-repairing, within certain limits; and yet, it is thoroughly dependent on the integrity of the etheric body and the balance of energy currents running through it.

The health and feeling of well-being we have in the physical body relies on this reservoir of vital energy, and its function as a transmitter of influence from the more refined and subtle vehicles in the make-up of the human unit. This brings us to the description of the seven features of this complex. The lower three of these are the solid, liquid and gaseous elements. The Etheric is the fourth up the ladder, forming a link between the lower three and the higher three spiritual ones, reflecting in a profound and mysterious way the septenary (7) basis of the cosmos, a theme to be enlarged on further.

There are three currents of energy running through the etheric body, this energy is usually called prana or chi. The main pathway travels from the feet upwards behind the body to the top of the head and down to the feet in front. There is also a lateral current flowing sideways round the body in a similar fashion, and the third goes in a tight spiral from the feet upwards.

Disturbances in the dynamic balance of these energy flows results in physical discomfort or worse. The pranic energy is held to be of two types, positive and negative, and are the Yin and Yang of the acupuncturists, who use well-defined lines of points on the skin, which can be stimulated in various ways to correct any imbalance.

The aura is an extension of the field of energy around the body, and can be partly displayed using Kirlian photography, the appearance of which can fluctuate according to the emotional and physical state. Clairvoyants claim to be able assess the character and health of an individual according to the colours in the aura. There are vortices of energy in front of the body, and are an extension of the workings of the etheric body. These are the Chakras, described in books on Psychism and Yoga. The main centres are seven in number, each one influencing a certain endocrine gland, or sympathetic nerve.

The Etheric Body

The etheric body is a co-existent subtle energy duplicate and is separated from the physical at death, carrying with it the departing lifestream. It is allowed to disintegrate after a few days, and a corresponding body – the emotional or astral body – takes over the duty of conveying the deceased to an appropriate realm, to which it either gravitates naturally or is guided there.

There are exceptions, hauntings and certain phenomena are related to their reluctance to pass on. Angels and human volunteers are on hand for when they consent to be guided. Freewill still operates even there.

A peculiar exception is the black magician, who elects to maintain his etheric vehicle as long as possible. This results in being able to drain vitality from the living, and is the true meaning of vampirism. It is recorded by Blavatsky that the etheric vehicle will, if allowed, continue doing this even after the lifestream has had to abandon it. It is possible to do this in life.

There is an account of a woman who, having lived in India, had learned how to vampirise a succession of house maids to maintain her youthfulness, replacing them as they became sickly and weak. Fortunately, they were able to recover their health given the right care and nutrition. The romanticism expressed by books and films on this dreadful feature is to be deplored, although the actual bloodsucking feature is fictional.

During sleep, the etheric body is suspended three feet above the sleeping body. For its use in nightly excursions, a development approaching that of an Adept is required. At death, the other vehicles which are transported elsewhere along with the Astral are the Mental and the Intuitional or Spiritual (Soul). Each of these function on a higher frequency than the one immediately below.

It needs to be emphasised that the integrity of the etheric determines the health and duration of the physical. In the future it will be the basis of medical practice and is part of the chapter on Alternative Medicine.

The following diagram shows the reflection of the Trinity in the Three Divisions, and the connection between the different psychic centres and the Kabala.

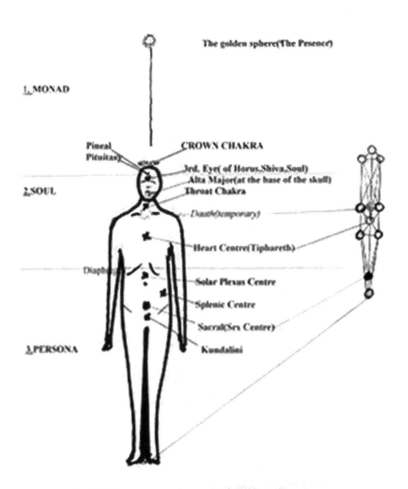

SHOWS THE REFLECTED TRIPLICITY IN THE HUMAN,
THE PSYCHIC CENTRES AND SOME SEPHIRA.

The Astral Body

Happiness has its seat in the emotions and is a personality reaction.
Joy is a quality of the soul realised in the mind.
Bliss is the nature of spirit, about which speculation is fruitless.

The Astral Body has a frequency of vibration higher than the Etheric. It is the core of the emotions. Its influence on the physical via the Etheric determines feeling of well-being and health. This is where emotional balance and control is important and is fully described in the chapters on Health. It exists on its own plane and wanders on that level during sleep.

This particular section which follows could be said to belong to the chapter on Metaphysical Philosophy. Because of the importance of the Astral in relation to our earthly existence, it is included here.

The Kurukshetra as typified in the Bhagavad Gita, is a battle within ourselves on the plane of the astral body. It is symbolic of the struggle to overcome the lower self and permit union with the Higher Self, which is synonymous with the Soul. This entails the sacrifice of freewill, which on close analysis is not really free at all. Needless to say, we are mostly a long way from that stage but will achieve this after many lives. This conflict is not only individual, but is of racial proportions.

It relates to the conflict between materialism and spirituality. Victory is the complete control of the emotions, a state which will herald the next quantum jump in evolution when mind will be most prominent. Then the mind, calm and still like a lake of glass, makes the biblical saying "there shall be no sea" understandable.

The Astral World is the place of emotions. It represents the most important phase of human evolution on this planet, wherein we are of the 4th Globe, in its 4th Round, of the 4th Chain and constitute the 4th Human Hierarchy (or the 9th, if the 5 gone before in previous cycles are to be considered). (Ref. under heading Globes and Rounds.)

It was on the lower astral planes where the most serious threats to our existence developed due to the principle of resonance inherent in the makeup of the Cosmos.

Reference to the following diagram of the Metaphysical Cosmos is recommended here, in the complexity of which the various levels can be identified. (from A Treatise on Cosmic Fire).

The astral plane of the solar system is the 6th subplane of the Cosmic physical. The Cosmic Mother controls the Devic Kingdom, and is closely linked with Devas of The Waters; water being essential to all life. The esoteric contemplation of the watery element sheds a lot of light on the significance of the 6th subplane.

The Solar Plane is in direct harmonic resonance with the 6th Cosmic plane, which is the Cosmic Astral with an interplay between it and the 4th, the Buddhic Plane.

The 6th Principle is the Love Aspect. It is the Force originating from the 6th Cosmic Plane. It is the Christ Principle working through these Astral energies, emanating from that area of space identified with the sign of Aquarius, they are already having effect and will ultimately "produce Universal Brotherhood and Unity after 1,000 years" (quoted from Alice Bailey's book, White Magic).

There are astral emanations in all social contact, just as there are etheric transfers with touch. The astral body can be made to reject all feelings of sentiment and compassion when it becomes cut off from the Soul. This is definitive of the Superman interpreted by Hitler. He is said to have had a vision in which he saw such a Superman, and was terrified.

In summation, therefore, the Astral is of the Emotions and is esoterically Watery, subject to calmness v. turbulence. It is, in a way, emblematic of The Primordial Chaos. In some ancient cosmogonies, The Cosmic Mother goes under a variety of goddess names, more recently of Mary: Note the inference from the word 'mare' (French for sea). The goddess has always been the patron saint and protector of mariners, and carried in effigy on the prow of their ships.

Before describing the remaining two vehicles (Mind and Soul) in our make-up, it is worthwhile considering some fundamental aspects of a human being and their components.

The lowest level is analogous to The Material Universe and subdivides from Seventh Cosmic into The Seven Solar and likewise from The Seventh Solar into The Seven Earthly. (See the diagram on the next page.)

There is a Relation Between the Same Numbered Levels of The Three System Resonance of Vibration in Their Respective Ethers, as in The Tonic Solfa or The Musical Scale of the Piano Keyboard. This is the Octave of Gurdjieff and The Workings of The Metaphysical Cosmos.

A DIAGRAM OF THE METAPHYSICAL
IN ITS SEPTENATE CONFIGURATION

COSMOS

1---------------------- The Top Three are Abstract Levels,

2---------------------- the Trinity and the Three Supernals

3-------------------- of The Sephiroth.

4----------------------

5----------------------

6----------------------

7------------------This subdivides into The Solar

SOLAR

1----------------------

2----------------------

3----------------------

4----------------------

5----------------------

6----------------------

7-----------------This subdivides into The Earth...

EARTH

1---------------------- Buddhic

2---------------------- Mental

3---------------------- Astral

4---------------------- ETHERIC

5---------------------- Gaseous

6---------------------- Liquid

7---------------------- Solid

The seventh Cosmic subdivides into the seven Solar and the Solar seventh in turn divides into the seven Earthly levels.

The Principle of Resonance effects a connection between the same numbered levels, and their subdivisions.

The Human Constitution

We are very complicated creatures based on the ultimate simplicity of the monad.

An attempt is made to show this as simply as possible in the following tables, which have been taken from "The Soul," a compilation of the works of Alice Bailey.

1. The Monad
   Reflects the Three Aspects of The Godhead.
   1. Will/Power   -   Father
   2. Love/Wisdom   -   Son
   3. Active Intelligence -   Mother (Holy Spirit)

2. The Ego
   Reflects The Monad   -   The Higher Self (Soul).
   1. Spiritual Will   -   Atma
   2. Intuition   -   Buddhi
   3. Higher Abstract Mind   -   Higher Manas

3. Personality
   The Lower Self.
   1. Conscious Mind + Subconscious Mind (Mental Body)
   2. Emotional   -   (The Astral Body)
   3. Material   -   (Dense Physical + Etheric)

These Three are a reflection of The Primary Trinity, and the Upper Three of The Kabalistic Sephira. There is nothing which does not have the Three Aspects inherent, and gives rise to the enigmatic assertion that "1 + 1 = 3" as a reflection of polarity in action.

The Three Aspects are the three basic qualities derived in philosophical analysis. In Hindu philosophy they are The Three Gunas.

The Three Pathways

In the Human Unit, there are Three Pathways of energy inherent in its makeup: The Sushumna, The Sutratma, and The Antahkarana, reflecting the Triplicity running through All Things.

The Sushumna is the path through the centre of the spinal cord, the Ida and Pingala being fore and aft, the one downwards and the other upwards. Take an analogy between this and the DNA double helix with its central axis.

The Sutratma is that connection between successive lives and is compared to a string of pearls, a pearl being the sum of evolutionary achievements of each incarnation, and connects the three centres of the head in later development, and exits through the crown of the head at death, taking the individual lifestream. The Sutratma is also called The Thread of Life. At the seventh year, it has divided into three branches, reaching into the three centres. It has a connection with the Antahkarana, in a potential sense.

The Antahkarana is a bridge between the Personality and the Upper Triad, which constitutes The Higher Consciousness. It connects with the Sutratma in an increasing degree during spiritual development, along with the three centres in the head. It is The Rainbow Bridge, in an interesting analogy with The Bifrost of Nordic Mythology. There is a corresponding link between the conscious level of the animal and that of the human, and is called The Bridge of Sighs.

Consciousness

The consciousness does not change. It is by definition in the Cosmic Logic of abstruse reasoning the centre and origin of all things, and therefore inherent in all things.

In many books, it is customary to express the idea of consciousness as evolving. This is an error, it is only Mind which is changing. There are levels of mind consistent with different phases of evolution, during which the sense of individuality becomes strained in our comprehension. The present mode of thought is linear and dependent on the passage of Time, and presents serious difficulties in trying to imagine anything different. I suggest that outside Time, thinking may be in kaleidoscopic patterns.

Consciousness can be described as Awareness, or Being Aware of Self. In its pure primordial state it is The Only Reality, Oneness, The Monad, The Absolute. This divides into The Duality, which is at once The Trinity and The Tetraktys from which Creation proceeds. This is aptly referred to as The Big Bang in scientific parlance, and yet there are numerous worlds in the subtle realms that occur before the material physical in the downward path from the Abstract. There have been countless millions of such events followed by their creation/ dissolution cycles and there will be countless millions more, forever.

IT is The Absolute and the Source of All Manifestation.

This is a mystery which denies rational explanation. Consciousness can be said to be the same as Spirit, and as such is intended in the rest of the book. The definition of Consciousness is a cause of never ending debate, but for this work the one given will have to suffice. The Absolute, therefore, is Pure Undifferentiated Consciousness, or, if you like, pure Undifferentiated Spirit. It has to be so, before the Duality on which all manifestation is to be based. Most students of metaphysics agree on this approach. Duality in Manifestation produces the Third member of The Trinity, and is the Force of Evolution.

Pythagoras taught the theory of creation by the use of geometric forms. His concept of the Triangle is reflected as The Trinity by Three Supernals on the diagram of the Kabala. From that we have The Law of Three, and hence a Fourth which is the "Emanation" of the Three. Thus we have the Law of Seven which results in the Metaphysical Cosmos built on the Octave for connection between all levels of existence.

The hierarchical levels of godliness and evolution are depicted thus, from Alice Bailey's "White Magic":

The Absolute (Godhead)
Brahma (Jehovah)
Supreme Lords of Creation
Supreme Lords of Karmic Law
Galactic Lords
Solar Logoi
Planetary Logoi
Cosmic Masters and Adepts
Human (Human stage is where separateness developed)
The Three Lower Kingdoms

Consciousness and Personality

Each night dying and on the morn reborn

Individual Consciousness is Immortal and unchanging.

Throughout the endless cycles of existence it just IS, and is regarded as SPIRIT. It is termed (for the need of naming things) the **monad**. This is the same as "**The Monad,**" which is the Primary Source of All Things. Actually, a name is pointless because it is All Qualities, All Knowledge, everything existing, and all that could exist. I would venture to say then, Consciousness is a Thing in itself, a Singularity independent of change. This is pure philosophy untainted by religion.

Personality

The use of the word ego is liable to cause confusion, as it has different meanings in different systems of thought (as in Freudism vs. Theosophy). In the theatre of the ancient classical world, the players wore masks distinctive of their role. The only way they could be identified was by their voice, hence a derivation of the word 'persona' or personality (from Latin; per, through; sonare, to sound). The personality is in a continuous state of change. After each day and night there is a renewal. Each situation during the day is unconsciously analysed and a suitable masks are adopted. There is a mask deemed appropriate for every encounter, whether it be for a friend, a stranger, a child, etc.

Facial expressions are important communication. Cosmetic surgery tends to produce an inability to do this, due to the tightening of the facial tissues.

Change is essential for Life and Evolution. The ego, which I think of as the personality, is never constant. The Higher Self also evolves and can be said to be the same as the Soul.

"That Which IS" in terms of pure Undifferentiated Being, is changeless and is the divine spark in all life. It applies to all things, because there is nothing which is not alive. But we, as units of Three Inseparables, with the monad as the foundation, are here "To Become, not just to Be."

The personality is a temporary thing and becomes a repository of experience, together with all that from numerous lives. The total becomes something of an Entity when the incarnation cycle is completed.

Are we a Social Experiment?

There is a theory rife in some metaphysical groups, that the situation on this planet could be a result of a social experiment which went wrong, and in the beginning we volunteered. This is proposed to have been much earlier, even millions of years at a time before Freewill was offered.

Was this then, a scenario in heaven before birth on this troubled planet? Imagine being presented with forms in triplicate, the basis of which stated, "I agree to being a volunteer in this holy venture and agree to lose all memory of this incident. I accept the risks of negative experiences and misfortune in many forms. Repeated rebirths will be necessary but the experience will be rewarding." I guess we have all signed up and still wonder about the rewards. Just how we went wrong is a long story.

Mind (manas)

Mind (or Manas to introduce the term for the cosmic totality of this), comes from the Logos of the Sun, as do all forms of energy in the solar system, "mind" being a very subtle type of energy on a scale dependent on the particular plane and subplane of existence.

Manas, therefore, is an attribute of the Logos at the foundation of the Creation process, and also as the mystery which constitutes The Mind of The Absolute in the Abstraction of the Primary Trinity. This energy although coming from the Sun in this solar system also derives largely from the star Sirius which esoterically senior to our sun. There is a hierarchical feature even in the progression of evolution in stars.

Furthermore, beyond that there is an apparent infinity of galaxies which are also conscious beings. Ultimately, there is a phase which is entirely abstract and is the home of the Super Gods. They are the Creators of Manifestation (Ref. The 11th Blessing).

Mind (manas) exists independent of the brain. It is an energy. There is nothing which is not energy in some form or other. The solidity of matter is an illusion, every particle is a complex of subatomic units of standing waves in seven dimensions. The energy of manas varies according to the level of existence. Its power is greater as we proceed up the ladder of evolution. Fundamentally, it is the organiser and planner of all manifestation of that which we conceive as the Mind of God.

The Mind of The Absolute Godhead came into being with the Causeless Cause and The Fiat Create, with the Primary Duality breaking into Triplicity.

Behind All That there was another element which is deemed WILL, an elusive thing which is present along with Mind. We know nothing about this, but it is a philosophical concept which has to mentioned. And so, it is the Will of a Supreme Deity which is behind Creation.

The formation of Manas was secondary to the energy which is LOVE (ref. The Nine Freedoms). It is the driving force in Manifestation and Evolution taking all life back to the Primary Source as conscious gods, over inconceivable eons of time.

MIND is the Vehicle of The Soul, in both the universal sense and the individual, and is present in all forms of life and inseparable from consciousness. To use our minds to analyse mind, is a formidable task. This is from the "Treatise on Cosmic Fire" by Alice Bailey, which is recommended for reference and as a textbook.

The Description Of Mind

An element of Manas exists in every form of life together with the two other essential elements, Spirit and Soul. It does not have to be active and may be only potential for eons of time.

Before the input of Individuality and Freewill into terrestrial humanity, awareness was in the nature of a Group Mind, and representative of a Group Soul. Civilisation existed, but of kind which we would find strange. The souls of those times derived from the Moon Chain and were unable to achieve the level of awareness needed for the further development of mind.

A sacrifice was made by certain inhabitants of Venus (their Group name is Prometheus). They came to Earth and mated with women, bringing that part of manas into the race required for individuality and freewill. The date given is 18,618,847 years ago. There is a mention in the Old Testament to this effect. According to that, a race of giants ensued, both in physique and mental power.

During this phase there was an unfortunate and perhaps unforeseen result in that mating with other species was indulged, giving rise to mutations, of which the only one which has come down to us through time is the simian population. Animal hybrids occur in myths and probably existed. "There was great confusion and mental turmoil in the beginning" (Blavatsky).

The account of this is taken from the ancient archives known as The Stanzas of Zion, inscribed on indestructible material and hidden in the secret recesses of the Himalayas. There are 340 of these, the substance of 40 or so which were deemed relevant to this humanity were communicated to Helena Blavatsky, and written into "The Secret Doctrine." According to this, the search for a missing link in the origin of man is fruitless, because there never was one.

"To get a true and accurate appreciation of manas is not possible for the finite minds of mortal man. The true significance of manas can only be achieved when the conscious mind is transmuted into the higher," quoted from the book "Treatise on Cosmic Fire."

This is because mind is a link between the abstract and the concrete. In theosophical terms, mind is "fiery," hence the title of the book by Alice Bailey: "A Treatise on Cosmic Fire." Manas (mind) has various connotations such as Intelligence, The Fire of Divine Impulse, Force of Karma, Originating Cause, Operating Will, etc.

In another quote from the Treatise on Cosmic Fire, "Until the faculty of Intuition is better developed, the very principle of manas forms a barrier to its understanding." This enigmatic saying is clarified in the following description of the human mind. The Absolute uses Manas in creating the Totality of the Plan, from its inception to the end in that Abstraction we have come to refer to as The Trinity.

An infinity of possible worlds exists in the Abstract of Universal Mind, which exists in the metaphysical realties (of which the physical is only one) of this particular Grand Cycle, and does not exclude the possibility of parallel universes; and what is more, the possibility of alternate Timelines.

MIND is WILL working Itself out in the Planes of Objectivity.

The Human Mind

Only through humanity can the Divine Plan work out.

The Subconscious, Conscious, Higher Conscious are levels of Manas (mind energy).

The Subconscious

This part of man's mind, although efficient and complex in its control of all physical and metabolic functions, is limited in so far as it is programmed and automatic. A study of the human organism reveals its sheer complexity in the mystery of its nervous system, cellular chemistry, hormonal and genetic. In this sense the human body is a very sophisticated organic robot, which can heal and repair itself (within limits), grow in a predictable fashion and reproduce.

The subconscious mind is a true and faithful servant due to thousands of years of evolutionary development, but is still liable to dysfunction subject to negative influences, such as: shock, severe physical and psychic trauma, and negative suggestion from the conscious mind. Otherwise it is a very good self-maintaining and healing source. Thus, it is the inadequacies of a psychic nature which lead to psychosomatic disease.

In regard to the aging process, we have been conditioned from childhood in expecting to grow old, become sick and die, becoming weak and changed in the process. In other words, to become looking old, ugly and dying prematurely. I suggest that the subconscious mind obliges in fulfilling these expectations! This is an idea which I have not encountered anywhere else. This does not mean that we should live forever. It is thought that an age of 120–150 can be expected in the future, dependent to some extent on an adequate diet and the limiting effects of global pollution.

However, on the other hand, the subconscious is receptive to positive suggestions. A person who thinks health and is not looking for sickness, is more likely to thrive and keep a youthful appearance. I think enough has been written by others about this under the headings of positive thinking, self hypnosis, auto-suggestion etc., to make any further comment unnecessary. Animals function, for the most part, on the subconscious level, the conscious mind being still latent. Recent work suggests that the dolphins and whales are exceptions, being more evolved as conscious beings.

In man, the subconscious is associated with the psychic centres below the level of the diaphragm. Much of our physical activities are subconsciously controlled, giving rise to ritual and habitual behaviour in our daily lives. This led Gurdjieff to assert that, "From a spiritual view we are asleep."

Morphic Resonance

In relation to this particular aspect, the subconscious as a function in animals is the newly found Morphic Resonance factor. Its description is attributed to Rupert Sheldrake and can be found in the book, "Paranormal or Normal" by Alan Radnor. It was discovered in 1988 through experiments in Howard University, and repeated in Edinburgh and Melbourne using rats. When put through a regimen of training they somehow managed to transmit the learned faculty to rats in other parts of the world. The inference being that there is a collective racial memory or "morphogenetic field," which is inherent in individual units, and can repeat itself in a non-material realm.

There is a similar process involving the hearts and minds of Humanity in "The Hundred Monkey Effect," which states that when a sufficiently large core group learns new behaviour it quickly spreads to the majority (Keyes, 1981).

This theme is enlarged on by Owen Waters in his book, "The Shift: The Revolution in Human Consciousness," and in his website, www.InfiniteBeing.com, in which a new cultural awareness is being born and spread throughout this humanity.

Carl Jung, in his life's work on the role of the subconscious postulated the existence of a racial subconscious, which fits in neatly with the Sheldrake hypothesis. An interesting analogy can be drawn in the idea of all that has happened in the long history of the race is in the Akashic Records, and exists on a certain level of ether in relation to the racial subconscious.

The Conscious Mind

The Conscious mind is a tool of the Freewill, in contrast to The Higher Self as representing the monad. Nevertheless, it serves that unit of consciousness in man. In the population at large it is used in varying degrees, and by some it may be said, very little apparently, exhibiting a behaviour which is more automatic in character controlled by impulse and desire in a predictable way.

This enables modern influences to manipulate and control public opinion, and is remarkably effective through the press and television. The most effective way would necessitate the implantation of a chip which would ensure compliance. Researches into more subtle yet scientific ways of control are said to be proceeding in secret laboratories. Experiments were made by the Russians during the cold war by aiming certain frequencies onto the American embassies. The health of the staff suffered and some were sent home.

The conscious mind is often obstructive, especially in the exclusively pragmatic so that the imagination and the ability to consider ideas beyond the sensorial are inhibited. That is what is meant by the quotation: "Until the faculty of the intuition is better developed, the very principle of manas forms a barrier to its understanding."

In the evolution of man's mind there have been three stages of development. These occurred in the 3rd, 4th and 5th root races. The next two stages will not be reached until the 6th and 7th rounds in a higher state of consciousness. At present we are only a little way past the halfway mark of this, the 4th round (ref. Globes, races and rounds, as in relation to Gaia). The majority on Earth are of the 4th root race.

It should be emphasised that Manas (mind) is a subtle type of energy and has its origin through the Sun, which is Aspect of Brahma, and has different features and potencies relevant to the level of existence.

The Sirius system influences our entire planetary system through the Sun. The three synthesising planetary schemes,

Uranus, Neptune and Saturn contribute; the latter being the focal point for the transmission of manas to the seven planetary chains of Earth.

In the days of Earth's prehistoric humanity, the gift of manas in the form of Freewill came from Venus (ref. Genesis ch.6 v.2-4) by the introduction of a new genetic strain. The period before this was perhaps the "Big Dreamtime," relevant to the Aboriginal tradition.

The Superconscious Mind

The Superconscious, or Higher Mind is still latent in Earth's humanity, with the exception of certain highly evolved members such as Adepts of Yoga, and the occasional rare Natural Mystic. It requires a higher level of the "mindstuff" we have come to call manas. All we have is an inadequate description of its function and powers from those who have deigned to make the attempt on attaining that level, language being woefully lacking in this respect.

It appears that it is the part of mind, which is actually a vehicle of the Soul, assimilation with it brings an end to freewill. At that stage, the individual identifies with its Group Consciousness, has command of the psychic faculties and can reach Cosmic Consciousness. There is a mode of communication between the superconscious mind and the conscious mind by way of the subconscious, all being available to the higher conscious. The Polynesian Shamans are said to be aware of this, and able to make use of it.

The Power of Mind

We use the power of mind when we create. By this we use our imagination as it is our creative faculty, even as the Mind of the Absolute behind all Creation creates in response to Will and Intent. In the microcosm man, it is subject to the will and intent of the individual monad, but the higher mind to which that applies is not being heard, because the conscious mind rebels at the prospect of sublimation and assimilation into the higher mind. There are methods of training which allow the mind, when fully concentrated and pin-pointed, to achieve that which would seem impossible. This faculty is misnamed willpower, although the will behind the mind is the promoting factor, and is increased in potency by such exercises.

In the realms of elevated consciousness, as in the Adepts and Masters of Yoga, the power of the mind is tremendous. This becomes further realised in the case of the Cosmic Masters such as Jesus, and allows the performance of miracles and the direct control of matter with apparent ease. The highest intelligences of the planets of this solar system are able to split their consciousness into numerous parts, and create bodies suitable for any environment simultaneously, each united in complete consciousness.

Measurements of the brain waves of humans show that the brain produces electromagnetic waves, which lie in the range between 1 and 40 Hz. This spectrum is divided into four ranges, which accompany different levels of consciousness. This relates to waves which resonate through the Earth, and may be significant in the transmuting effects being endured at the present, of which there is more under the heading of "The Schumann Waves."

Thought

The spelling of the word thought is due to the derivation from thoht, the past participle of thenken (Old English, to think). The similarity between this word and that of the name of Egyptian God Thoth and also the Norse God Thor is quite striking.

The Cosmos is a Manifestation of Thought, as conceived in the Mind of The Absolute, perfect and complete in timeless abstraction but imperfect in the manifestation of the evolutionary process. In the view of some, this suggests that it is an elaborately controlled system of chaos. A miniature example of this is the weather.

The nature of thought in relation to man's mind is somewhat analogous, as it produces thought forms on a certain level of ether, the careless results of which have produced a morass of undesirable thought forms in the mind belt around the Earth, and indirectly is responsible for chaotic conditions generally.

There is power in concentrated thought and is greatly enhanced by group cooperation, and can be used to transmit healing energy. The Adepts can use their minds to produce a thought form, and send it forth imbued with a sort of life to scout remote areas and situations, reabsorbing it afterwards. This faculty was used by George King in his first tentative ventures onto the planet Venus.

As already intimated, words and emotions are always producing thought forms, and over the centuries have affected the weather patterns of the globe. This is because the Devic agencies whose task is to control the weather, depend on such emanations of humanity, the quality of which is so reflected.

The energy of manas which forms our minds comes from the 5th Cosmic plane and constitutes the 5th Principle (see diagram).

That energy of the Superconscious mind relates to the 6th Cosmic plane, which is that of the Christ, and is only concerned with unselfish impersonal love and service. It is the realm of the Soul.

The Place of WILL

"WILL" is the presumed intent behind all Mind, and is often forgotten in works on the Mind. There is an element of this in all levels of existence, reflecting the Will of The Absolute, and associated with what we call Freewill. There is not much to say about this, and not much in the literature which confuses it with mind. Perhaps it is because WILL is an aspect of the monad.

The Prometheus Myth

Thinking is a dangerous activity. It can change your whole life.

The Prometheus Myth is identifiable with Lucifer, and is a myth pertinent to the subject of Mind. From time to time, I included in my lectures metaphysical references to the Greek Myths, and this one directly concerns the introduction of manas (mind) into humanity. It is noteworthy that esoterically Mind is Fiery, and is particularly relevant in this context.

The name Prometheus means Far-seeing, it is synonymous with Lucifer in respect to the introduction of Fire, derived from the Latin (lux and ferre), and so therefore, Lightbearer. This may be a bit of a shock to churchgoers, who have been brought up to think of it meaning the devil, but this is an unfortunate part of the attempt by the Church to maintain the doctrine of fear by creating this personage.

The term Lucifer is also the same as The Demiurge of Theosophy, and is that Force from the manifesting of the Trinity, as the Primal Energy of Creation and an Aspect of Brahma. The War in Heaven is an allegorical theme of the conflict of Spirit with Matter, which is the same as the Polarisation implicit in Duality. That is the first level of the Myth. The second level is the introduction of mind into ancient man in the Lemurian Phase, over eighteen million years ago. This was a time of great distress and confusion as the concept of Freewill was introduced.

The Swastika is a very old symbol of Evolutionary Force and Fire; it is also Thor's Hammer by which "sparks" were struck at the Fiat CREATE in the diaspora of the monads. It can be seen as a symbol of the Fire (Manas), Mind being the instrument of Creation and Evolution. The Swastika which is commonly associated with Hitler and Nazism was reversed in the anti-clockwise direction, signifying the idea of stasis and opposed to any change and evolution, a true negative and a perversion of an ancient and sacred symbol.

The early root races of mankind were shadowy creatures, highly spiritual and long-lived but not having the gift of mind and a sense of individuality. According to the most ancient tradition, the most highly evolved beings transferred to the Earth from the Moon chain in an early attempt to further the evolution of these "men," but they were unable to gain the faculty of mind as we know it. To compensate for this failure, Spirit Beings came from the Venusian chain; their group name was Prometheus.

Note that the concept of mind, in the metaphysical sense is fiery. Thinking, therefore, is like playing with fire. Some people seem to be afraid of thinking, especially if it means questioning the beliefs imposed by a religious dogma. It is a very profound concept.

The idea of vultures eating the liver of Prometheus chained to a rock, is interpreted as being imprisoned on Earth, and subject to the desires and conflicts which plague humanity.

It is worth noting, that the influx of Venusian influence is in the Old Testament, in the sense of a genetic input, "The women of Earth were seen to be fair." (Genesis)

Speech

Because words are so closely associated with thought, they need to be considered in association with speech. Thought precedes speech, and every word produces a reaction in a certain wave band of the ether, and can be made to create a potent thought form. Apart from that, words can hurt and once released cannot be recalled.

The apostle James seems to have been particularly keen on this, regarding the tongue is an unruly organ needing continuous control, (ch. 4, v.8–10). We are known, and often judged by what we say and how we say it. To realise when to be silent merits attention and applies to us all.

There is a peculiar dynamic in the use of words. Certain charismatic individuals realising this have often come to power based on its use. Such people are very dangerous as proved in our recent history, otherwise having the 'gift of the gab' is very useful for con men and salesmen.

The clever use of words is even more important as radio and television are mediums for political propaganda and lies. There is only the Internet to counter this, but it requires keen discernment.

Pythagoras made it a rule for all applicants to his school to maintain complete silence for two years before acceptance. As to himself, he did not address students directly, but through an intermediary acting as his mouthpiece, who stood close to a curtain behind which the master would speak through a hole.

A Yogic Master, may at some time abstain from speech for a number of years and only communicate in writing, as mentioned by George King from one of his encounters. The significance of speech relates also to the practice of Mantra. These are short phrases which must be in Sanskrit. The continued pronunciation of a mantra has a profound effect in energising the etheric body, and is an important part of Dynamic Prayer.

The peculiar Enochian language was introduced by Dr John Dee, who claimed to have received it direct from an Angelic source to allow communication with the Devic Kingdom. It was adopted for use in Ceremonial Magic in which the names of gods, principalities and powers are invoked. It has to be articulated in a sonorous and "vibratory" fashion to be effective, requiring some practice. It is available on the Internet complete with its 22 letters.

Truth

The Truth will set you free (John 8 v.32)

Truth is "That Which Is," because "That Which Is Not cannot Be True." The Whole of Truth is The Ultimate Reality which is changeless. It is represented by a circle, which is boundless and all-encompassing. It includes Infinity, Abstractions and Paradoxes impossible to comprehend. It has many dimensions and can be conceived as a multidimensional sphere, yet it is impossible to imagine a sphere of only four dimensions. Taking a sphere of three dimensions, imagine that it has innumerable flat surfaces making it appear round.

The knowledge we have available to us is only a few of these facets, one comprises that which is metaphysical knowledge, and another is sensorial experience, supplemented by that accruing from scientific investigation of the mysteries of number and abstruse mathematics. The symbol of the circle is to be found wherever there are archaeological findings relating to Man, and often as seven concentric rings. The Totality of Truth, is to be found in The Concept of The Monad, as The Primal Source of All That Exists, as even That Which Does Not Exist, but Could Exist, has Been, and Will Be.

The problem of Consciousness and Individuality centres on the monad, that part of The Monad, which dwells silently in all life forms. In the human it is associated with the centre of the heart, but is not part of that space but behind it in the abstraction of a perfect vacuum without dimension. In stories handed down to us, there are discernible certain mythical references such as Tom Thumb and Jiminy Cricket of Pinocchio, as the monad is that from which we get our conscience. The multi-dimensional diagram crudely depicts the Cosmos in configurations of 7 levels. It is Jacob's Ladder and Jack's Beanstalk, representing the path of evolution along the multidimensional spiral. I have attempted to show this in a diagram, which is to be found in the relevant chapter.

Freedom

The struggle of freedom from tyranny is the picture of man's turbulent history. This is the political type of freedom, but there are many varieties. We can categorise the types of freedom. In the same way, it is reasonable to say that there are an equal number of, and categories of, types of slavery, just as a glass is either half-full or half-empty.

When the peak of endeavour has been reached, it is customary to say, "that man is Free." However, the constraint of security measures and tax problems leaves the rich man still hampered by forces with which to contend. Take, for example, the opposite case of a man who has devoted his life to unselfish service, and is unconcerned with the money factor but is still limited by his human form and desires.

An extreme is the austere life of a Buddhist monk, or an Indian Fakir. These men are not free, as they have material bodies in which they are still imprisoned, and are ever-faced with controlling the Mind.

We are all living in degrees of slavery, in this way. One aspect of slavery is Religion. Many are afraid of thinking independently as a result of the conditioning received by tradition and dogma. I hope this book will free some from their restraint.

The pressures of life impose an implacable routine of ritualistic behaviour. For most, every day is the same, apart from minor differences. We are actually prisoners in a life of regularity, to the extent that we have been referred to as organic robots. It is difficult to argue against this idea, as it refers especially to city life. The routine of the peasantry can be seen as more natural in the seasonal rhythm of nature, but it still applies.

Only last year, there was an article in the scientific magazine, The New Scientist, emphasising the robotic characteristics of life, and compared it to being prisoners in a vast and complex hologram. The analogy holds under detailed debate. There are films in which the actors portray this theme, the keynote being as to how they can liberate themselves after their minds have been locked inside a computer with its sophisticated program of a replica of city life. This may not be impossible, as seen in the ability of the Alien Android which could create an environment 48 square miles in extent, which was indistinguishable from the natural environment.

There is reason to take this seriously when the philosophy of existence comes under scrutiny. The metaphysical aspects delve into spiritual considerations, and come to coincide with the ancient doctrines of Plato and Pythagoras. The more ancient doctrine, as revealed in the Bhagavad Gita, echoes this most precisely, raising the possibility of liberation from bodily imprisonment contended by Arjuna, and echoed by the words of the Buddha.

After all that, there remains Freewill, which is sacrosanct on its own level. In the words of Isaac Asimov (professor of chemistry and author of books on science, but more famous for his excellent stories of science fiction), they were, "The Last Freedom is to go to hell in your own way!"

There is only True Freedom when Freewill is recognised as not really free, it will be abandoned eventually, although the sense of individuality will remain; but, by then, you will be enjoying Soul Consciousness.

Knowledge

After Mind and Thought, here are a few aphorisms on knowledge from Alice Bailey:

"Truth is arranged in sequences by knowledge."
"Truth is the mirror of the soul."
"Knowledge is the life-aspect of learning. It is not Wisdom."
"Wisdom is Self-Knowledge and belongs to the Real."
"Knowledge belongs to the Unreal."

In my own limited view, there are only two kinds of knowledge: Apriori Knowledge, which relates to the faculty of Intuition, and Knowledge gained through Experience.

Ignorance

It is possible to envisage a theory, as to the way ignorance afflicts man using a little of what is known of metaphysical principles. The difficulty encountered when exposed to new ideas may be due to significant changes that have taken place in the subtle composition of the human unit underlying the physical. It is well known that some old people get "rather set in their ways," and become very conservative and reluctant to change their habits, particularly their views of the world.

It can involve a hardening of the auric envelope, so that the outer layer becomes impervious to new ideas penetrating and entering the mind from the World of Ideas of Plato, which is also The Noumenal World of Kant, containing all possible ideas.

In this solar system, everything arrives via the Sun, as in the old adage "There is nothing new under the Sun." The closed mind makes it more difficult to consider new information whether in the ordinary course of things, through reading or more personal contact. The result is its total rejection as foreign and incompatible. It may be just uncomfortable, or heretical and so threatening cherished beliefs. The result is total rejection and ridicule, and sometimes downright hostility.

The notion that our minds are in three tiers of development, Subconscious, Conscious and the Higher Conscious has been dealt with in some detail in earlier chapters. It should be remembered that the pathway of ideas from the higher mind to the conscious mind is by the subconscious. Most of us are not on too great familiarity with our subconscious, and some cut themselves off completely. In Jungian terms, this can give rise to an inflated ego and a hubris of such proportion that all feelings of morality and compassion are submerged, as in Hitler's version of The Superman, derived and misinterpreted from the philosophy of Nietzsche.

It is the same as a psychosis in its extremes, without compassion or moral sense. "Peace falls like the gentle rain from heaven," to quote a poetic expression of the Master Jesus from The Twelve Blessings. We are urged to offer no resistance to this flow, "as every cell in your body will rejoice 'neath this light."

If the auric envelope is closed by having developed a hard exterior, there will be no penetration from above, sealed off in such a way that all reception from more mundane sources is likewise rejected. One should try to guard against this and preserve that sense of wonder which we had as children, so that the new, however outrageous, needs to be mulled over and savoured by Intuitive Discrimination.

In the more serious cases of "ossification" of the mental sphere, there occurs a failure in maintaining that thread connecting the higher and the lower aspects of the human complex, and to all intents and purposes leaves the individual so afflicted cut off from the subconscious and the higher, producing what amounts to a mere shell of a man functioning in a purely robotic manner. In the words of Helena Blavatsky, "You are rubbing shoulders every day with some who are more dead than alive."

In addition to all that, any help from the Devic Kingdom which could be solicited is shut off by the closed mind.

Soul

"The Gods themselves are facets of Soul requiring attention." (Marcilio-Ficino, secretary to the Medici, who sent him to purchase the ancient texts on which mediaeval magic became based.)

There is no scientific evidence for the existence of Soul. We can only rely on the information from the forerunners of the human race, such as Adepts, Masters of Yoga, Saints, and Mystics. Ancient Stanzas were handed down orally from generation to generation, before being committed to writing. The feats of memory by the ancient seers was extraordinary. Eventually, these were written down, and are often referred to. As they are attributed to Avatars such as Patanjali, Krishna, and more recently Jesus, such information on Soul needs to be seriously considered.

The Soul is an unknown, and has to be accepted on faith, which is the intuitive knowledge of the philosopher, and not the imposed "faith" of dogma. Information from those with direct experience is available, but language has proved lacking for this purpose.

The Universal Soul, or Anima Mundi, is a direct emanation of the Manifesting Trinity.

Here are some Metaphysical definitions of Soul: A Vortex of Twelve Energies held together by the Will of the Monad. The Result of The Relation between Spirit and Matter. A Mediator and Middle Principal between the Manifest and the Unmanifest.

The Soul has many names: The Christ Principle, The Form Building Aspect, and The Essence of Individuality. It appears that a list of the properties and functions of Soul is the nearest we can come to understanding It. The Universal Soul represents The Force of Evolution and is the 2nd Aspect, The Son. It is Unified Sentiency of which the Human Soul is a part, and is That Force which is Impersonal Love, propelling all lifestreams back to their Source through Karmic Experience.

It developed the human form over millions of years, to form a link between the Upper and Lower Triads. At the same time, it is also an instrument of Law through the use of Manas.

As the Principle of Intelligent Activity, it is more under the influence of The Feminine Aspect of The Logos, giving rise to the many names of The Goddess. In the constitution of the human unit, Soul is synonymous with the Higher Self, and provides the Faculty of Intuition. It is not generally aware of the personality, but is conscious of, and active within, its own group on the Buddhic plane. Until stimulated by unselfish action and spiritual exercise, it is not normally aware of the personality.

It can be completely disassociated, to sever its connection in cases of prolonged and extreme depravity. In the event of unsuccessful encounters with combined Dark Forces it can be sent into a kind of spiritual shock which will cause it to seek refuge in the void for a very long time before it resumes activity. This is a hazard peculiar to certain Adepts as warriors of light.

The next phase of evolution will be Soul Consciousness, and is the inevitable goal for all humanity, and beyond that is Ascension and True Freedom. The ceremony of Ascension was witnessed and described by George King in "The Nine Freedoms" during a visit to The Third Satellite.

There is much on the Internet and in some publications of ascension being imminent for all humanity in the year 2012. This is thought to be a minor form of ascension, is assumed to be an elevation into a higher level of vibration, and is a process which has already started. Some will take advantage of shortcuts to this end, using the various methods which have been made available. The metaphysics involves the raising of the Kundalini Power, which is described in the pages on Yoga Philosophy. It is through the etheric body and its vortices of psychic energy that Soul contact occurs.

The Soul is sometimes called The Solar Angel, and The Angel of The Presence. There are many other names given to this most mysterious part of the human unit. In order to function in the cosmos, the Soul creates a suitable vehicle called the Causal Body. During the intervals between incarnations, the lifestream spends years on the Plane of the Soul (The Buddhic Plane), depending on karmic factors and the associated ray of the monad.

The Causal Body is virtually immortal in our conception of time, but ultimately is left in favour of a Spirit Body on the realm of Monadic Consciousness, which seems to be way beyond the Adepts. These 'bodies' are entirely unlike our notion of what a body is. They are pure energy, egg-shaped, and free to move with the speed of thought. They can take on form of any kind, anywhere.

The Third Eye is the Eye of The Soul, dormant in man until some degree of soul awareness is present and tangible. It is The Eye of Shiva, the organ of clairvoyance and the exercise of magical powers.

In the Hindu pantheon, Indra is Lord of the Buddhic plane, the Home of the Soul the symbol of which is that of Air (Aquarius), just as Agni is Lord of Manas and the Mental plane, Fire and Kundalini.

Twin Souls in Existence

The quest for the perfect lover has been described as a reflection of the search for union with the Soul, which is in opposite polarity. This idea is prevalent in romantic novels, but to meet the opposite can be a hindrance in every sense of the word, even as far as being an enemy!

Much was revealed about the "other half" of ourselves in a transmission by Sananda, through the mediumship of a lady named Lisa Smith, in 1999. This information taken from the Internet, describes many different facets of the Soul Concept. It is quite complicated, and is only a summary of a comprehensive treatment by Sananda (who is, or may be, another manifestation of The Christ Force.)

Here is the new information taken from the Internet:

Sananda deals with the separation of the soul from its beginning on higher dimensions, and classifies these as from this base:

1. Twin Ray
2. Twin Flames
3. Twin Souls
4. Twin Mates
5. Divine Expression
6. Soul Mates
7. Divine Complement

7. Starting from the base at number 7, we may meet with our opposite number several times, which mirrors yourself, and may reflect negative vibrations. One result is the tendency

to have more than one sexual partner throughout a lifetime, as partners age and change. "It is worth remembering that relationships on Earth are in preparation for moving you to a higher level of being."

6. A Soul Mate is arranged for each rebirth. An encounter is likely to occur at important stages and make a profound effect on life. They rarely join in marriage, but a journey together in several lives is not unusual.

5. A Divine Expression makes a great impression, and promotes a right attitude and action. It may be unpleasant. It is a guidance from above. In my opinion, it must be from the Higher Self reflecting the Twin Ray.

4. A Twin Mate is not likely to be concerned with romance. It is part of a group consisting of at least 144, working in the Galactic Core or on the Earth. They form a composite unit of togetherness. We are all connected in this way with our Group.

3. A Twin Soul is part of the Twin Mate grouping, and each individual has Twelve Twin Souls. They are close to the Earth work. The ratio of male/female in the group is not always equal. Romantic encounters occur within the group of twelve.

2. A Twin Flame is on a higher level, and is a being you have to work with closely from the Galaxy down to the Earth life. This relationship lasts for eons. There are Seven Twin Flames to which you are connected. Integration has to be reached before union with The Twin Ray. The Twin Flames are four of the opposite polarity, and the other three the same of the

indwelling earth unit. These may exist elsewhere than on the earth. The group of Twin Flames are above sexuality in a bond of communal devotion to their work.

1. The union of The Twin Rays is the ultimate stage as understood by the Cosmic Masters. However, there is a seemingly endless range of groupings beyond and above that.

Thanks to Lisa Smith, who channels the Lord Sananda.

The Seven Twin Flames could be the same as the Seven Rays of Theosophy, in association with the Seven Lords of Creation.

Health

There are many ways which are taught to maintain health. I will only deal with those with which I am familiar. Essentially, there is a need for the right attitude and this involves an acceptance of certain truths.

Because, if we are to accept energies of a healing and sustaining nature, we have to recognise their existence. The matter of which our bodies are formed is basically not solid in the fundamental sense, because all matter consists of standing waves of energy in seven dimensions, and all micro-atomic units are such. And so, solidity is an illusion, but a very real and effective one for those entrapped in it.

The second and most important truth is the acceptance of the Intelligence behind Creation. It is also helpful to recognize the Hierarchical nature of Its Powers, on which we depend for the continued stability of our environment, and that within ourselves which is the basis of health. These powers are the energies themselves, intelligent, and for the most part formless. They are The Devic Kingdom, which comprises individual units just as in that part of the manifested kingdom which is Humanity.

Our dependence on the efficiency of the devas cannot be over-emphasised. Fortunately, they are effective in keeping the variations of climate and steadiness of the Earth, but only within those limits imposed by Karmic Law. This insists on such extremes as demanded by the quality of the conduct and thought throughout the long and terrible history of this humanity.

The constitution of a human being is very complex, and although the physical anatomy has been described and understood, there is an underlying energy foundation which consists of a circulation of energies in an envelope of subtle matter, based on a series of vortices in relation to the endocrine and parasympathetic centres. It is the balance on this level which determines health, longevity and a peaceful frame of mind. It is Mind which is the key.

MIND is a type of energy, and contrary to orthodox opinion, exists independent of the brain, which is the vehicle for the exercise and application of Mind. There are three levels of this energy, the most important of these for the maintenance of physical well-being is that portion we call the subconscious. This faithfully directs the complex orchestra of endocrine balance and the regular function of the different organ systems. It does this throughout the whole of a life. It never rests or falters in its work.

Life is subject to assaults of various kinds, injuries which demand repair, diseases which call on the immune system. Sometimes, the protective mechanism meets that which it is unable to counter effectively and is unable to fight it off. Then the whole system succumbs and ceases to exist in spite of medical science.

Apart from all that, there is another way in which the subconscious is hindered in keeping the balance of health. This involves the emotions. When we are upset, this reflects on the mind in such a way that the balance is disturbed, and a condition arises which is now known as Psychosomatic.

All functional ailments derive in this way, and constitute the vast majority.

Emotional control therefore, is very important. That does not mean you do not have to feel. I think there is no escape from that, it is what makes us human. It is rather difficult to describe, but an effort needs to be made not to be overcome by what Shakespeare called, "The slings and arrows of outrageous fortune." There are ways in which a correct attitude can be cultivated and the effect on the subconscious mitigated considerably.

Anger is most dangerous in this respect. Anxiety, jealousy and hate all have to be consciously transmuted and eliminated from the mind. Underlying all this is fear. The whole of western society seems to be subject to this factor. It is important not to let fear dominate your lives.

There are well-known methods of dealing with these problems, the most popular and I might say most expensive, is to resort to a professional psychologist. There is a fashion in some cities for the wealthy to consult their psychologist weekly for analysis and understanding of their emotional problems. It seems to work, but may take years. If I seem to be somewhat sceptical of this practice, it's because I am.

The Conscious Mind can be educated to deal with emotions. It requires a bit of self-discipline, and regular and simple exercises. There is an infinite source of energy in the universe and some of it is available on demand. You have to believe in it, or at least accept its possible existence. This is where it becomes a bit spiritual, in that we are involved asserting the existence of a Primary Source of Energy, which in our case comes through the Sun, which is the medium for ALL energy in the solar system. This energy is on levels of different frequencies, some are accessible to us and used all the time, and if we know how we can manipulate things to access more when we feel the need. Attitude is all important. Expect to BE WELL and so you will be.

If illness occurs, you then you are better equipped to overcome it. The Subconscious Mind readily responds to Positive thoughts, but unfortunately is also inclined to recognise morbid and Negative thoughts and may even oblige by providing such a disturbance, which it may consider you to be submitting repeatedly. It is necessary therefore to maintain a healthy and positive outlook, and you will be better protected against common things like colds and 'flu, and even the more serious diseases.

In these days, it is all too easy to depend entirely on the medical system, to not take any interest in self-maintenance, and to reach for medication at the slightest hint or suspicion of disorder. To be sure, a prescription is all too readily available. I should know, because I had that responsibility as a doctor, and was careful to restrict prescribing by the indication of each diagnosis. I think I was perhaps bit mean when it came to tranquilisers and sleeping capsules. Needless to say, such restraint is not recommended for developing a large practice! Without the discovery of broad spectrum antibiotics, many would not be alive today, and I, myself, would not have survived without them. However, the lavish and often unnecessary use of antibiotics soon gave rise to resistant strains of penicillin. Let it be clear, therefore, that resorting to medical science is not something to be denied, and I am proud to have been part of it.

We can ourselves do more to maintain our health by adopting a positive and cheerful attitude. There will be times which are depressing. No one is entirely exempt from negative experiences. Life demands a balance for any experience to result.

Depression, if it occurs, should be regarded in the light of philosophy, and in most cases eventually passes. Nowadays, there is a counselling service for any kind of affliction or communal disaster, but to subject a school to this after some pupils are killed in an accident seems to be just a little in excess. There is of course the severe form, Endogenous Depression, that can be life-threatening and requires close medical supervision.

An amusing anecdote comes to mind. There was the occasion when I was waiting for the consultant psychiatrist and looking out of the window there was this brilliant pink car. I exclaimed to the patient's General Practitioner doctor, "To whomsoever that car belongs should see a psychiatrist!" Just then the door opened and someone said, "It so happens that is my car." I turned round to confront the man for whom we were waiting— it was the psychiatrist himself!

He was an excellent fellow, a Scot of the traditional dour mien that is more adaptable to the stresses of the specialty that has the highest percentage of suicides in the medical profession. For the best method to counter the pitfalls and hazards of life, the sovereign way is the proper approach and practice of YOGA, and I do not mean the physical contortions and exclusive attention to the physical body that goes under the name of

Hatha Yoga, which in itself is an excellent form of physical development and mental discipline, but needs the balance of breathing exercises and meditation to supplement it.

In fact, the most experienced and Master of all forms of Yoga taught a system exclusive of Hatha Yoga. If you can maintain the suppleness and joint mobility of a ballet dancer, Hatha Yoga is then appropriate. Not many of have the necessary flexibility, and to indulge without close supervision may cause injury. In the same way, the practice of standing on the head needs to be approached with caution and ceased if it causes dizziness. The neck is not intended for supporting the weight of a heavy build as the cervical discs receive the full pressure of the inverted posture. The elderly should not try Hatha Yoga. The position of sitting on a low seat with crossed legs is sufficient, as the yogic asana is impossible for all but the young and athletic. The use of a high-backed dining chair in the posture to be seen in the pictures of the pharaohs has been recommended.

The best times for the practice of this ancient science, in my limited personal experience, is in the hours between 2 and 4 am. Traditionally, the hour before dawn has been advocated. Others may find it too inconvenient, the times most suitable and practical need to be found, but it is best to use the same time each day. The periods can be short in the beginning. Ten or fifteen minutes done well, is better than a long and irregular pattern. After a year or so, it will be easy to double this time comfortably and gain access to the knowledge of Mantra Yoga.

The midnight hours are best for the following reason: The group mind of local society is quiescent in comparison to daytime and is more suited to meditation. An empty stomach is also more conducive to successful practice, as you will see. Any details in the actual methods are left out purposely, because I am not qualified to so advise. There are numerous books on the subject, and classes in every locale.

Personally, I find that group meditations are unnecessary. I find a solitary mode is the only way for me. There is no way in which meditation can be taught satisfactorily, it just needs to be learned by yourself. We all have our own built-in teacher, which is the Higher Self.

However, there is one tip which I will venture to submit. It is useless to command the mind to shut down all thought. By allowing the thoughts to pass through the mind in a disinterested fashion, it will settle down into slow activity and after a variable time, of several minutes, will cease, and then meditation may be attempted. Then, Entering The Silence becomes possible. It is worth bearing in mind, that the whole idea behind this ancient system is to Know The Self, and is only another term for Soul. Without acceptance of The Source of All Energy, there is less likelihood of success.

Know that the Sun is the medium and giver of the life energies as an Aspect of The Supreme Power in this solar system, and, in fact, all energy in all the spectrum of the known frequencies and many more which are not known. The Egyptian Pharaoh Akhenaton introduced this concept and built a new city devoted to the Aton (sun disc). After he died, the old gods were replaced and his memorials erased.

Spiritual energy is the KEY to all the problems which plague this humanity. We just need more of it, and you will get more of it if the practice of Yoga is followed diligently. You will have better health, you will not worry about things so much, and altogether you will be a better person and easier to live with. All it needs is that little bit of self-discipline, and here it is where we fail as the pressures and demands of life and family are formidable obstacles, as I found so myself in the early years.

The Wands of Horus

I have included this chapter, as it is relevant to the foregoing regards the balancing of subtle energies which are an essential part of Life. The pictures of the Pharaohs are often depicted holding a short cylinder in each hand. Until two of these objects were found in the tomb of Pepi, the 6th dynasty, 2278-2184 BC, it remained a mystery as to their purpose. These were cylinders made of copper and zinc, the copper to be held in the right hand and the zinc in the left. Relating to the positive and negative energies they were to maintain a healthy balance by their use.

This was shown to be the case in a research instituted at the Polyclinic of the Medical Centre of the Russian Federation in Moscow. The wands, held for a few minutes induced the Alpha Rhythm evenly between the right and left cerebral cortex. The wands need to be hollow, and tuned to the frequency of the Earth, and conform to the proportions of The Golden Mean. The length is 151mm and the diameter 28mm, in resonance with the height of the great pyramid before it was damaged. The mathematics can be found on the following websites. The materials must be pure, not less than 99.96%, and are being made in the exact proportions by Dr Valery Uvarov.

You can refer to the website (www.neilos.org) for downloading of his book, "The Wands of Horus," from the site's Library section.

Longevity

There is an ancient Chinese text, "The Secret of the Golden Flower." The translation is a small book of 160 pages, of which 20 comprise a commentary by C.G. Jung. As in all the esoteric traditions, this material was transmitted orally until the printed version of 1,000 copies in the eighteenth century. The translation was made by a missionary in China, Richard Wilhelm (1873–1930), who also translated The I Ching. His book has the title, "The Secret of the Golden Flower, A Chinese Book of Life."

The origin of this teaching is said to have been Persia and some associate it with Nestorian Christianity, but the elements of Taoism recur throughout the text. It is essentially a book of Chinese Yoga and has similarities with the Indian, but without any reference to the physical exercises. Meditation and breathing form the core of this work with some notes on its practice.

In order to maintain life it is recommended to visualise the energy flowing from behind, upwards to the crown of the head and down the front of the body and so on, at the same time breathing in on the upwards movement, and breathing out with the downwards movement. In this way, the balance and support of a healthy etheric body is preserved.

Students of Yoga and metaphysics will recognise the path of the Kundalini, but the Chinese system makes no direct reference to this and is apparently not intended to involve it. There arose an enthusiastic following by a sect devoted to this teaching, which at first flourished and was tolerated. Almost inevitably, it became suspected of political aspirations and was cruelly persecuted by the Manchus, just as with the Falun Gong in present day China.

There is also a similar system, based on The Kabala, described in a book "The Middle Pillar" by Israel Regardie. In this, you imagine yourself centred in the Tree of Life. Israel Regardie was a great enthusiast for analytic psychology. In his opinion, this should be a preliminary to all studies and practice of the occult. Although I disagree, it should serve as a reminder that it is a serious study and not suitable for the dilettante.

Alternative Medicine

Disillusioned with orthodox medicine, many have turned to alternative methods.

These can be described, but I am not fully acquainted with all such systems and the list may be incomplete. Of all the various methods becoming increasingly popular, it is Acupuncture, which I practiced myself for a number of years and found it to be effective, at least as much as the more conventional medicine and without the worry of possible drug reactions. That is to say, in selected cases. Not all conditions are so readily amenable to this ancient method. The most dramatic and satisfying results were with migraines, allergies, sciatica, backache and rheumatic problems, with the exception of cases where there was the legal complication of accident compensation!

In my enthusiasm I approached the local hospital by letter, offering my services freely to the outpatient department. The facilities required being so meagre, I thought it would be readily accepted. However, this was not to be, and my offer was turned down somewhat curtly with the inference that my intention was to use the hospital to increase my general practice! The lot of a pioneer in medicine is not a happy one. Anyway, since then others have followed, and now there is free use of acupuncture in some departments, particularly in midwifery.

The bogey of transmitted infection by needles is prevented by using disposable ones, which I used freely soon as they became available. For those with a morbid fear of what is essentially a painless insertion I used a weak laser beam, a cumbersome and expensive device that eventually broke down, and could not be repaired. There is now a new model on the market, which is battery operated and the size of a larger type of mobile telephone.

Other methods are in use instead of needles, and one widely used in the US is by applying an ultrasonic beam to the acupuncture points. Electro-puncture uses the direct application of a mild electric current, and some specialists in the field apply electricity to needles in situ, but there are small handheld models which can be used to apply different levels of current to points on the skin. A sophisticated method is by finger pressure called Shiatsu, a procedure perfected in Japan. It is often performed by Japanese girls in Shiatsu clinics, which are in most five star hotels in the Pacific area.

In addition to the more commonly practiced acupuncture there are a number of microsystems, which duplicate the bodily surface points in localized extremities. For example the hand, on which points have been localized and defined to produce a replica of the whole body surface in miniature. In like fashion, there is a system confined to the foot, and this is the basis for the rapidly increasing popularity of Reflexology, using acupressure on areas on the sole of the foot, duplicating the science of Acupressure of points on the body. It does not end there, because there are similar microsystems on the nose, on the scalp, and the gums adjacent to teeth. But the one I have been most interested in is that on the pinna of the ear.

The points on the ear have been mapped out by the French scientists with remarkable accuracy. They have written books describing new ways of conveniently stimulating the aural points, a method originating in China. One of these requires sticking on the ear a minute (1–2 mm), low-strength magnet onto the relevant point for the part needing treatment. A chart of the points on the ear is appended below.

Very small wire drawing pins are sometimes used, or small beads.

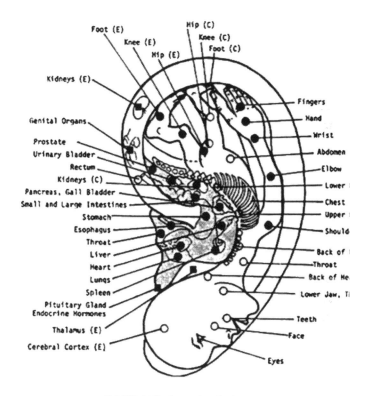

C = Chinese Ear Acupuncture System

E = European Auriculotherapy System

The magnets used are small, secured by a small piece of sticky tape. The ancient Greeks were familiar with use of magnetism, but had to be satisfied with lodestones, which they tied to the affected part of the body.

Acupuncture is at least 3,000 years old and is based on the principal of balancing the positive and negative energies. The Yin/Yang balance is thought to be similarly preserved in exercises of Tai Chi.

Acupuncture was used on elephants 2,000 years ago in Sri Lanka, where archaic maps have been found illustrating the acupuncture points on an elephant. I have seen a duplicate of such a map, which was printed on strips of bark. The use of these techniques in veterinary medicine is quite common nowadays, especially on dogs and horses, for which the laser method is generally preferred.

The practice of acupuncture has become simplified for western use, especially by Dr Felix Mann of Harley Street, London. When specialists from Helsinki visited Melbourne, I was also able to learn their techniques. The emphasis was on the selection of areas sensitive to pressure, or reactive to mild electric stimulation.

This is much to the disgust of those well-trained in the oriental way, which, for the Western practitioner, is frightfully complex and over-systematised, and relies on the ability to diagnose imbalance between the five elements by feeling the pulse. This technique, is said to require fifteen years of training, but which if done properly may only need one to three strategically placed needles. I knew of one elderly doctor in Holland who was reputed to be able to do this, and he ran his own training school.

In China, many needles are used, especially for anesthesia during which the patient remains conscious and comfortable during major surgery. I was very impressed when I saw a Chinese surgical film for the removal of a lung. The patient was calmly chatting and had an occasional drink throughout the operation.

However, at the risk of appearing to be bragging, I frequently obtained good results using only one needle in one spot on the dorsum of the foot (Liv 3, for those acquainted with the technique). I learned this from Dr Felix Mann of Harley Street. Twenty years ago I cured my sister-in-law (who among others, were cured of migraine headaches), by briefly needling this point.

Homeopathy

My investigation into alternative medicine brought me into contact with Homeopathy, which is undoubtedly effective and has a wide following, the most loyal adherent being Queen Elizabeth. She is reputed to carry a collection of homeopathic remedies on all her travels, in which case she is an excellent recommendation for Homeopathy. It is also spoken of highly by the Cosmic Master Aetherius.

I have no firsthand knowledge of this method, but among my acquaintances at a seminar on the gadgetry, which was claimed to be 21st Century medicine, there was a young doctor who was using one of these electronic machines for use in Homeopathy. It appears that the initial consultation is usually a lengthy one in order to arrive at the most specific remedy, after which the follow up treatments using the latest technique only requires a few minutes.

This chap had a large and lucrative practice. It involved the testing of various substances, which were put into a metal container connected to the electrical contraption in circuit with the sufferer. The correct material to be used was then taken from reading the dials. By testing for the most general, and working to the more specific, one arrives at the right substance. The fully-trained practitioner of Homeopathy does not need such a device.

The specific material, having been identified, is diluted in water many times until there is literally nothing left chemically detectable, yet this produces the most potent form. This is the reverse of the orthodox Allopathy. So how can this have any effect? The answer lies in a metaphysical assumption that there remains an etheric shadow of the material, which allows it to be more therapeutically effective, dependent on the curious properties of water. Perhaps it s triple molecular constitution of two hydrogen atoms with one oxygen atom as reflecting the Trinity allows this property.

It is a mystery, but there is no doubt that good results are obtained. There are schools all over the Western world offering courses for full qualification. It is the only system of therapy which has been invented by one man, Samuel Hahnemann (1755–1843). He was a German physician, and based his theory on the principle that a substance which can cause the symptoms of a complaint will effect a cure when greatly diluted in water. It is a safe method and has no toxic effects.

An increase of symptoms may happen for a few days prior to cure, and is referred to as a healing crisis. There are two ways of practicing it: The traditional one of finding and prescribing the proper solution, or the modern one by which a complex machine finds the right substance to use.

Colour

It will have be apparent to the discerning reader how the Triplicity Factor is in everything and applies equally to the phenomenon of colour as evinced by visual recognition of the Three Primary Colours in Light of Red, Green and Yellow, as detected by the retina. The colour Blue is formed from the mixing of the two pigments Green and Yellow.

Our vision is limited to a very small part of the electromagnetic spectrum. The Seven Colours of the Rainbow (Red, Orange, Yellow, Green, Blue, Indigo, and Violet) represent the Seven Rays of Creation and the Seven Laws. The colours of the lower seven Kabalistic Sephira on which Metaphysical Cosmos is based, have different colours for each of the Four Kingdoms.

On the higher levels of existence, the number of colours in light is of the order of three hundred plus! How I know that, is a result of being familiar with some of the sayings of a Cosmic Master: In a taped recording, the visitor to George King commented on the colours he could see of in a glass of water.

It is well known that there is a genetic disorder transmitting colour blindness to males. There is said to be an island race in the Pacific, where colour blindness is endemic and extreme, in that only different shades of grey are seen. Unless colour blindness is detected early in life, it can have devastating effects on a career, if considered in the armed services, or the art world. An Englishman named Dalton was the first to research into colour blindness after realising he was colour blind. He was convinced that it was a defect in his eyes, and insisted that an eye should be removed on his death and examined.

Dogs see in shades of yellow, blue and gray (Wikipedia), and have better night vision. Some insects seem to have good colour vision. Colour concerns both the artist and the metaphysician; the former is more concerned with the practical application, whereas the latter is interested in its application to the structure and function of the Cosmos. The distribution of colour in the Tree of The Kabalistic Sephiroth is briefly mentioned under that heading.

The colours of the Kabala are different according to which of the Four Kingdoms (mineral, vegetable, animal, man) it represents. (Ref. The Golden Dawn volume.)

In regard to the Devic Hierarchy, there are colours associated with the particular realm or function. According to the Tibetan Master, as quoted in The Treatise on Cosmic Fire, "In the Devic Kingdom ideas are expressed in terms of colour which can be heard, and sound which can seen, the reverse being the case in man."

In the tradition of The Ancient Wisdom, the development of hearing preceded that of sight, as sound preceded colour. Colour is especially associated with the Fourth Ether, which is our particular ether connecting the three lower levels with the three higher in the constitution of the human unit.

The use of colours and sounds are of great significance in the Practice of Ritual Magic, in which the four corners of the compass are associated with The Four Archangels in the form of Telesmatic Figures showing their particular colours. In the days of Atlantis, the methods of controlling the elementals was by exploiting their knowledge of Colour and Sound. Eventually this was lost, due to its misuse. Some remnants of this science have persisted, or been rediscovered, and can still be used for good or ill.

Colour can be used for healing, but does not seem to be practiced very much. The trick is to find the right colour. An operator who has the faculty of seeing the colours in the aura has a ready indication of which colours to use. Exposure to the correct colour relieves discomfort of the more common functional ailments quite readily, and according to George King, can even be used to cure serious diseases such as cancer, but would needs the use of special lamps and an intensity of light. It was his intention to write a book on this use of colour until he was moved to devote his energies to the metaphysical during the world crises of that period.

A friend of mine in New Zealand professed the ability to associate a particular colour with the basic colour code for embryological tissue and used this as a guide towards selecting the right colour. By a putting a sequence of coloured slides in a projector, he would change it until a feeling of well being resulted. He claimed dramatic results in cases of migraine, and that animals always responded well. Equipment for this method is now advertised on the Internet.

Green taken from the middle of the spectrum, has a calming effect and is used at the beginning and the end of a treatment. It is also suitable for establishing the correct ambience for meditation sessions.

Yellow is useful for mental disturbance and is the colour of wisdom, and, apart from its therapeutic applications, is popular for decorating schoolrooms.

Orange is a stimulating colour when applied to areas corresponding to the various organs, and is selected treatment involving the circulatory system.

The colour Red, concentrated on rheumatic joints, is very beneficial, but is not recommended for any other conditions.

Blue has the effect of cooling and relieving emotional stress, and a subdued blue light is helpful in some people with insomnia.

Violet is the colour of transmutation, and stimulates the flow of energy between the chakras. It streams from the Logos of the Earth whenever requested, and forms an essential part of the Ritual of The Presence.

This is a very brief summary of the indications for colour in therapy. For more information, there are number of books on the subject. This account is based on the book by George King and Richard Lawrence, "Realize Your Inner Potential."

Alien Medicine

Adrian Dvir – born in Hungary 1958, died in Israel 2004.

Do you want to know the weirdest of all systems of healing? Well, there is a website of Adrian Dvir for you to check this if you are so inclined (www.etmedical.com), on which there are videos by enthusiasts who were cured of diseases regarded as incurable. Adrian Dvir was a computer engineer in Israel with remarkable psychic faculties. He had communication with aliens from different parts of the galaxy and parallel universes. Since his death in 2004, his website is being maintained.

According to information on his website, The Alien Council's purpose is to include planet Earth as a member in their organization of 17, 45 and 68 Alien Planetary organizations, which have made their presence known on Earth for collaboration, with 54 of these in medical activity. This all seems very fanciful, but evidence lies in the cures by the insertion of very small prostheses, and the videos of those who were cured of what were otherwise incurable conditions.

There is more in the book by Adrian Dvir, "Healing Entities and Aliens." This extraterrestrial activity started in Israel in 1995. Alien medical teams from other realms or dimensions cure humans at Healers-Mediums' alternative medicine clinics. Patients feel strange sensations during the treatments (itching, heat or cold, increase or decrease in gravity sensations and many more) and some even see and communicate with the alien medical teams.

The number of clinics has increased steadily and, as of 2003, there were 50 clinics in Israel, and 464 in the USA (according to the aliens). Alien alternative medicine clinics also exist in other countries England, Denmark, Australia. ET medical activity helps to raise public awareness and increase acceptance of alien existence.

The aliens treat humans in alternative medicine clinics only after the patients give their full consent. No abductions take place. In addition to the alien medical activity, they willingly collaborate and answer questions on different issues including: information about aliens and their activity on Earth, general science, astrophysics, and even Earth events.

Alien information about Time describes the difference in the Time Scales in different parts of the universe. The clinics are quarantined during the visits of one group, because the time difference of their environment in which they operate is several times faster than on Earth.

Information on the Soul and pathologies involving its diversity, constitute interesting case histories related by an alien physician, and forms part of the book by Adrian Dvir. It was some months later that I learned of the Lord Sananda's treatise on the multiple nature of the soul.

Spiritual Healing

There are a number of healing methods under the category of "The Laying On Of Hands," sometimes called "Spiritual Healing," and this literally allows healing power to be transferred to the sufferer from and through the practitioner.

To heal from one's own store of vitality will cause the operator to feel run down and is not recommended. The correct way is for the power to be requested from that infinite reservoir of energy held in the workings of the Cosmos, and, in this solar system, comes directly from and through the Sun. Anybody can function in this way, with the correct attitude and expectancy of channelling healing power. It is free and should remain free of charges, although a modern trend is to charge a fee. if only to cover rent and expenses.

I only know of two principal methods. One is by an exercise of mind and ritually charging one's self with the ability to transfer healing power, applying it to areas of the body from above downwards. This can be learned and practiced by reading the book "You Too Can Heal" by George King, my mentor in all things spiritual as well as the metaphysical.

The other system, which I investigated and learned from a friend who was a Reiki Master, is similar and more like the traditional laying on of hands. In this one, there is usually a requirement for personal initiation, and a certain fee for a weekend seminar. It has a very interesting history and was developed by a Japanese monk, who had a very mystical experience leading up to his learning it. There is no doubt that it is a potent method, but has the disadvantages of taking longer and the need for a suitable couch. The fee-paying structure which has developed leaves me feeling bit uneasy. It is apparent that it is now regarded as a career. On the other hand, it is practiced gratis in many cases.

Both techniques lend themselves nicely to the way healing can be transmitted in absentia, for which distance is no barrier. There is only one essential requirement for this type of healing, and that is the acceptance of a Universal Power being available on request. You can also heal yourself.

The following practice, called "The Ritual of The Presence," was given by The Lord Aetherius as a preparation for meditation or healing. This balances the energy channels and has a transmuting effect.

The Ritual of The Presence

Stand erect, or sit on a wooden chair. Put the left hand over the right hand placed over the solar plexus. Imagine a brilliant white light descending from above, filling the brain and penetrating the body down to the lower end of the sternum (breast bone). It is possible to feel a tingling in the head when doing this.

Next, imagine the Deep Violet Transmuting Flame from the Logos of the Earth ascending through the body up to the chest, amalgamate the two forces and send them up to the Golden Sphere 40ft. above the head.

Then, summon its Golden Light down the body through the feet, filling the auric envelope. You can then send it back up to the Golden Sphere as advised by Aetherius.

Ayurveda

This account would not be complete without mention of other ancient systems, notably the use of herbs, a knowledge of which in the West is rather skimpy nowadays, compared with that of the East where it is used in connection with acupuncture. Often, both are used as an adjunct to modern methods.

The ancient Indian system of Ayurveda also relies heavily on herbal lore, and uses certain coloured minerals in their connection with the Five Elements. To learn the Ayurvedic system one had to be to be fluent in Sanskrit, which was only taught in India.

It is now taught in metropolitan cities without having to learn that language. I once went to the university in Tasmania on a two weeks course to learn the rudiments of Sanskrit. The written form is outrageously complex using an ancient alphabet without any spaces between words. From the position of a linguist, it has been described as the most perfect language. I would say it is the most difficult.

On a historical note, the medicine practiced in Europe was for centuries based on The Four Elements, going under the name of The Four Humours following the teaching of Galen in the tradition of ancient Greece. This led to the practice of bloodletting which probably never benefited anyone, especially women who were often anemic. An interesting exception is a disorder which makes an excess of red corpuscles requiring the regular removal of a litre of blood. Such a person can live to a ripe old age.

The ancient Egyptians developed a system of surgery, and their instruments compare closely with those of modern times. The constraint on practitioners was that they were taught to recognise and leave those conditions known to be incurable, lest they be subjected to the accusation of causing death.

Some Metaphysical Aspects Involved In Eating

The food we eat is essentially a vehicle for the element of prana, just as is the air we breathe. Food prepared by a cook who is feeling angry and resentful, may well alter the pranic content in a negative way. There is a lot to be said in favour of home cooking. The Master Aetherius gave a little formula to correct this when eating out.

All direct contact transmits a minor exchange of personal prana, as in hugs, handshakes, etc. When you are fingering the ripeness and desirability of fruit and vegetables in the supermarket, you are actually leaving a bit of yourself there, but do not feel guilty as it is so minimal and subtle as to be insignificant. Some people wash produce anyway, and this is considered worthwhile for removing any pesticides.

I am not a vegetarian. My younger son decided to avoid eating meat when he was about eighteen. I have learned some vegetarian dishes for when he makes his weekly visits. It may contribute to the development of paranormal faculties, if that is what you want. The little connection I have with the unseen worlds has been a mixed blessing, and an embarrassment at times.

Fasting

A 24-hour fast at the New Moon and the Full Moon was recommended by George King. Some Shamanic training involved fasting for three days to allow the spirit to leave the body, an experience related to me by my old friend the magician in New Zealand in his recollection as a trainee in a previous life as a Maori.

It has been shown that it is possible to live without eating. However, this faculty is the prerogative of Saints and Yogis, who by some divine privilege have been granted this in the course of advanced yogic practice. A number of such instances are recorded in Yogananda's Autobiography. They take energy direct from the Sun or the planetary Logos. This also applies to inhabitants of the other planets.

St Teresa of Avila is a well authenticated example of a Christian saint who, after permission by the local bishop, had an X-ray examination showing that her stomach had shrunk into an appearance of tube, consistent with her diet of only a wafer of the sacrament daily. This is added to illustrate that the force of prana is all that is required, and is peculiar to the advanced states of spiritual evolution common on other planets.

Ordinary types like you and I have to rely on the prana in food, but the merit from Yoga breathing exercises is heartily endorsed for healthy living. I must say, I quite like food, and have no desire to live on prana in that way. In any case, I will have to wait until elevated to that phase of existence living on pure energy in some life in the remote future.

The food we eat is essentially a vehicle for the element of prana, just as is the air we breathe. Its quality varies in the different foods. In the principles of Chinese Acupuncture, a diet is advocated consisting of a balanced intake of Yin and Yang foods. Red meat, dairy products and eggs are very Yang, and also beans and cereals. Processed foods, sugar, alcohol, fruit and root vegetables are Yin. Tiredness and lack of energy are blamed on too much Yin. Over action and excitability result from too much Yang food.

At one time, it was a practice to balance the Four Elements in the choice of foods. This is the subject of a book "The Physiologia of Jean Fenel (by Jean Fenel, 1567)," originally in Latin of course, as were all literary works in those days.

Human Evolution and Pre-History

We are very ancient beings and did not always have human frames.

Darwinism proposes that mankind derives from an apelike predecessor and, supported by various skeletal remnants, remains the accepted scientific theory. The missing link has been sought in vain, and one item particular proved to be a hoax regarding a certain skull fragment. The controversy between the Darwinian enthusiasts and those adhering to the Biblical version continues. Neither is correct. Some chapters of the Bible shed some light on the problem, particularly in The Book of Genesis, if it is read in an allegorical sense.

The most satisfactory version for the metaphysically inclined, is to be found in the Stanzas of Dzyan, and commentaries in "The Secret Doctrine" by Helena Blavatsky. There are several hundred stanzas, hidden and preserved on imperishable material in the fastnesses of the Himalayas. Only a limited number are used as pertinent to the esoteric history of humanity and its preceding phases.

During the geological upheavals of the Earth, the continents have changed many times, so that much of the archaeological evidence lies below the sea bed or mangled beyond recognition in convoluted layers of rock.

The early stages of prehuman existence were of an ethereal substance, and so left no possible traces. According to this ancient tradition, the earliest root race was of a highly spiritual nature and conscious of its divine origin. They lived for thousands of years, and in all probability inside the Earth when it was still in a semi-gaseous state (according to Rudolph Steiner). These beings had spheroidal bodies of ethereal substance. They reproduced by budding a replica of themselves. It made them virtually immortal during that particular epoch, which lasted probably, for the duration of the first globe in the series of the seven globes of this chain. The next two root races related to the second and third globes. (Ref: The Globes and Chains of Earth.)

During the second phase, individual buds separated and were left to mature in the rays of the sun to form a hardened shell-like covering, to emerge after some years. It was not until the third cycle, on the third globe of the earth that an androgynous being evolved. That is, after recapitulating the previous stages. These creatures were still only conscious in a very rudimentary sense, yet were conscious on a spiritual level inconceivable to us.

It was not until this, our fourth Earth (or globe), that the separation of the sexes occurred and, again only after the mandatory recapitulation of previous stages. You can see now, how the whole process accelerates from globe to globe, and millions and millions years are encompassed in the early stages of development.

It was much later that the separation of the sexes occurred, and something resembling the human form developed. And so, the Lemurians and then the Atlanteans, huge in size and mental capacity as they were, much of which today is hard cognition and thought was instinctive to them, which made them magicians par excellence. Some glorified themselves to

the degree that they refused to acknowledge their divine origin
and tried to perpetuate their physical existence indefinitely.

This was the beginning of black magic on this earth, and
resulted in the destruction of both civilisations in atomic wars
between their different factions. Lengthy periods of mutation
and barbarism ensued, as a result of radiation pollution.
Therein lie the foundation and cause of present-day distress,
compounding the effect of destroying our previous planet. The
asteroid belt is all that remains of what was once an Earth-like
world.

Evolution proceeds regardless of hiccups and temporary
reversals, and is built into the manifestation of objectivity
and its laws. There is no escaping the eventual emergence of
intelligent life from the three lower kingdoms, and nothing
to stop the metamorphosis of the human phase into the
superhuman.

This is analogous to that of the caterpillar into a butterfly,
but for man it takes thousands of different lives. Each, in its
personal integration develops into a superconscious unit of a
group. This occurs when the lower self becomes united with
the higher. At that stage, freewill is abandoned as a useless and
selfish thing, and the whole essence of action is to sense and
assist those lives linking the lower levels of the evolutionary
path in service to Cosmic Evolution. Individuality is preserved
and even accentuated.

The human phase is quite brief in comparison to the superhuman
condition which follows in a seemingly never-ending ascension
into levels of existence still to be achieved by the Perfects of

Saturn. The Cosmic Plan forms an ever increasing integration of groups, into bigger and bigger groups, up to formation of the Logos of a Planet. To continue this idea further, it is envisaged that Planetary Logoi eventually, after millions and millions of years, which may well extend into successive cycles of creation, become Solar Logoi.

Even beyond that, there is a vast number of galaxies which are themselves conscious beings. Look up into the night sky, and see the myriads and myriads of stars, which in a timed exposed photograph of a small area, reveals an even greater condensations of stars and galaxies. Therein lies the remote destiny of humanity and Life in general. But, long before that, we will achieve interstellar travel to patrol and investigate the galaxy and beyond.

There Were Giants In Those Days
(Gen. 6, v 1–4.)

There is more to the history of prehistoric man. Large footprints have been found in both Australia and Texas dating back 140 million years. These would appear to belong to a different race of Man, just as the Neanderthal variation made a relatively brief appearance. This all started in 1943 by paleontologist Ralph von Koenigswald, who discovered fossilised teeth in China which proved to be like the human molars but six times as large. Fossilisation takes thousands of years to form. Chinese apothecary shops had been using these as an aphrodisiac when ground into powder.

After massive hand tools were found in digs performed in a dried river bed north of Bathurst (Western Australia), this led to the finding of a large quartzitised fossil of a human molar. A giant tool-making race must have preceded the Aborigines by many thousands of years. There is reference to other races of man in their folklore including giants.

When Koenigswald transferred his researches to Java he found a fossilised fragment of an enormous jawbone with three human teeth The estimated height of this specimen was calculated to be 13 feet. Similar finds were to show up in other parts of the world in China, Africa and Southeast Asia. The contention as whether these were giant apes or humans continues.

It is now established that Aboriginal man came into Australia over 40,000 years ago. Sometime later, approximately 20,000 years ago the land bridge connecting Asia with Australia was covered by the melting ice.

A geologist, Rex Gilroy, decided to investigate the ancient dried river beds for signs of a prehistoric man predating aboriginal man. That there were many animals of giant proportions suggests that there could have been very large men. The areas researched were believed to have been lush forests and swamp lands supporting many large species.

The section of the original Macquarie River (Australia) which once cut a gorge 100 feet high, created similar conditions in East Africa where Louis B. Kealey discovered fossil remains millions of years old. It was in this region of New South Wales (NSW) that the hand tools of great size and weight were unearthed. There were three phases of fossilised human remains described by Gilroy in that region of Bathurst, NSW.

The latest phase was not more than 10,000 years old. Deeper, there were signs of giants 60,000 years old, and approaching 30,000 years aboriginal remains in the same sites. This constituted the Mid-Phase. The lowest level revealed fossilised skull fragments compatible with a body of height 25 feet and estimated as 240,000 years old. It is well to note that these were not bony specimens, but because of the extreme antiquity had actually fossilised. The stone hand tools of the successive layers had weights varying from 8 to 25 pounds as deeper excavations proceeded. A fossilised human molar was discovered in a layer which was geologically 500,000 years old.

Fossilised footprints of giant feet are the next to consider. These also vary in size and could be related to particular geological times. The most outstanding of these (and from the attitude of some academics, the most outrageous of all), was the finding of human footprints preserved in volcanic lava from eruptions which occurred millions of years ago. These measured 2 feet in length and were 6 feet apart, indicating a stride of a 12-foot giant, and are in a place south of Penrith, NSW.

Human footprints 25 inches long have been seen by the side of dinosaur tracks on the banks of the Paluxy river in the dinosaur park near Glen Rose, Texas. The implications of human prints contemporary with dinosaurs contradict the notion that mankind was not to evolve for another 75 million years, or more.

There is enough evidence to revise the theories of ancient man in the face of discoveries made in the last few years. These findings are not exclusively Australian, and have been duplicated in other parts of the world.

To conclude this contentious theme, there is the case of the petrified finger, which was found in cretaceous limestone. It was part of a finger broken off below the middle joint. The full length would be 15 inches of a normal proportioned hand. CAT scans and chemical tests confirmed the bony features of a normal finger.

All this was taken from the website of Rex Gilroy (www. rexgilroy.com), who has written a number of books on this topic. His detailed researches into the historical accounts of the numerous recordings of encounters with the Yowie from both Aborigines and European settlers, suggest a remnant of the above may persist on a different level of vibrations and have access to some means of transference permitting intermittent visits and foraging. There are similar accounts in the US, and the districts of the Himalayas of an elusive creature of similar proportions. So far there has been no photographic evidence and the videos are obviously faked.

There are a few more geological findings worth of mention. A gold chain was found embedded in a coal seam. Elsewhere, a stainless steel screw was found embedded in rock. Microscopic examination of ancient soil samples have revealed nano-sized bits of metal, cylindrical in shape with closely coiled markings in helical pattern on the surface.

Were we visited by time travellers or cultures in the remote past who left these things? Of course you can always say that it is just another hoax, in which case the efforts to produce them deserve acclaim.

PART THREE

Being

Totality of BEING can only be vaguely appreciated, and for this purpose we resort to the Pythagorean Numbers and Shapes, which illustrate as fundamental any understanding of The Deity Concept. It is The Be All and End All of Existence in The Noumenal World of Kant, and which is The Ideal World of Plato.

Everything is represented as Perfect and Complete in Abstract Potential. Consideration of this idea will show that nothing there discreet of itself, but merges into an infinity of concepts.

This World of Abstraction exists in the Mind of The Absolute, and IS NOT before The Fiat "Create!" This is confusing, even to those who have spent a lifetime in the study of Philosophy, so do not be dismayed if it is not readily understood. Science is involved in the mysteries of the three-dimensional world. Metaphysical Theory tries to cover the multiple dimensions and the role of consciousness in evolutionary development over successive eternities. Although hopelessly inadequate because of our limitations in linear thought, it does a reasonably good job of it, producing an explanation of the working mechanisms of the Cosmos and its Laws. It helps to have imagination and a grasp of symbols in their implications.

It is a difficult exercise for many due to long held illusions, acceptance may be too uncomfortable to even contemplate questioning. It is a pity, as the only thing wrong with the world is ignorance. The irony is, that we have willingly contributed to it all ourselves.

In Truth lies Freedom, freedom from fear and prejudice, or I should say in the Study of It as far as we are concerned, seeing things, "As through a glass darkly," (Corinth 13, v.12)

As you are to be confronted with my version of things, let us clear up the misconceptions of what I prefer to call The Deity Concept. Those who are familiar with the ideas of Pythagoras, Leibniz, Spinoza and others, know they came to similar conclusions after a lengthy process. By such methods, it can be shown how the Deity Concept provides a framework on which the Cosmos operates in what is essentially a Manifestation of Law, and any personification of the agencies involved is made by ourselves. These agencies are beings vast and impersonal, of which the Highest in the Hierarchy exist largely on abstract levels. They effect streams of energy on different frequencies to keep things going in a finely-tuned fashion for life to exist in many different forms. They, in turn are part of the Will of the One in the Centre, Brahma, Jehovah and various names in the Hindu Pantheon.

The Hierarchical structure of Deity in Action has been described, and, for those so inclined, there are methods to invoke such energy as may deemed desirable for unselfish purposes. This commonly goes under the name of Dynamic Prayer, which is really a means of transferring energy. We are referring here to prayer which is in itself is a metaphysical exercise, requesting and radiating the power through the heart centre and the palms of the hands, in contrast to the Christian Church method of holding the palms together which holds the energy within and is thereby restricted. Do this after reciting the New Lord's Prayer (see later) and you will feel the heat as you maintain this posture. Hold it as long as you can. George King was able to do this for long periods and suffered burns to the tips of his fingers.

The energy foundation of the human organism allows it to be both a receiver and transmitter of spiritual power, especially during the Magnetisation Periods (ref. The Third Satellite), and allows it to be the foundation of Prayer Power.

The Ancients used this (ref. Exodus 17:12, Moses in the battle of Amalek).

Meditating

The purpose of Meditation is to unite with The Higher Self.

There is the complete silence before dawn. Not a leaf in the trees move. There are no clouds to create shadows of the bright moonlight. Then, there is the warbling of a magpie heard faintly in the distance, heralding the first light.

Such conditions lead the mind to thoughts challenging the nature of personality and the self. The persona is an ephemeral thing and only serves something greater, which is the Lifestream, which in turn experiences all that is demanded by that core of life conceived as Soul. How many incarnations are involved? Thousands? Perhaps millions.

At the end of repeated incarnations in different environments and, for all we know, on different planets, there is the completion of a circle. The summation of all lives becomes an Entity now fully aware and conscious as a Soul. It is neither male nor female, but an amalgamation of opposites. In addition there is the Third, which is neither, and this is the Divine Spark which has been present throughout.

This entity is no longer human, and is aware of the eternal Now outside of Time and can see Itself as Complete in the fullness of the Grand Cycle from Beginning to End. It recognises itself as a developing reflection of the Primary Trinity in a vista of evolution which recedes into realms of possibilities. The consciousness is that of a Group Soul, but in a paradoxical fashion Individuality remains forever.

If this is so, then why should I not invoke the assistance of my Higher Self to this unit of the lifestream? Power is transmissible throughout the Sutratma into the past and from the future by invoking the godlike SELF.

In the makeup of the human there is a sphere of golden light situated above the head. Mysteriously, this is a reflection of the Sun and ever at one with a Divine Spark central to the human body. There is an exercise to imagine this golden sphere, and feel oneself rising up to meet it. This is not so far-fetched as it seems. We know that there is such a thing as the transposition of Mind into faraway places, called Farseeing or Remote Viewing, which can be cultivated by a system of training. This was used for spying by both the US and Russia during the Cold War.

When the officers so employed became redundant, some of them set up in business to teach this technique. It is very much to their credit that they test you first to see if you have the potential. This is written about in the book, "Cosmic Voyage" by former Emory University professor, Dr Courtney Brown, who calls it "Scientific Remote Viewing."

The exercise of imagining yourself rising up through the roof and meeting The Golden Sphere is also described in the book by Mouni Sadhu. It is your Real Self. Sending the Mindstuff up to the Golden Sphere*, therefore, plays a part in involving and identifying with the Risen Self, and allows a request for uplifting power to surge throughout the lifestream, from the future and even from the end of time. You can then identify with the monad in the Eternal Now, and demand power from the Infinite Source of Power, and send it through time down the Sutratma connecting the different lives of your lifestream, for encouragement, love and guidance.

*Endnote. This forms part of the "Ritual of The Presence."

A Fantasy?

There are many questions which arise in my mind during the perambulations demanded in the interest of essential exercise. I am a lazy person and it requires considerable effort. On the basis of it being possible to make a fetish of such regular exercise, I do not make it a daily practice.

But on such an occasion I had these thoughts: The mystery of Time presents many paradoxes. ALL is in the ETERNAL NOW, so why do I have to wait for the results of my numerous lives to gain Enlightenment and Ascension into godlike status? As a unit of Consciousness, which is my indwelling monad, it is my right to ask for the privilege of accessing this state in the NOW, where I am also.

In the limitation of my present condition I did not think it likely to be able to receive any reply, but faintly and more gradually I felt that I was receiving an answer:

"THAT which determines the course of evolution in the myriads of galaxies and alternate universes and the Law behind All That, is quite capable of granting your request, which as being in possession of the monad is your privilege, as you have perceived. However, to grant your request would not give you the satisfaction you imagine, and would result in returning back to gain experience. There is also danger in prematurely gaining Mastership. All has been tried in the Outbreathings of ALL THAT in former Great Cycles, sometimes the results were disastrous and created monsters. I am only a voice and a minor official in the great Scheme and a server of IT, and know of these things. Rest assured your aspirations are noted, but you will only advance in accordance with the Law, and how long it takes is up to you."

You can never be too forward, if tempered by humility and respect in asking pertinent questions. We have minds, and are expected to use them in lively curiosity. There is no other way to Truth. Don't be afraid of it. You may find certain aspects you do not like, but that is because you are human with limited appreciation of what IS, or as one celestial group channelled, "You are ever limited in the linear (as an expression of Time)."

Polarity

Polarity is inescapable at every turn and is also inseparable from a third aspect, which is the monad, a feature to be emphasized in consideration of all metaphysical themes, and Chaos is at the Root of All Things before Time.

The whole of manifestation is founded on this principle if we take its origin from that stage of Primordial Chaos, preceding the formation of matter. In that inconceivable condition of Eternal Now in the mind of the Absolute, which we associate with the Trinity as resulting from Duality and its Polarity, All Things are created that have been, are, will be or even could be in a Static State of Potential. This is The Parabrahman of The Vedanta, the actual manifestation comes via the Divine Tetraktys, as Brahma in the Infinite Force of the opposing polarities. This is symbolised by the triangle inside the square surrounded by a circle.

Brahma in the dual role of spirit and matter, produces that which is a rarefied homogeneous primitive substance, which then becomes agitated and condensed into a state analogous to milk, from which particulate matter is precipitated. Eddies form masses of whirling gases, which become the galaxies of the visible universe. The ancients, in their peculiar imagery, made the concept of milk and the cow sacred symbols, and the bull in turn the embodiment of creative impulse.

These ideas are found in the Egyptian and Cretan civilisations. The cow is still very important in India, and is allowed to wander and forage freely. In a very picturesque fashion, the ancient Greeks visualised the Mother of the Universe arising from the Primordial Froth, as Venus born in The Foam of the Ocean, and is I believe the subject of a classical painting.

Chaos and the Source of Evil

This is bound up in the concept of polarity.

This idea, therefore, of a state of Chaos preceding Creation is a fundamental concept in metaphysical thought. What follows, is that chaos must still be around, always held in a state of balance by the Will and Mind of The Absolute, but still a factor to be reckoned with in the course of evolution in that lowest of the seven levels in which human development takes place. In this way, it can be seen why some of the scriptures relate the origin of evil with the creation of matter, giving rise to the mythical notion of the war in heaven. That is one level of it, more detail is to be found in the chapter entitled, "The Prometheus Myth."

Chaos is more apparent in the lower kingdoms, and has power due to their increased involution. In the higher levels of existence it has no power. We equate Chaos with Evil, as it obstructs the evolutionary process. It has limited reserves of energy in comparison with the Universal Source, but it is still formidable and greater on the astral levels where it is strongest. On this the material level, evil is more limited and ingeniously uses the failures and weaknesses of the human condition. It feeds on suffering and so promotes it – endlessly.

In this way it has been responsible for serious lapses in the history of the race, and goes back thousands of years into the remote periods of the Lemurian and Atlantean wars; and much further back before coming to Earth, after destroying their planet by tinkering with atomic power, and its use in war. These events resulted in very long periods of mutation and savagery in between, and have left us lagging behind in evolution in comparison with the other planets, a theme enlarged on elsewhere in the text.

There is mention in the texts of the Ancient Wisdom, of The Lords of The Dark Face of God, as being an essential feature of the universal maxim, "As Above, So Below." It comes from the very foundation of Creation, and is further symbolic of the so-called War in Heaven. It relates to the formation of matter, and is an ongoing thing.

The balance is maintained by The Will and Intent of The Mind of The Absolute, using the totality of manas (mind) in its multiple gradations and facets within a system of hierarchies. These are The Devic Hierarchies, some of which have been named in the old books of ceremonial magic, together with their demonic counterparts. These names are very important in the rituals of ceremonial magic in the invoking of such powers, whether light or dark, that is to say for good or ill.

The principal agencies of chaos dwell in the lower astral regions, and have learned how to prolong their lives there for thousands of years, thus avoiding for as long as possible the prospect of a succession of rebirths in severe limitation in response to the Law of Karma. Meanwhile, attempts to recruit those interested in the occult and the web of black magic continue, and are assisted by the growing drug culture which blunts the moral sense and the ability to see danger.

The principle weapon of the forces of evil is fear. By inducing fear into man it is possible to foment wars. Elements of evil feed off suffering.

The more wealth, the more the feeling of insecurity necessitating more armed guards, more electronic devices to protect possessions and to avoid kidnapping and extortion. The insecurity and fear in the very rich must be ever-present.

Rock music, is you can call it music, often comes with strobe lighting and voodoo rhythms. The shouting and raucous rendering of lyrics is often disruptive and disgusting in some rock music. It stultifies and obstructs all the uplifting emanations being released at this time. The effect on young people is disastrous, promoting mass hysteria and the adulation of the artists, who often present unwholesome appearances and foul mouths. Their drug addictions and drunkenness are bad examples to young minds already rebellious and lacking self-discipline, which is the result of misguided, laissez-faire upbringing, advocated by social scientists and psychologists.

This type of entertainment is the direct result of inspiration by the agents of chaos. Apparently, the numbers devoted to the corruption of humanity is limited so that a mass effect is obtained through a type of popular music.

Petty tyrants, greedy for power, are readily corrupted and lay themselves open to suggestions and dreams of conquest and power. All the famous tyrants of history have fallen for this path. Some even sought the inspiration and help from the main powers of hell, not knowing they were to become pawns, to be drawn and trapped in a web of evil. Hitler is a prime example by inviting his nemesis.

In conclusion, therefore, I suggest that the whole of manifestation is in a state of finely tuned control, of increasing perfection towards that which is abstract, and (as we behold it) is in a continued state of conflict. The same applies to the galaxy, in which there are space pirates and slave traders, raiding peoples with an advanced technology far better than ours. Some cultures are based on a policy of expansion and plunder, and make attacks on other planets. The galaxy is large with trillions of worlds, many harbouring intelligent life, humanoid and non-humanoid. We had escaped attention until quite recently, as in tale(s) related.

The Law of Three

Following the dissertation on Chaos, it seems appropriate to reassert the principle of Triplicity which is basic to All which is manifest. I have shown the origin of Chaos and the how the concept of Evil is associated as an essential opposition to Good and Evolution.

The principle of Triplicity is used to further advancement by the Powers behind the Law of Karma. I refer to the Sankhya doctrine of "The Three Gunas." In this part of Hindu philosophy the Three Gunas represent the three basic qualities of The Trinity, TAMAS, RAJA and SATTVA . The first two are the polarities, opposing forces held apart by the third, Sattva, and which can be called the Will and Intent of The Monad.

This Law influences all stages of life as part of the Inseparable Three, and is present in the circulation of energies between the trios of heavenly bodies. SATTVA is representative of The Son in The Christian Trinity, and is offset as opposed by a 4th Factor, which is the remnant of Chaos from the formation of matter.

Sex and The Monad

The attraction between the sexes can be regarded as a reflection of the Primal Polarity preceding Creation, and the flame of passion as that between the lower self and the higher. Their union is only achieved in the final surrender to the Soul, when all desire is sublimated, transmuted or merely exhausted, whichever way you care to look at it. This final Initiation of a human unit comprises a foreshadowing of a greater contact of the endowing lifestream with its integral component the monad. Complete union is deferred until the End.

I feel that I must point out that union with the monad is not properly effected during manifestation. This will not happen until the End, when the Grand Cycle is complete and All return to the One Source in the Abstraction of Being Not Being (As in "The Day Be With US" from the Stanzas of Dzyan in Blavatsky's Secret Doctrine).

Meanwhile, lasting contact is made, not union. This is often overlooked in the literature. Theoretically, the removal of one monad from its integral place in any lifestream, would cause the whole edifice of manifestation to collapse back into Itself. I wonder if it has ever happened, as we would never know.

The Soul is in opposite polarity with the human unit, so that for men it is feminine and for women it is masculine. Thus we have the phenomenon of nuns regarding themselves as Brides of Christ as representing the Church. Monks have to be content with devotion to the Goddess, in the person of The Mother of Christ. It should not be surprising, therefore, that the harsh suppression of the normal sexual impulse led to some bad habits in this otherwise saintly calling.

Not that this suppression was ever complete, as there are authentic reports of tunnels between convents and local monasteries. Numerous baby skeletons have been found in excavations around some old nunneries in Europe, according to Blavatsky. Sins are forgiven at confession, easing the conscience by imposing penances. These became a few prayers in latter days, but indulgences at one time could actually be bought. It became a source of wealth and extravagance in a corrupt priesthood. A redeeming factor is the presence of the beautiful cathedrals to which they contributed.

Money left in trust for the saying of Masses for one's soul is not unknown today, and, until a few years ago, were still being held for King Ludwig of Bavaria, famed for his magnificent palace and mysterious death.

The Devic Kingdom

The Angel motif is inherent in all myths. In Christianity, we find numerous references both biblical and historical. The name derives from a root meaning messenger, but esoteric information covers much more than that.

In the ancient texts of the Wisdom Tradition, they are called Devas, and there are described hierarchies of different orders in Hebrew, together with details of their opposing numbers which have been copied from other sources like Babylon and Egypt.

Four Principle Orders are commonly under the guise of the Four Archangels: Michael (south), Gabriel (west), Uriel (north) and Raphael (east). Each of these is associated with a direction of the compass and one of the four elements respectively – Fire, Water, Earth, and Air.

But our particular interest is more concerned with the role of the Devic Kingdom in the function and control of the metaphysical universe, and of course includes the physical material universe. Coincident with the monadic diaspora of Life, as we can perceive it, there was also that of the devas. There are the two types of monads, the same by definition but issued on a different ray, closely related yet effectively separated from communication. There are certain rituals by which contact can be made with the lower orders comprising the elemental kingdom. Anything higher requires high initiatory status, although they can be invoked by group ritual in the purity of intent. The evolution of men and angels run parallel. Human evolution is along the path of karmic experience, which is harder yet shorter than the devic.

The existence of the Devic Kingdom and knowledge of its nature and function, are fundamental to the appreciation of the metaphysical world. It is in negative polarity to the human kingdom and in the very remote future there is to be a union between the two.

The devas are the custodians of Prana. Mankind is the custodian of Manas, and as regards prana the devas are the energy of prana themselves, which they embody in some way, being basically of two types, those with a form and those without. Some books have been written based on information from individual devas through mediums. Any attempt to contact the devas presents the hazard of misinformation by astral intelligences representing themselves as devas.

In the past, communication was more common and could be safely invoked, but because of a resurgence of ritual magical practice of a disreputable nature, this avenue was virtually closed down somewhere around the 14th Century. Communication with angels remains possible, and in recent years seems to have become much more frequent, if the mass of information offered on the Internet is anything to go by, and is mentioned later in the text. One effect of the changes produced by metaphysical operations has been the opening of the gates for this type of channelling.

By means of ceremonial magic it is possible to persuade an angel to manifest itself. I met a man who claimed to be able to do this. He said they always had wings. He was a minister of a Christian church, and I said, "I hope the Bishop does not hear of your practising Ceremonial Magic." He said, "What if he does? I can always say that I am researching the Ancient Judaic Religion."

He demonstrated the method of invoking an Angel before a group of theosophists, complete with assistant and appropriate robes in the Pentagram Ritual. Unfortunately, nothing happened. I was not surprised. The atmosphere of scepticism which is likely to be present in any public gathering will create a barrier.

Here are a few aphorisms relating to Devas and Man from the from The Treatise on Cosmic Fire by Alice Bailey:

"Man demonstrates aspects of Divinity, Devas demonstrate attributes of divinity.
"Man is evolving the inner vision and must learn to see, Devas are evolving the inner hearing and must learn to hear.
"Both are imperfect, and an imperfect world is the result.
"Man aims at self-control, Devas evolve by being controlled.
"Man is innately Love, a force which produces coherency;
"Devas are innately intelligence producing activity."

The Devic Kingdom controls stability in the Cosmos and, in the Microcosm, Man. By sending out Love and Power to these divine agencies, they are helped in their work to stabilize the Earth as well as ourselves.

They are also agencies of Transmutation, a process which is now being speeded up.

The Storm Devas

In their role of the Devic Kingdom controlling the weather of this globe, they use the thoughts and emotions emanating from humanity, the quality of which determines in turn the quality of the weather patterns all over the world. Because of our centuries of uncontrolled thought and emotion, their corresponding effects are floods, droughts and storms.

In New Zealand, I was friendly with a couple of elderly magicians. They told me of a ritual performed in their house by visitors who proposed to cause an Angel to appear. This was not successful because one of them thought it was a cheek to make an Angel leave its work for the satisfying of someone's vanity in such a demonstration, and put up a mental barrier in the works. The rite did not succeed, in spite of an impressive ceremony and tuneful chanting.

Her husband was a grand old chap, he suffered badly from arthritis of the hip-joints, which nowadays is commonly relieved by a hip replacement. He bemoaned the fact that in spite of his extensive knowledge and training there was so little he could do in Practical Magic. Nevertheless, he was able to relate how he summoned the Deva of a great storm which threatened to demolish his house. The entity appeared as a face in the centre of as swirling cloud; after the appeal to slacken the intensity of the storm it disappeared and things immediately improved. I do not know if he realised the tremendous risk he was taking. Faltering, or a serious error in the ritual, is likely to cause the death of the magician in such an enterprise.

He related how another member of the brotherhood used to engage a fire elemental for drying the laundry outside on dull days. He berated him as he thought this was irresponsible and could have resulted in his house being burned down.

He recalled his previous life as a Shaman in the Maori tradition, and his wife had recollections of being murdered by a Welsh tribe when she was a Christian missionary during the Roman occupation.

Two other anecdotes relating to Storm Devas

Driving in severe weather a man realised that he could see the Deva of the Storm. He said by "By God, I can see you!" Then he heard a voice say. "You can see me, can you? Now feel me!" and the car was bounced about by the wind in very alarming way. Perhaps the devas are not devoid of a sense of humour. The man who told me this story is a Reiki master.

George King once summoned the Storm Deva during an unusually severe thunderstorm over London. The storm suddenly abated and drifted out to sea. In his account of this he emphasised the danger of this exercise, which could be fatal if there was a mistake in the ritual or even any hesitancy in its performance.

The Kabala

The full name is The Kabalistic Sephiroth, and is often called the Tree of Life. It is regarded as symbolic of the Microcosm (man) and The Cosmos. It is very ancient and was transmitted in oral fashion for thousands of years. The recorded version is of Judaic origin, but its origins are Babylon and Egypt.

An illustration of the Kabala shows ten circles, numbered from 1 to 10 in descending order, these are the Sephira and are intended to represent the formation of The Creation, The Three Supernals at the top of The Tree represent The Trinity and are abstract. The manifestation of the Creation is in the numbered sequence from above, Kether down to the lowest, which is the physical world Malkuth. The lower seven Sephira are related to planets, as shown on the diagram. The uppermost, Kether, is The Absolute, followed by Binah as the Primordial Chaos and the Zodiac. These three represent The Abstraction from which All is created and the Force of Creation derives.

The Right and the Left Columns are of positive and negative polarity, identical with the idea of Yin and Yang, and are called The Pillars of Boaz. The Middle Column is the path of the Kundalini Power situated at the base of the spine. When the Tree is super-imposed on the human frame in a diagram of the human body, the various Sephira are shown placed on the shoulders, hips and knees in the Judaic texts, together with the particular planets and their astrological symbols.

There are 32 Paths formed by the lines connecting the Sephira which, from below upwards, represent the grades of Initiation in the Mystery schools. The number of initiations required has been reduced to three by one of the most ancient Orders of Chivalry, in which I had the honour of being initiated while in New Zealand. The ultimate is a 33rd degree, alleged to give Total Freedom by either White or Black Magic. Some authorities say there are yet other grades higher than this.

The Tree of Life

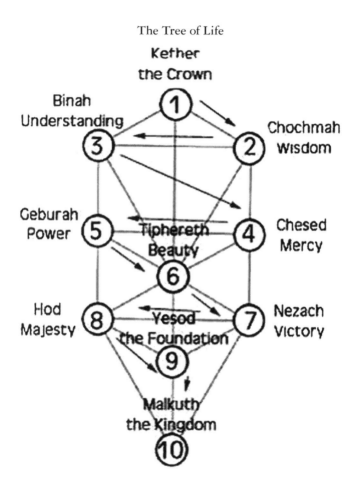

Each Sephira has a colour thought most appropriate to its heavenly symbol and, in the same way, so has each connecting line (or path). In the text of the Golden Dawn (Vol. 1), these colours differ according to which of The Four Kingdoms (mineral, vegetable, animal and human) is represented.

The Caduceus of Mercury is formed by twin serpents coiled three times around the Sephira, and the heads separated at the upper three facing outwards. It has been adopted worldwide as emblem of the medical profession. What is not generally known, is that contemplation of The Tree of Life inspired the notion that the pituitary gland was the controller of the endocrine system.

Regarding contemplation of The Tree of Life, it is possible to imagine the Sephira imposed on the physical frame, and is called The Way of The Middle Pillar, and is a form of Yoga. It is fully described in the book of that name by Israel Regardie.

An explanation of what appears to be an 11th Sephira on the Tree is in reference to a temporary psychic centre situated between the shoulders at the base of the neck during yogic development, called Daath or Daas, and is usually shown in dotted lines as it is not part of the Tree, or it is left out altogether.

The centre named Tiphareth is related to the Sun. It is the Heart Centre and the largest, more of which can be read in the chapters on Yoga and Soul. Suggestions for reading on the Kabala are, "The Middle Pillar" and "The Tree of Life" by Israel Regardie, and "The Golden Dawn" (Vol. 1).

There is a mass of information about The Kabala on the Internet. Alchemical websites show mediaeval art including many paintings representing stylised forms of the Kabala.

The Tree of Life can be used to represent the microcosm man, and the Universal Macrocosm.

Theology

I make no apology, for what may appear to be a bold and authoritative dissertation on this controversial topic, which encompasses the most profound of all religious and philosophical thought. This is the base and foundation of world religion, but rarely expressed because of the difficulty of expression, and the distortion presented by those who should have known better.

There is a tendency to avoid such terms as God and Religion in philosophical discourse, due to the misconceptions of what constitutes the Deity in Its anthropomorphising tradition. That is, the idea that IT has the qualities of being human, and even projected as an old gentleman with a flowing white beard, and a bad-tempered and impatient disposition towards human failings. This is due to certain aspects of the jealous god of the Old Testament, and the influence of the classical Greek pantheon, in which Zeus was father of the gods, and this was repeated in medieval art.

The name Religion, has the unfortunate connotations of historical strife, and an excuse for war and persecutions, and so the term Spiritual Philosophy is advocated for an approach to things of the Spirit, and the nature of Man as the Microcosm in its relation with the Cosmos. We have the written accounts of various Mystics and Cosmic Masters who have visited this planet throughout the ages. As far as the latter are concerned, they never wrote anything down themselves, and so we are reliant on the versions of their contemporaries, and often the memories of following generations.

To complicate things further, there have been successive copyings and translations from the original, such as Aramaic to Greek and Coptic, then Latin and finally into English. Herein lies the weakness of scriptures, the more ancient traditions were always transmitted orally for many years until somewhere about 2,000 BC. The weakness of language is only too obvious if we consider the profound misinterpretation which can result in the omission or obscuration of a negative prefix. The worst has been the misquoting of a passage in the Bible relating to Witches, and resulted in the cruel persecution and deaths of thousands of women.

In the last analysis we rely on our own judgement of what is perceived to be The Truth, and not what we would like to be The Truth, and this requires the Intuitive Faculty. This particularly applies to the most widely read book in the world, which is The Bible. The validity of much of the New Testament is being challenged by scholars researching the sources of the gospels, supplemented by the discovery of gospels which had been rejected by the early Church. How the Four were adopted makes interesting reading.

How the Four Gospels Were Chosen

There is an account of how the Four Gospels were chosen for the foundation of Catholic teaching. Some writers of the period asserted that the council of Nicea comprised 318 bishops who were illiterate, apart from two named who were well known to be scholars, and of course, the Emperor.

Quoting from the book, "Isis Unveiled" by Helena P. Blavatsky: "Notwithstanding the grandiloquent eulogium of Constantine, Sabinus the Bishop of Heraclea affirms that, 'Except for Constantine the emperor, and Eusabius Pamphilus (bishop of Caesarea) these bishops were a set of illiterates, simple creatures that understood nothing.'"

Quoting further from the same chapter of Isis Unveiled: In his Synodicon to that Council Pappus says: "Having promiscuously put all the books that were referred to the Council of Nicaea (June 19th, 325 AD) for determination under the communion table in a church, they (the bishops) besought the Lord that the inspired writings might get upon the table, while the spurious ones remained underneath; and it happened accordingly."

The divinity of Jesus was the most contentious of the Nicaean debates, the side that said he was God won over those who denied it. Eventually, reference to reincarnation was forbidden. In recent times a number of the so-called spurious gospels have been discovered including one by Philip, and others by James and Judas. There is also one by a woman, thought to have been Mary Magdalene.

The Deity Concept

And so, what is God? This is the most delicate and profound question of spiritual philosophy, as embraced in metaphysics. To emphasise the Primal Oneness as The Godhead is not enough. That which we maintain as being responsible for All That Is, in relation to our individual existence requires elucidation.

For this, we have recourse to the principle of The Monad, and is the favourite of those metaphysically-inclined philosophers and mystics who have bothered to consider the origin of consciousness. The Monad is to be regarded as synonymous with The Absolute, The Godhead, Spirit and Consciousness. Monads are inherent in all life, even in the atomic particles. Everything is destined to proceed into evolution through the lower three kingdoms, then into the brief human phase of thousands of lives, to higher forms of existence back to the One Source.

More than one cycle of Creation/Dissolution may be needed for passage from the lowest to the highest. The human phase passes into a condition of freedom incomprehensible to our limited conception of freedom, which, for the most part, means self-indulgence and pleasure. In the light of philosophical analysis the ultimate freedom is to be free from the restriction of form and bodily imprisonment, and is only possible after the surrender of Freewill, but only when the stage is reached where it is no longer required.

From a personal view, the closest relationship to Deity is The God Within. This is the same as the monad; that part which was released at foundation of the universe in what I call the

Monadic Diaspora, coincident with The Word as expressed in the Bible.

This divine spark is associated with the centre of the heart, in a place of completely empty space, as distinct from ordinary space, which is full of activity and those subatomic particles inferred by science. Herein lies a mystical significance of the heart, which is the power centre of the body and the core of its vitality. And so, the individual monad is a fragment of The Godhead, and the whole aim of life is to realise union with IT.

This requires eons of time and transition through the human phase, which is only a step towards higher states of consciousness. Millions of years of Soul Consciousness, in a body of pure energy called the Causal Body ensues, which permits free movement throughout space, in any form adapted for the occasion in the ethic of service.

Eventually, even that vehicle is abandoned and reduced to its basic units, and a Spirit Body is acquired compatible with Monadic Consciousness. Even then, complete union with the monad is only possible at the end of time, in "The Day Be With Us," as phrased in the archaic Stanzas of Dzyan (Blavatsky). Lasting contact, however, is made in the interim through the accession of Cosmic Consciousness.

The Highest aspect of God in our present concept of manifestation is the Solar Logos, which is the source of all life and energy in the solar system, and includes the most subtle of all energies – MANAS, which is mind, and only secondary to LOVE.

This is applicable to every level of existence. We are advised to remember this and to turn our faces to the Sun and invite its transmuting force, for which we are ever in debt for life and experience. I have this on the word of a Cosmic Master, Jesus himself, during the 8th of The Twelve Blessings, that the Sun is our highest expression of Deity. Call IT Brahma or Jehovah, as you like. This may come as a bit of a shock. It certainly was to me as I was fortunate enough to be present at the time that this Blessing was delivered. This is all you really need to know about Theology, unless you wish to delve into the mysteries of the Trinity and the Tetraktys, symbolised by using geometrical forms after the style of Pythagoras.

Salvation

It seems appropriate for this to follow as it forms the core of spirituality as envisaged in Christianity. I use the word Salvation to describe the condition that lifts the cloud of ignorance and suffering which bears down on us when we are unable to see that we are all gods, albeit in the embryonic stage. We are units in what is a racial entity, which is also a part of something greater still which contains ALL.

Salvation, therefore, is to be regarded as that spiritual state associated with Enlightenment, or degrees leading up to it, as in the case of man. The key for those wishing to hasten this process of upliftment and freedom is very simple. It is difficult although simple, and yet attempts should be made as there is nothing accomplished without its beginning. When an individual achieves that which is Enlightenment, there is some perception of Truth and inner knowledge of The Oneness from which All derives.

This becomes a small step to Universal freedom. Another light has been lit, illuminating that which is The Group Soul compounding the whole of humanity. Asked how this individual transmutation can be hastened, my feeling of ignorance and inadequacy forbids any specific answer. The age-old exhortation of The Masters of Yoga and past Avatars, who have tried to educate us in this matter from remotest antiquity, has to suffice: "Know Thy Self ."

The methods are various, and are basically founded in the metaphysics of Yoga as means for developing the ability to meditate, thereby subjugating that which is our personality and basic self-interest to become united with the higher level of consciousness which lies in potential within us all.

From this, you will perceive the idea of self-sacrifice and concern for others in unselfish service. This is Karma Yoga, the most powerful Yoga in these days. If you read The Twelve Blessings, it becomes apparent that Salvation is a theme central to it, and it is a tribute to those who sacrifice their Salvation on our behalf.

Worship

Great store is held in the minds of religious teachers of the importance of worship. Whether it is the worship of a Hindu Deity or the One God, it is of doubtful value in terms of getting enlightenment. In my opinion, IT does not want your worship. What IT can be perceived as wanting, if you like, is some effort to show Love in action towards fellow men and to Nature. There is no better way of doing this than by unselfish service.

The recognition of The Supreme Deity is also better achieved by Gratitude for Life and experience. There is only one prayer you need and it is, "Thy Will Be Done," and feel it when you say it. There is a universal and never-ending Blessing in the Love which is pouring through all manifestation. Our problem is not having accepted fully this tremendous power. We have closed off our minds by the strictures of the written word, and by being concerned with accumulating symbols of wealth.

When you send thoughts of thankfulness and love to Logos of the Sun, and repeat this every time you awake to another day, you are worshipping in the most effective way. When there is effort to realise your essential Oneness with IT, you are exciting the activity of your Soul, and herein lies the virtue and merit of Yogic practice. Singing hymns, and mouthing prayers in Church every Sunday, may make you feel good in church and forms a worthy social exercise, but do not register with the Lords of Karma.

The Cosmic Mother, The Creative Force, is Feminine

Yogananda's favourite conception of Deity was The Cosmic Mother.

The Primary Force is the Force of Evolution, and is also the Force of LOVE. IT is The Cosmic Mother, and like all good mothers does not brook any foolishness, and has arranged for LAW to be incorporated in manifestation. By this, mistakes are noted and suitable, just reactions result in a most precise training system throughout numerous lives. There is no judgement, other than that imposed by ourselves, in the most precise of all educative systems.

Spirit is regarded as Masculine and positive. Undifferentiated, it will not create, and has to have the opposing aspect for the unbounded facility of Creation as an expression of the Divine Will. There are groups of women who feel that the Paternal Aspect has been emphasised extravagantly, and promote the idea of Mother God. The idea of the Creative Force being Feminine does not sit well with orthodoxy, being conditioned to interpret The Father as fulfilling this role.

To try and attribute human qualities to the Divine has been the custom for thousands of years, and is called Anthropomorphism. IT is so far above the gods, it is ridiculous to associate IT with human features and emotions. IT is LOVE in ACTION as the force of evolution, and is the monad which dwells silently in everything and the same as that Singularity, The Absolute which is ALL.

This is the core of Metaphysical Philosophy. It is beyond Religion.

Operation Prayer Power

Operation Prayer Power was devised by George King, and was inaugurated on June 30th, 1973. Two years later (September 2nd, 1975), it was accepted as part of the Cosmic Plan for terrestrial salvation.

It is a fact that Prayer is a form of Magic, as when practised properly it is effective in the transfer of energies. Because of this it is important for prayer to be used with discretion, and never used in a manner to the detriment of anyone or group.

Prayer Power is used by groups in The Aetherius Society to invoke the energy and store it in radionic batteries to be released periodically, and in times of catastrophic events. Groups are trained in the technique. The leader receives the combined effect of prayer energy directed to him and in turn directs into a radionic battery, to be stored for discharge in a controlled manner.

The periodic discharge from the batteries is effective in reducing mortality and the number of casualties from disasters throughout the world. It is possible in this way to mitigate or even avoid and sometimes postpone these, until we are better prepared to deal with them. The prayer power of lone individuals, wherever they may be, is also used through the co-operation of a division of the Devic Heirarchy.

There are pilgrimages to some of the charged mountains throughout the year to practice The Twelve Blessings, during which ALL the other charged mountains release energy. Prayer Power is magnified 3,000 times during the visits by The Third

Satellite. The details of this metaphysical development are being freely discussed in this work.

Jesus gave a New Version of The Lord's Prayer, to allow the dissemination of spiritual power throughout the world, in these difficult days.

There is nothing wrong with the original Lord's Prayer, and will remain part of the Christian liturgy. The phrase "Thy Will Be Done" is the essence of all true prayers. (But THAT which is addressed would never lead you into temptation).

This is The New Lord's Prayer given by Jesus, through George King on Dec. 20th, 1961.

Oh Divine and Wondrous Spirit!
Oh Everlasting Lord of Hosts!
Send forth, now, through me
Thy great and lasting Power.

Allow me, oh mighty God, the lasting privilege,
Of radiating to all the world Thy great Love,
So that those who suffer may be given the
Power and energy to rise above their weaknesses.

Oh mighty God, in great humility do I ask you
To send forth Your Power.
To give to me this great lasting privilege,
Of being a channel so that my suffering brothers
May be helped and guided and healed and
Lifted into Thy Light.
So that they who know not may look up,

And in doing so, receive through their Higher Selves,
Your Divine Counsel.

Oh mighty God, this day have you granted me,
A Divine privilege.
I ask you, now, to give to me the strength,
So that never again will I turn from my inner vision of you;
Om Shanti, Shanti, Shanti.*

In praise of your Greatness, Oh God,
Doth my Soul sing.
Grant it energy to sing on
Forever and forever.

*(Shanti means Peace).

The singing of the soul is I think, an expression of its devotion
in service to the will of God.

Chivalry

The debt men owe to women is considerable. We seldom think of the risks and personal sacrifice involved in bringing new life into the world, and overall we have not treated them very well. There is karmic debt there, and all men should be aware of it.

The Concept of Chivalry dates back to the time of Henry II and his wife, Queen Eleanor of Aquitaine, who encouraged the idea of platonic relationships between the knights and ladies of the court, through the medium of poems and songs of travelling troubadours. This was further influenced by Mallory's version of The Arthurian Myth.

The knight was nothing without his horse, hence the name chivalry, from the French cheval, for a horse. An affluent knight travelled with three horses, one for travel, another for carrying personal effects and armour, a third was the destrier which was a heavy breed capable of carrying an armoured knight and had a temperament suited for battle. In addition, there was a pony or a mule for his squire (knight's attendant), if he was lucky.

The idea of nobility was associated with horsemanship. The privilege of knighthood became politically entrenched in recognition of the oath of fealty, and the prerogative of royal decree. It was adopted by some of the mystery schools, designating a certain level of initiation, and is used in the higher echelons of The Great White Brotherhood. Otherwise knighthood is relegated to the recognition of rock singers, football and cricket players, and, of course, politicians. Occasionally, the merit of someone who has been of great service to humanity is so rewarded. Now that the tradition of royalty is under public scrutiny in the UK, and confined to a small number of countries, it does not seem so important any more in public life.

In the more ancient times, predating the classical period, there was the idea of woman being sacred to the Goddess as a reflection of Nature and The Source of Life. Originally, in the more primitive eras, it was very important for a tribe to so protect its females to ensure the propagation of its members and thus have numerical viability. Failure to maintain adequate numbers in the tribal group was the most likely cause for the disappearance of the Neanderthals.

Unfortunately, nothing has prevented the abuse and exploitation of women throughout the ages, and is more apparent in some parts of the world than others. Our own society, which we are pleased to consider more enlightened, is not entirely blameless.

The Code of Chivalry survives in the hearts of all true men. The traditional courtesies, which are due to woman as the vessel of the future race and reflection of the Goddess, will be sustained. Women are allowed to become members and officiate in some Chivalric Orders. There are 14,200 sites on the Internet under the heading of Chivalry, and some approved by the Vatican.

The ancient principle of Knighthood is preserved on Shamballa. This ceremony was performed on December 5th, 1978, when George King was made Grand Knight Templar of The Inner Sanctum of The Holy Order of The Spiritual Heirarchy of Earth.

The Grail

This dissertation on Chivalry is not complete without a word on the Holy Grail. The Grail is a corruption of the expression Sang Royale, meaning Royal Blood, and is in reference to the cup used in The Last Supper. There is a mythological analogy in the ancient idea of the Greek Cornucopia, The Cauldron of The Celts, and the Argha, which is the ceremonial vessel of the Brahmin priests. Mystically, it is The Causal Body, the Vehicle of The Soul.

The Grail has also become emblematic of a bloodline supposed to have originated from the offspring of the family started by Jesus, and perpetuated in the line of the Merovingian Kings. This is a modern feature and is associated with the idea promoted in books describing the importance of a psychedelic mushroom being used in the sacred rites of the Essenes. I don't know if there is any truth in this, but it is well known that it forms an essential role in the training of a Shaman in Mexico.

It is held that the royal blood is, or should be blue! This is also bound up in the myth of an ancient bloodline. An interesting suggestion has been put forward, that the prevalence of copper required for blue blood is due to the appearance of such aliens in the kings of Atlantis and perpetuated in later times.

There are some very interesting stories on the Internet in this vein! Search for Merovingian kings for some good yarns.

The Grail became the essence of The Quest in the Arthurian myth, and derives from the Crusades, which we now know produced a disgraceful rampage through Eastern Europe on the pretext of freeing The Holy Land. A saving grace, one might say, was the effort made by The Knights Templar and The Knights of St John in their protection of travelling pilgrims and setting up of hospitals, fostering the concept of chivalry and knightly conduct.

The Quest is symbolic of the effort to attain a higher state of consciousness by the lower self, analogous to the battle of Kurukshetra in The Bhagavad Gita, and is essentially an inner conflict.

The Knights Templar, by the way, were not guilty of the excesses attributed to them. It was all lies spread by the church, and supported by the inventions of the interrogators, to which spurious admissions were made under the most frightful tortures, to make them reveal the secrets of their order. They made the mistake of being too influential and wealthy, by becoming the bankers of Europe and a source of finance to kings, notably the King of France who, at that time, was instrumental in their persecution at the behest of the Pope. I suspect that the king may have had a considerable debt, and welcomed the idea of not having to pay. Records also say that he was refused another large loan because he did not pay up.

The Templars were originally Christians, but they became adherents to the doctrines of the Essenes and Gnosticism. The outward show of Christianity was upheld as a necessary façade. They were on friendly terms with some of their Muslim enemies in the Crusades, who were of like disposition under Islam as Sufis.

Some of them escaped the persecution of the Spanish Inquisition and Henry 2nd of France, with their fleet and an appreciable amount of treasure, and settled in Scotland where they were welcomed by King Bruce. The modern version is not that of the early Templars, and, according to Blavatsky, was only allowed to exist under the shadow of the Jesuits.

Some of the Templar ships adopted the skull and crossbones as their flag, and raided ships of France and the Vatican in Mediterranean. They were the first to use The Jolly Roger.

Mysticism

This is an important part of metaphysics, and can be defined in various ways. We commonly associate it with the supernatural, but it is essentially related to the subject of UNION. This Union is that which occurs when the individual becomes conscious of being AT ONE with The ALL. Vulgarly, it is called God, but is a term I wish to avoid because of its many different conceptions. To appreciate the basics of Mysticism, it is necessary to know about the metaphysical aspects of both the Cosmos, and the Microcosm which is Man.

To begin with, the description of the Human Unit is founded on the idea that at the CORE of All Life, there is THAT from which it issued, and therefore by way of definition, IT identifies with The SOURCE as the Divine Spark present in every particle of existence.

This is The First Paradox. It is the MONADIC PRINCIPLE and has to be accepted before progress can be made. It is the Monadic Theory, familiar to students of Metaphysics, and the Philosophies of Plato, Kant, Spinoza and Leibniz (it was the latter who made use of the term monad).

Although I have written theory, it is more than that to the metaphysicist. It is a principle and axiomatic. The Mystical Union encountered in literature, both secular and religious, presents attempts to describe the indescribable. The authors have not experienced it, or if they have, are unable to find words. It is said be a beautification of wonder and ecstasy. There seems no doubt it leaves the experiencer forever changed.

Mostly, it is only an isolated flash or a dream in which time stops. For this to be sustained, we have to discuss Comic Consciousness, which I can mention as being familiar with the writings of one who was able to access this elevated condition. Regarding the actual experience, words fail, but the train of subjective experience of the phases leading up to it have been graphically described by George King in "The Nine Freedoms," which I believe is unique.

The procedure for obtaining Cosmic Consciousness is well known, but success is confined to those with the knowledge and experience of previous lives devoted to Yogic Practice. It involves a technique viewed as dangerous unless guided and closely supervised by the personal attention of a teacher advanced in Yoga. This is because it involves raising The Serpent Power residing at the base of the spine, which is The Kundalini. A course of Yoga, leading up to the method of raising the Kundalini, is to be found in the recent publication of a book, "Realise Your Inner Potential" by George King and Richard Lawrence. It was written after due consideration of its implications and possible risks. Of course there are other books and teachers who advertise. I advise caution in accepting such tuition. There is a variety of symptoms associated, even when it occurs spontaneously, but mostly of a minor and temporary nature.

Cosmic Consciousness is the acme of mystical experience. An Adept advanced in the technique is able to enter the trance-like state of Cosmic Consciousness in two minutes, under any conditions. It was done before the television cameras in the U.S. by George King, and I was present on such occasions during The Twelve Blessings in 1958. How this happens requires a more detailed description of esoteric anatomy; but let it suffice to say, that raising the Kundalini is not easy and if forced may produce its own range of pathologies, which are numerous and various – and some quite serious.

In the chapter on Time, I have presented a theory of how there could be a possibility of achieving The Now Moment, and consequently Cosmic Consciousness, by an understanding of the nature of Time.

Mysticism of Christianity

Mysticism through Christianity, by which I mean the Orthodox form to which it generally refers, is by the devotion to Jesus and in a monastic existence. Many Saints are so recorded, so let us not decry that which has been successful and ever worthy of praise. Although I criticise the Church, it remains a great source of spiritual power in spite of the errors in its dogma. The devotions and sacrifices of thousands have made it so. When a ritual, such as The Mass, is widely practised for over a thousand years it becomes a force.

The core of Truth that existed before the formation of the Church under the control and approval of Constantine was lost. It then became heresy to teach reincarnation, and fear became the prime feature of the dogma. Transubstantiation of the Host during the Mass became a necessary belief and free thinking was effectively discouraged. The word of the Pope is absolute. I was reared in this atmosphere of unquestionable belief.

Because the outdated doctrine the Church is under threat, the idea of being told what to believe without question becomes increasingly rejected. But the fear of dying without the final rites has caused some famous intellectuals to re-embrace this doctrine. There is nothing like a bit of insurance.

Mysticism comes directly from the appreciation of Truth and Spiritual Philosophy, and is better sought through the practice of Yoga and Meditation.

Love

LOVE is a Universal Force. It has as many degrees of power as there are levels of existence. It is the Force behind Evolution. Our emotions represent the lowest aspect of LOVE.

This power LOVE emanates from That which the Source of ALL things before Mind. It is Pure and Impersonal, and is the Will of God in action. To stay in tune with IT is the goal of all life in the higher states of being, and is the condition of Cosmic Masters. Being out of tune is the state of Humanity in the exercise of Freewill during the quest for experience.

The Power of Love cannot be rejected, by which all Life must return to the Original Source as conscious gods. When used for a definite purpose it will repeat its action increased four times if it is rejected, until the target complies or is destroyed. As such it is a transmuting power in the hands of gods and Cosmic Masters. An example of this is the defeat of the Entity in the planetoid that was transmuted by George King. Because of this, caution is needed in the use of this power. For example it must never be used to influence political leaders or to change anyone in their convictions.

LOVE is the medium to be used in prayer, it is then a transmission of this Energy. The commonly held notion of love confined to the idea of sentimentality and sexual attachment is not pure love.

The nearest thing to Love is that which necessitates unselfish sacrifice for another, or sacrificing one's life for some complete stranger, or even your enemy. But the greatest sacrifice, more than that of physical existence, is the Sacrifice of Salvation.

This is the cessation of spiritual evolution, giving up peace and bliss and the prospect of regaining it for many years. To take on physical limitation after the bliss of higher existence is the sacrifice for which there are no words. This is true impersonal LOVE, as exemplified by Jesus, and also by The Planetary Ones of the 4th Blessing.

In the metaphysical and the spiritual sense, Love is much more than that conceived by society in general. It is a Force which guides and propels us through seemingly endless cycles of rebirth along the evolutionary path. The goal of all living things is to go back to The One Source in an enhanced degree of consciousness, through the enrichment of karmic experience and unselfish service. This human phase, therefore, is the essential pivot of the evolutionary spiral.

This Energy LOVE is the healer and the answer to all the world's problems, without exception. It is not possession. It brings freedom. It is also sacrifice made in service, to help and uplift life into higher levels of consciousness. Everyone is capable of using this power, and to do this during the day permits its use sometime during the hours of sleep, but will not, as a rule, be remembered.

The Force of Love is The Christ Force and the manifest power of The Goddess, which is that aspect of The Trinity creating and evolving life forms. In the world today, there are some who have sacrificed themselves, giving up everything to be able to transmute the basic energies of Nature into that of Love and to give it freely to those in need. They are the subject of the Third Blessing. The full description of LOVE is included in transmissions by Mars Sector Six, and contained in the book "The Nine Freedoms," by George King.

We are fortunate to have incarnated in these crucial times, during which special spiritual opportunities prevail. The transmuting effect of LOVE is being released now as never before in the history of the Earth! Unless an effort is made to acknowledge and accept this power, most of it just passes through; but, even then, there is benefit by just being here in these strange and wonderful times.

If we fail to use these energies, we will not encounter these opportunities for spiritual advancement again for many generations: 287 lives, according to the Cosmic Master Aetherius.

The Mexican Sorcerers

(As adapted from the books by Carlos Castaneda.)

This deals with an ancient system of initiation used by adepts of the Yaqui Indians of Mexico. It predates the Toltec civilisation which was much earlier than the Aztecs, and, being unlike any of the better known techniques, seems worthy of including in these dissertations on the metaphysical. It is a Shamanic system.

Candidates for initiation are chosen according to the appearance of the aura, described as a doubling of the etheric body. After accepting the invitation (or in some cases conscription!), the candidate is subjected to a variety of confusing experiences, which eventually may take on a menacing aspect, even to the point of being life-threatening.

The aim of the nagual, or teacher, is to convince the pupil of an alternate reality. It would appear that initially the use of psychedelic drugs are used, as in the case of the author during his attempts to engage the nagual, Don Juan, to disclose information for his thesis on anthropology at the University of California. There were two substances used, a weed and a particular mushroom.

In the aim to achieve spiritual enlightenment, the novice is encouraged to think as a warrior in the role of stalking, which in essence is a relentless course of self-observation to overcome the lower self, truly reminiscent of the Arjuna situation in The Bhagavad Gita, and also the teaching of Gurdjieff. At the same time, effort is made to destroy any feeling of importance until a stage is reached called The Place of No Pity (i.e. self pity), and is associated with moving The Assembly Point. This notion of the assembly point is peculiar to the system. Everyone has it in a certain place in the auric complex, and by its shifting allows a different conception of reality.

From time to time, the nagual will unexpectedly smite the novice between the shoulders, which effected a shift in the assembly point and precipitated him into another world. Castaneda describes his confusion and resentment when subjected to this and a variety of strange experiences, including confrontation with women who were adepts in the techniques.

Some of the situations contrived were exceedingly complex. They were calculated to entrap the candidate into pursuing a tedious and systematic course of training, which could involve an incredible amount of theatrical subterfuge, sometimes over a number of years.

The method varies according to the type and predilection of the nagual, which could be classed as severe or gentle, in the degree to which the nagual is prepared to "indulge his folly," and sacrifice his impeccability by enduring the ignorance of his protégé. There are many facets of the system which defy equating with metaphysical thought, and make it all the more intriguing.

The adepts of the ancient system of Mexico refer to themselves as sorcerers, a term that has unfortunate connotations in the West with black magic, but I think this relates to translation difficulties from the Spanish dialect.

One of the sayings of his teacher, Don Juan was, "The condition of man is as though he lives in a large house of many rooms, is unable to get out, and can only perceive a blurred and distorted impression of outside through the windows, which is vague and misleading." And so it is; cf: "As through a glass darkly." (Paul: Cor. 13 v.12).

Carlos Castaneda is a pen name. His name was hidden until after his reported death in 1998. There has been much criticism of Castaneda's books, notably discrepancies on the impossible geography of certain journeys, during his trips to and fro with his mentor. Nevertheless, it remains for the reader to judge.

Magic

This is an important part of metaphysical lore. It is an ancient science, incomplete and a relic of Atlantean times, but still formidable in the right hands and continues to be practiced to this day. It persisted in the various mystery schools in secrecy under different names during persecution by the Christian church. In Europe, this led to its attrition and fragmentation. In the East, however, and particularly in Tibet, the tradition of Ritual Magic was able to continue undisturbed for centuries, and became grafted onto Buddhism.

Let it be understood that we are not referring to that which is Stage Magic, which is a form of illusion ingeniously contrived by the use of technology, suggestibility, and allowed only by the limitations of the human eye. The Magic herein referred to, is a system which utilises ancient knowledge and rituals, to achieve higher states of consciousness. This power has always been present, since the inception of polarity at the dawn of Creation, and is not to be trifled with as its use is strictly governed by Karmic Law.

Some of the ways in which it can be used will be alluded to, in what must be a brief account owing to the vastness and esoteric complexity of the subject, and my limited knowledge.

The classification of method is along the lines of purity and altruistic intent of the operator(s), as against the absence of it. Usually, it is performed by groups trained in the tradition. It is a brave soul who undertakes to go it alone. And so, there are two kinds of magic: White and Black, and, in between, degrees of Gray. White Magic uses that particular energy which is Impersonal Love, and is only directly accessible by the Soul, meaning that Soul Consciousness is necessary to wield this power by the sole operator.

The energy of magic is under the control of intelligences (these are the Devas who are the energy themselves) capable of the manipulations of energies commonly spoken of as miracles, under the direction of an Adept. As in all energy, it is Prana and can be used mitigate conditions and to manipulate Karma, and is so used in personal sacrifice and accepting temporary limitation. Jesus is the classical example of this.

For us lesser mortals, we are restricted to performing those rituals and affirmations, reciting names of principalities and god names, in a paraphernalia of vestments and amulets etc, which constitute the performance of Ritual Magic. This is performed by groups well-versed in the routine, with a modicum of secrecy and discretion. The aim is to See and to Know and to become as we should Be.

White Magic is a form of Yoga to assist in Self Realization, and if performed properly, invokes a power which enters those present. One aspect in the mystery schools is a social one of brotherhood and mutual assistance, and is most pronounced in one which is the most famous. This also applies to The Wicca, an ancient Celtic system involving herbal lore and spells. It is usually the prerogative of women, and was originally a fertility rite invoking a lunar deity, and recognising the importance of the Earth Mother.

Witchcraft (Wicca) has seen a resurgence in recent years, and is openly accepted. In its pure form, it is a good and beneficial force for the members, and the Earth Itself. In ancient times, human sacrifice was sometimes used to ensure good harvests. A parallel theme can be applied to the Druids, but they were more concerned with Sun worship.

Black Magic's modus operandi is much the same as for White Magic, the difference being that of intent, which is essentially for selfish purposes, or calculated to do harm.

Satanic rituals are of a revolting type and may include a human sacrifice. It so happens that the devic agencies employed, and which manipulate the powers invoked, are not particular as to the purpose. Such exploitation of these agencies carries a heavy karmic debt.

A sophisticated form of Black Magic is prevalent in India. There is the account of a man who fell afoul of an important personage when he was living in India. A magician was employed to arrange his death by some mystical means, which is quite possible to do at a distance. It is usual to allow the victim to learn of this, as fear is important to ensure success. However, the man sought the advice of a Yogi, who gave him instruction how to ensure that the evil energy dart was reflected. As a result it was the magician who died.

The psychic centres amenable to activation by ritual magic are those situated above the diaphragm in White Magic, and those below in the case of Black Magic. The black magician is a pawn of Adepts of Black Magic residing on the lower astral realms, and aims to become as one of them and prolong existence there for thousands of years. The role of the Black seems to be an integral part of the balance of chaos in the material world, which, together with the astral, is the battleground of evolutionary endeavour, which is being heavily contested in these days of change. The study of Chaos in scientific thought has become quite prominent in recent publications, and worthy of reference for the philosopher.

In **Gray Magic**, the degree or shade is determined by the quality of intent and an estimation of whether harm is involved. The intensity of projected thought can have a devastating effect when used by concentrated trained minds.

To this end, peculiar methods of potentiating this are known to be used in certain communities, and involves the making and abusing of dolls and images of those who are to be the target. This goes under the name of Sympathetic Magic, which may only be an aid to the concentration of the operator, but is definitely black magic.

It is a fact that prayer is also a form of magic, as it involves the transfer of energies. We are told that, when performed diligently, passionately, and with concentrated entreaty, it is a potent method for healing and spiritual uplifting of the world. It is then part of White Magic. On the other hand, prayers devoted to the death or misfortune of enemies and their leaders is Black Magic! This bodes ill for all those congregations and church ministers who have so indulged in times of war, according to Karmic Law.

There is a program for individual and lone indulgence for an early achievement of Self-Realisation by Magic, which is the Ritual of Abramelin the Mage.

The Ritual of Abramelin The Mage

This was discovered and translated by a member of The Golden Dawn. It describes in detail how to achieve the goal, referred to as The Conversation With The Guardian Angel, which is regarded as the same as The Solar Angel, The Higher Consciousness and The Soul. Anyone over forty was said to be too old, but this can be read in the context of ancient times. The candidate has to shave the head and retire in seclusion to a rural area in close vicinity to a grove of trees and a brook.

A personal servant, of proven loyalty and an unflappable disposition, proficient in housekeeping and committed to six months service, is obligatory. The performance of the marriage rite is restricted to once a week. There follows a very rigorous six months regimen of spiritual exercises, prayers and meditation, and regular and frequent rituals, accompanied by vocal exhortations and appeals to The Angel. The whole experience is described in a book written by a man who had the courage and endurance to complete the course. He had a very difficult time of it. His book is a pocket sized paperback called The Sacred Magician, under the pen name Chevalier, and emphasises the danger and extreme trials of solitary experimentation in Ritual Magic.

Dr John Dee

The Father of Magic in England

This article on Dr John Dee has been included because of his profound influence on metaphysics in the Renaissance in England, in which he was responsible for introducing Hermetism and Ceremonial Magic. He was born on 13th July, 1527. At the age of fifteen, he enrolled in Cambridge University and, after graduation, was made a fellow of Trinity College and appointed as Greek Underwriter.

He rapidly became involved in academic society while travelling on the continent and lecturing on geometry between 1547 and 1551, during which time he was engaged in espionage and signed his letters to the Queen by the code '007,' which was used by the author, Ian Fleming, in the exploits of James Bond. On his return from Europe, he was given the post of teaching navigation to naval captains, and continued in this capacity for 30 years.

He narrowly escaped being burnt when Queen Mary Tudor accused him of sorcery, because of his researches into Alchemy. As it was, he only spent a few months in prison and soon gained favour when Elizabeth became queen. He became established as court astrologer, determined the date of her coronation, and advised the use of fire in naval battles after receiving tips from a spirit. This was used effectively by Drake when he sent burning ships among the anchored Spanish fleet.

However, John Dee became most famous for his experiments in the Occult and his attempts to contact the spirit world. It appears that he had some sort of psychic experiences and dreams which set him on this path. To assist him, he employed a gifted psychic named Edward Kelly, in spite of his being a con. man with a criminal record. This type of research became his main interest for the rest of his life and he had some success in raising spirits, in particular the shade of Appollonius. It was said to have been a very dreary and disappointing affair.

Like so many of his contemporaries, he dabbled in Alchemy in search of the mythical Philosopher's Stone. His fame in this respect led him in 1583 to Europe on the invitation of a Polish nobleman, but it has also been suggested that it became unsafe for him to remain in England because of activities which could be related to witchcraft.

Unfortunately, when his patron lost heavily by gambling, he could no longer afford them but kindly paid their fare to Prague (1586) with an introduction to Emperor Rudolph. He was well received there and spent several months in his researches until the Pope got wind of his activities and gave Rudolph the option of dismissing him or executing him. The Pope had an exceedingly long arm in those days. There followed a period of unemployment. They eked out a living on the streets telling fortunes, until they managed to convince King Stephen of Bohemia (Czechoslovakia) in a scheme to get rid of the emperor Rudolph. This did not last long and they were soon dismissed as an unnecessary extravagance, but were again lucky in conning another nobleman to finance their researches for two years. It seems that Dee had a partner in Kelly who could be very persuasive.

Both men took their wives with them on their travels, and it is recorded how this eventually ended the partnership. Edward Kelly insisted that they should indulge in wife swapping, which persisted for a time until Dee resisted and then left for England, where he was promptly appointed Chancellor of St Paul's. Later, in 1595, he left that post to become an official of Manchester College.

His retirement was spent in greatly reduced circumstances. When he returned from Europe he found that his house, the library, and laboratory had been completely vandalised. King James regarded him with suspicion as a possible sorcerer, and so he was not welcome at court. He died in 1608 in poverty aged 81. Edward Kelly had died in Europe in 1597, after he fell from a building while escaping from custody.

John Dee is memorable for introducing Renaissance-inspired Hermeticism to Britain and for his influence in the court of Queen Elizabeth as an astrologer. He had an interesting life researching Alchemy at the expense of certain wealthy persons in Europe, and was the first to indulge in Spiritualism with the assistance of his partner, Edward Kelly. He left five lengthy works on Magic which became the core of the modern mystery schools, using his discovery of the Enochian language. They are available, translated from the Latin in an abbreviated form, as "John Dee's Five Books of Mystery: Original Source Books on Enochian Magic," by Joseph Pearson.

Sleep

The purpose of this phase of existence is to wake up. Gurdjieff

The subject of Sleep has some interesting features in the light of metaphysical thought. It remains a mystery. We spend a large part of our lives in this unconscious state; without it we soon go to pieces. In effect, you might say, it is a way of recharging our batteries as we are basically electromagnetic. Some rare individuals, resenting this time wasted, decided to go without sleep. They always had to recourse to "cat naps" in spite of resistance, which, if persisted, result in brief losses of consciousness, hallucinations and gaps in concentration. Without a reasonable amount of sleep, accidents and errors of judgement occur. Prolonged sleep deprivation causes hallucinations and metabolic dysfunction. Regrettably, it is commonly used in interrogation by totalitarian states, and I suspect by some democracies.

Scientific electronic metering has provided some information about the brain during sleep. It is found that a low level of electrical activity is continued during deep sleep, and is enhanced in REM (Rapid Eye Movement) sleep associated with dreaming. This seems to be a normal sleep pattern, and does not happen during drugged sleep.

Occasionally, dreams of a numinous and startling character can be related to mythical themes and symbols used in the interpretation of dreams. Carl Jung, famed for his work on the subconscious wrote a considerable amount on this. Most commonly, dreams are merely a garbled rehash of the day's events interwoven with elements of fear and desire. On the darker side, such dreams may portray the hidden desires, passions and violent conflicts, which are never to our credit in terms of Karma.

During the hours of sleep, the mindstuff can travel into the future, and be recalled later to predict events, which are usually of a catastrophic nature. James Dunne, in his book "An Experiment In Time," described how he recorded his dreams meticulously in order to do this, apparently with some success. I am not aware of his research into dreams having been repeated.

The state of mind and physical relaxation, which can precede the sleeping state is a very suggestible one. It is exploited in hypnotism, which in essence is a form of suggestion, and can be performed on oneself with appropriate affirmations, being a potent method for engaging the power of the subconscious mind.

An intriguing idea is that we are all asleep in the sense of spiritual awareness. Gurdjieff based the whole of his teaching on this, and instituted a bizarre system of exercises to wake up his followers, many of whom belonged to the intelligentsia of the time, including some well known personalities of The Fabian Society. This idea was to become known as stopping the world, just as in the material recorded of the Mexican mystics. This idea of the Now Moment is central to an advanced mystical state.

One of Gurdjieff's methods demanded complete immobility on a signal, which was by blowing a whistle. I remember doing this as a child in a game we called "Statues." It caused a number of accidents in his disciples during gardening at his retreat in Fontainebleau. Nowadays, this activity is replaced by individual dance movements, according to a friend who attended one of their meetings in London. The idea that the condition of the population is one of "waking sleep" is not new, and refers to the lack of Soul consciousness.

The work of Gurdjieff is important as he was responsible for a new approach to the idea of Self Realisation, and as such deserves mention in a work of this kind devoted to the changing conditions of the age. His is the 4th Way, the three others being those of the Fakir, the Monk and the Yogi. There is a supplement to this book of material taken from the Internet, which outlines the mystery of the Enneagram (nine sided figure inside a circle). Gurdjieff introduced this into Europe. There is wealth of material about the Enneagram. There are groups all over the world using Gurdjieff's methods. It appeals to the mainly intellectual persons who are disinclined to adhere to any religious organisation, and live an otherwise normal life.

There are many books on this, and it is large on the Internet. The automatic, robot-like functioning of the human unit is a feature which we can all assess in our own lives of routine and individual habits. An extreme form results in what is tantamount to a spiritual death. It is associated with an obsession for wealth, power, and self-interest. The thread of soul communication then becomes tenuous, and can be severed for the remainder of that life. H.P. Blavatsky in one of her books stated that this condition is quite common and said, "You are rubbing shoulders everyday with some who are soul dead!" A similar reference is to be found in the New Testament: "Let the dead bury the dead," in words attributed to Jesus.

Now, to return to what happens during natural sleep. In the normal sleeping state, the etheric body is said to remain hovering three feet above the physical. It is the Astral, or Dream Body, which sallies forth, carrying the sleeper into experiences we seldom recollect. Those who are sufficiently advanced, are able to carry healing to the sick, or to appear as an apparition in places remote. To be able to move freely in the Etheric body during sleep is the province of yogi adepts, and seems to be central to an advanced mystical state.

However, there has been research into this sort of thing using electronic devices for exiting the body in full consciousness, as taught by the late Robert A. Monroe. He patented this, which he called "Hemi Synch," and founded the Monroe Institute in 1978. Establishing synchrony between the two sides of the brain through earphones connected to the machine allows an altered state of consciousness, which in this case can send the candidate to roam the astral planes while being monitored from the centre. There are books written by him, and a later writer named Bruce Moen ("Exploring The Afterlife Series") of his extensive experiences in the hidden worlds. They make fascinating reading and have revised somewhat my preconceived impressions of what life after death may be like.

The Science of Sleep

The ability of the brain to enter and maintain certain frequencies while sleeping may relate to physical wellbeing.

From The National Research Centre for Chronic Fatigue, there are FOUR main BRAIN STATES as measured by EEG: BETA, ALPHA, THETA and DELTA.

Each frequency has a characteristic blueprint and produces a distinctive state of consciousness, which they define as follows:

BETA waves (14 cycles per-second and above) dominate the normal waking state of consciousness when attention is directed towards the outside world.

ALPHA waves (8–13 cycles-per second) are present during dreaming and light meditation when the eyes-are closed.

THETA waves (4–7 cycles per second) occur in sleep and are dominate in the highest state of meditation.

DELTA waves (0.5 to 3 cycles per second) are experienced in deep meditation and deep sleep.

Beta waves range between 14–40 HZ. The Beta state is associated with peak concentration, heightened alertness, hand eye coordination and visual acuity, peak concentration.

Alpha waves range between 8–13 HZ. This is a place of deep relaxation, but not quite meditation. In Alpha, we begin to access the wealth of creativity that lies just below our conscious awareness. It is the gateway, the entry point that leads into deeper states of consciousness.

Alpha is also the home of the window frequency known as the Schumann Resonance, the resonant frequency of the earth's electromagnetic field is associated with being relaxed, quietly alert and introspective.

Theta waves range between 4 to 7 HZ. Theta is one of the more elusive and extraordinary realms we can explore. It is also known as the twilight state which we normally only experience fleetingly as we rise up out of the depths of Delta upon waking, or drifting off to sleep. In Theta, we are in a waking dream, vivid imagery flashes before the mind's eye and we are receptive to information beyond our normal conscious awareness. Theta has also been identified as the gateway to learning and memory.

Delta waves are associated with Detached Awareness, Healing, Sleep, and are long, slow and undulating. Delta is the slowest of all four brain wave frequencies and most commonly associated with deep sleep. Certain frequencies in the Delta range also trigger the release of Human Growth Hormone so beneficial for healing and regeneration.

There is something about this in the book by Adrian Dvir, "Healing Entities and Aliens." A computer engineer in Israel with unusual psychic abilities for communications with Aliens from other realms, he found that some claimed to not need sleep!

Sleep paralysis occurs on waking and makes it impossible to move, and may last several minutes. It is usually possible to see what is going on during this time and it is a frightening experience. My wife related how this happened when she was a nurse on night duty, and had fallen asleep in a chair. A metaphysical explanation is that the subtle body which leaves in sleep has not fully settled back in and connected up properly.

An interesting discovery into the circadian rhythm was the finding that it is more naturally 25 hours than 24. This occurs notably in animals, and is said to be due to the moon taking 25 hours to circle the Earth, although some would like to think it is because the Earth used to take 25 hours to make a complete orbit revolution.

There is much research going on into sleep, a condition in which we spend a large part of our lives. Some relation to melatonin secretion has been found in some parts of the brain, notably the hippocampus and the brainstem. The five different phases have been identified in the brain waves during a night's sleep, and may have a relationship with the Schumann Resonance factor, which is in another chapter.

The fact that I spend so much time in this state of sleep and have no recollection of my experiences, which I have reason to believe happen is very frustrating. Although I am lucky in the way I can drop asleep anytime if conditions are not adverse, and has always been my recourse in times of anxiety and stress. Getting up in the middle of the night for a house call, which would occur two or three times a week, sometimes twice in one night in those early days in the British National Health system, I was glad to be able to drop off to sleep afterwards within minutes of getting into bed, and never took sleeping tablets.

The Philosophy and Metaphysics of Yoga

The term Yoga is Sanskrit, meaning to yoke or join and traditionally refers to Union with God. It is both a philosophy and a way of life, and its purpose is to facilitate spiritual aspiration and self-knowledge. The effect is a transmutation. Its practise requires dedication and self-discipline, in what amounts to a Quest for the Soul.

Yoga is very ancient. When taught by a Master of Yoga, it is a science that can be modified to suit the candidate's life, and indeed his endurance.

In the Arthurian Myth, it is The Quest for The Holy Grail, and in the terminology of Ceremonial Magic, it is Union with The Solar Angel.

The methods are described in detail in an Eastern tradition as old as humanity itself, from the mouths of a succession of Avatars. The most brief and well-known written account is to be found in The Sutras of Patanjali, the translation of which is available in a little book by Charles Johnston.

Yoga was always intended to be performed under the direct personal tutelage of a Master of Yoga, possible in India but, in the West, reliance is upon qualified teachers who were trained in India. Most seem to have a preference for Hatha Yoga. It involves postures and contortions which are impossible for all but the slim and those who have very mobile joints. It needs to be combined with breathing exercises and meditation, which form an essential basis of all the different schools.

Complete withdrawal from public life was the original aim, and to practice yoga in seclusion. This is rarely practical in Western society and is no longer necessary. The ancient Brahmins, at the time of life when their children had become independent and were raising their own families, would abandon their material possessions and retire to the seclusion of a community devoted to the practice of yoga, or if preferred the isolation of a hermit.

A number of lives spent in this way may be required before any hope of achieving enlightenment, and even more for cosmic consciousness. Better health and mental poise are the benefits meanwhile. Family life does not preclude the practice of yoga, but it certainly makes it more difficult, if not impossible, as I found in the early years of raising a family. My wife and I then gave up the practice; but for me it was only a postponement.

There are a few practical details, or tips, regarding suitable positions for meditation. The Lotus posture is advocated in the traditional way, but is difficult and an unnecessary strain for anyone who is either not young or not flexible in the joints, and so a cross-legged sitting position on a low seat is generally used. In fact, sitting in a straight-backed chair in the classical Pharaoh appearance has been approved by a most prominent master of yoga. After all, the main reason for the lotus position is to fix the body sitting upright, so that in the event of a trance-like state you do not fall over!

The other advantage is to bring the foci of prana together. An advanced stage may manifest in levitation, as related by George King who left the evidence of his head coming in contact with the ceiling from his use of oily Brylcreem hair dressing, which was fashionable in those days. This led to an amusing anecdote about the effect that it had on his landlady.

Psychic faculties are sometimes aroused by the intensive practice of yoga, and are to be regarded as insignificant. Unless properly controlled they can be a nuisance, although the ability to see the auras is often prized. To seek psychic faculties has its own hazards. Having achieved an ability to see and hear other worlds can be a frightful nuisance. To control this to be turned on or off would be the next task.

In my opinion, to seek paranormal ability is not to be recommended, but if it occurs it needs to be tolerated in good humour as it can be very trying, and needs to be kept to yourself lest you be dragged to the psychiatrist's office and plied with tranquilisers, if not committed. For anyone wishing to achieve psychic faculties, The Aetherius Society holds training courses calculated to do this safely in their London establishment, the "Inner Potential Centre." Richard Lawrence of The Aetherius Society has written a book, "Unlock Your Psychic Powers."

Some of the different types and methods of Yoga are: Raja, Karma, Bhakti, Jnana, Hatha, Mantra, Mudra, Kriya, Agni, Tantric and Kundalini.

Raja Yoga is often called the Royal Road, because any advancement is preserved and carried forwards into the next life. It is primarily a mental form, concerned with emphasis on the concept of Oneness in meditation and affirmations of Unity with The Monad in its profound philosophy.

Karma Yoga is simply unselfish service to humanity, and in these days deemed the most important for the manipulation of Karma.

Bhakti Yoga is that of devotion, as exemplified by the Saints, and described in some detail in their writings and biographies. It is the Yoga of Love and devotion to The Divine.

Jnana Yoga is the way of knowledge. It is the study of Spiritual Philosophy as encompassed in metaphysics. It is favoured by the intellectual and the curious who have an open mind for ideas which cannot be proved. It is a study of Truth.

Hatha Yoga is the form most familiar in the Western world. It has an accent on the physical, in the way of emphasis on postures and contortions, and therefore, excludes those whose physique will not permit their performance.

Mudra Yoga consists entirely of hand gestures. It is virtually unknown in the West, except to those masters of Yoga who are familiar and proficient in all its forms. It originates in certain Tibetan monasteries and is said to be a very potent method. Books on this type of yoga are rare.

Mantra Yoga is a science of sound systems in the repetition of certain Sanskrit phrases. Repetition may continue for a long time, raising the vibrations in the subtle bodies. A mantra is given to the student by the master, with the admonition never to let anyone else have it, until such time as they are confident that "the mantra lives in them."

Kundalini Yoga is a powerful and dangerous practice without the close personal supervision of a Yoga Master. It involves attempts to raise the power at the base of the spine up the spinal column to the crown of the head. This leads to the accomplishment and realisation of Cosmic Consciousness. Unsupervised, this practice can cause all manner of physical distress, mental disturbances and various pathologies, even death or insanity. It is fiery, and not to be idly provoked.

Nevertheless, it is the goal and destiny of everyone to accomplish this feat. In fact, it is the only purpose of being here at all. Not to worry, some risks have to be taken in anything worthwhile. George King thought for a long time about this, and finally decided it was the right time to write details of a safe way to include the Kundalini in the practice of Yoga. Finally, after much deliberation, instructions regarding Kundalini Yoga were included in the book, "Realize Your Inner Potential" by George King and Richard Lawrence. Let it be said that the prospects of success for anyone accomplishing cosmic consciousness are still remote, unless they have been ardent practitioners of Yoga in previous lives.

Kriya Yoga was advocated by Yogananda, which he learned and practised from an early age. There are correspondence courses available from The Self Realisation Fellowship, based in Los Angeles. I understand that all are given a secret Mantra, not to be divulged to anyone else. I wonder if they are all given the same one?

Agni Yoga is not practiced much. It is another fiery technique, in which the candidate volunteers to submit to the transmuting effects of the combined minds of several Yogi Adepts. It is said to be quite an ordeal and not to be entered into lightly.

Tantric Yoga is mainly to be to be found in India. It is highly ritualised, with emphasis on those sexual aspects thought to reflect the origin and creation of the Cosmos. Ramakrishna who was one of the best of natural mystics was led through the highest initiations by a woman who was a high Adept. He endured it all with good humour, and, I wonder, perhaps in mild indifference.

Hermetism. This summary of notes on Yoga would not be complete without mention of those techniques peculiar to Europe. The principal group can be classified as Hermetism, and covers the Masons, Rosicrucians, The Golden Dawn, The Knights Templar, and many others. All these schools are based on ritual varying only in complexity, and founded on the remnants of Atlantean principles, handed down through the Eastern, Middle Eastern, Egyptian and Grecian priestly castes.

These schools vary in size from worldwide to single, isolated, exclusive, small groups. Breathing exercises and meditation are used. A Ceremonial Initiation is the rule. There are rituals relevant to the particular initiation and the stage of advancement determined by the elect, often requiring some study into the traditions and knowledge of Occultism. There are many books on this subject, usually under the heading of Ceremonial Magic.

Another school was started by Gurdjieff. He wrote a number of books including "In Search of The Miraculous" and "Beelzebub Tales." He was of Russian origin, and had picked up esoteric teaching in his travels in the East. His influence was mostly in the period following the First World War in the nineteen twenties, and was financed by a wealthy group of intellectuals. He strongly emphasised the notion that we are all asleep in the spiritual sense, and claimed to have invented what he called the Fourth Way. His version of cosmogony is a bit different to most in some respects. The reference to what he called the shock effects of slowing between elements of the octave remains an enigma to me.

This dissertation would not be complete without a word about the Yogis themselves. They are the forerunners of the human race, and have had to spend a number of lives devoted to the practice of Yoga. Some have only half-completed the course, as it were, as described in Yogananda's autobiography, in that they become stuck at a level of psychic accomplishment. Some Yogi-Adepts can appear in two places at once, and walk through a solid door, as confirmed by the experience of George King.

The Masters of Yoga have no personality as we understand it. They have renounced all that is material, and have no selfish motives having sought and achieved liberation from the three worlds. They often take on limitation, accepting negative karma to help this humanity. For them, Service is a Soul Instinct, just as the urge to satisfy desire is a characteristic of the personality. The urge of the Soul is to Serve. "Service is the Jewel in the Rock of Attainment" became the motto of the Aetherius Society.

Perfection

Be Ye Perfect as Your Father in Heaven (John ch.30, v.10)
Know Ye Not That Ye Are Gods? (John ch.11, v.34)

That which is perfect must be without blemish, pure and uncontaminated by other elements; also, in the ultimate sense of the word, timeless, immortal and, if having any form and shape, symmetrical. To look for this type of perfection in the physical world is pointless. Perfect as a flower is in full bloom, it is transitory and fading as you look at it. The most perfect diamond may have hidden flaws. The most holy and mystical of all saints will not be perfect on close scrutiny. The fact of being human inevitably implies flaws.

We have animal bodies and are vulnerable to the desires and impulses of our animal nature, and it is a battle to control and sublimate our baser instincts. This is "The Quest" and the "Way of the Warrior" in the esoteric sense, and is essentially non-violent and subjective. The saints of old tried cruel ways in their attempts to "mortify the flesh" on themselves and on each other through a misguided and ignorant doctrine in which they thought that they were purifying the Soul. The Soul is not amenable to such improvement as it is, by its own nature, already pure and active on its own level. It is only influenced by those attempts to contact it when the lower vehicles are sufficiently clear of those qualities by which it is denied.

Perfection in the ultimate sense is elusive as in art, as any artist will confirm regarding his work. The Spiritual Perfection aimed at by the Mystic and envisaged by the Occultist is a goal that is not readily attainable by mortals, requiring a seemingly endless road throughout time. There seems to be degrees of perfection in this sense, which makes a paradoxical denial of what I have just said. The Masters of Saturn are referred to as the "Perfects" by the Adepts. Absolute Perfection exists only in the absence of manifestation.

Before leaving this subject of Yoga, there is a New Age system that originated in Jewish Mysticism.

The Merkaba

The Merkaba is an interdimensional vehicle of two tetrahedra (four-faced solids), interlocked with a common centre. One tetrahedron points up and the other down. This is conceived as being superimposed on the human frame.

A whole system of Self Realisation has been developed around the Merkaba. Breathing exercises and mudras, combined with certain eye movements are aimed at activating a saucer-shaped energy field around the body and imagining the Merkaba as the centre. This vehicle is anchored at the base of the spine, and its field may be as much as 50 feet across. When activated it is able to travel into the higher dimensions.

This system is taught by Drunvalo Melchizedek and is very much a New Age Yoga. It is based on an ancient Jewish system associated with Melchizedek of the Bible.

The origin of the Merkaba is to be found in mystical Jewish writings, and means the "Chariot," and is mentioned in the Talmud. But the name is obviously of Egyptian origin: Mer-Ka-Ba (pyramid-spirit-body).

The Merkaba opens up a whole new avenue for study in metaphysics. Like all the methods for Self Realization, it requires study and dedication and appears to be fairly complex. There are courses of instruction on The Merkaba available on the Internet.

Karma

The moving finger having writ moves on, and all your tears shall cancel not a word of it. Omar Khayyam.

The Law of Karma is The Law of Inevitability. Every cause has an equal reaction. Even as it is true in the physical world, so is it true in the metaphysical world throughout all its septenate (7) ramifications and holds for all moral and ethical considerations.

This principal of Karma is of particular interest and importance to everyone. All unselfish deeds in the spirit of love and service have the effect of achieving merit for the positive and good things of life, but not necessarily in the present one. In the same way, an evil life motivated by selfishness and regardless of the harm to others, will result in physical limitation and negative experience in future lives, if not in the present.

It can be seen from this that repeated lives in different personalities and environments are an inescapable conclusion for The Law to work out. Even thoughts are subject to karmic scrutiny day and night.

The suffering of the world is due to the actions and attitudes of the race as a whole over the centuries of recorded history and long before that. The purpose of human life is to learn and it seems we are still at the bottom of the class in the solar system doing it the hard way.

I have heard it said that the reason suffering and distress of all kinds is so rife in the world today is because karmic debts are being called in before for the next imminent phase of human development. It is also likely that the terrible mass suffering and privation and the great increase in the world population is due to a great influx of souls requiring negative experience, suggesting that some may originate from other solar systems.

The spiritual energies are greater now than ever before in the long life of the planet, rendering conditions attractive and practical for advancement. From the position of the gods, our earthly existence in the totality of its numerous lives is only a brief episode in the experience of an individual monad. In the Cosmic Plan, it is a mere blink of an eye in Cosmic Time.

However, as explained elsewhere in this text, opportunities for shortening the process are available in what could be regarded as an escape clause in The Plan. Such is included in the various systems of Yoga, of which the most potent of all is Karma Yoga in the form of service to humanity. In these days, we are being subjected to increasing evolutionary pressure by the transmuting radiations from above.

Karmic Law

The Law of Karma underlies all the other Cosmic Laws, and there is no escape from it, as it is written into the very fabric of the Omniverse. It is an essential part of evolution, sweeping all life into higher states if existence, in which the human stage is the transition between the lower three and the higher three worlds. The Force behind it is The Impersonal Love of That, which the Mystics call the Cosmic Mother.

For the benefit of those who might like a bit of Biblical confirmation of The Law: "Vengeance is mine" sayeth The Lord, and also from the Old Testament, "An Eye for an Eye," etc, which unfortunately, have been used as an excuse for feuds in misinterpretation ever since!

Also, in The New Testament there is: "Not one jot or one tittle of the Law, but shall be fulfilled." In a saying of Jesus, but most of all "As you sow, so shall you reap!" – a most emphatic reference to Karmic Law. The Christian Church has replaced the teaching of Karmic Law, by the Washing Away of Sins by The Blood of Christ, and ritualised in The Confession.

This is contrary to The Law and does not happen, in spite if some misconceptions by the writers of the gospels. According to The Law, there is forgiveness but NO Forgetting and is ministered impartially by ourselves. Universally, The Law is supervised by The Supreme Lords of Karma at the highest level of The Celestial Heirarchy. They maintain the balance between the Forces of Evolution and Creation against the tendency to revert to the Chaos, from which All arose in the Beginning.

The Conscious Mind has a natural resistance to the idea that we are prisoners of Illusion. This makes of a perfect prison in which the inmates are unaware of being imprisoned. Our task is to realise this and try to escape. It is almost like a game to which we consented and contributed. I like the concept of being imprisoned in a sort of divinely designed hologram.

When we use selfish pursuits and harm ourselves and others we resist the Force of Evolution, which is the direct Force of Divine LOVE. This indulgence is the source of all our troubles but results in valuable experience. Remember what Isis said to Hermes? "Out of my great Love for Man, he may need to be afflicted by all manner of tribulations, in order for him to be driven back to Me, to enjoy the Bliss of his Divine Heritage."

There is no Divine Judgement. There is Law which sets the parameters of conduct, but the Deity (or whatever you call IT) is not really interested in what you do. This acknowledges how the framework of manifestation is LAW. However, what does attract attention in a subtle but powerful and impersonal way is the attempt to know the Self, that mysterious thing which is the undifferentiated consciousness within all life. This is the basis and reason for Creation, for ALL Life to become conscious gods. What if you were to ask The Creator why it does these things? I imagine IT would say, "I Create. Through Love I Create."

At the core of Evolution on a time scale so vast as to be beyond comprehension, control is effected by the Karmic Lords. This acknowledges how the framework of manifestation is LAW. It is irrefutable as being the nearest thing to a Concept of Deity even for the Adepts and Cosmic Masters, who sacrifice their bliss and take on negative Karma on our behalf. For there is compassion, in that sacrifices are made possible for elevated beings to take on limitation and suffering to help this humanity struggling under its colossal karmic debt. We should acknowledge this and send them our Love.

You can take power from the Universal Source in the performance of the New Lord's Prayer and send it out to suffering humanity. The transmission of the Force which is Love, always benefits the sender. It brings peace, better health and influences future lives. Regular use requires a little self-discipline, and may be a little difficult in the initial stages. After that, it becomes a comfortable and rewarding routine and you will feel the benefit.

It is well to remember that the Force of Love is such that it will not be denied. Eventually, it will ensure that ALL Life will return to Its Source as conscious gods through the natural process of evolution. My friends, do not concern yourselves unduly over your misdemeanours. You set the terms for your ultimate Freedom yourself. Mistakes will be made, however good your intentions, sometimes even *because* of your good intentions! On the other hand, if you decide to be a very devil and ignore the bounds of civilised conduct, you can expect the repercussions of "negative experiences," if not in this, then in future lives.

Sexual practices do not attract retribution unless you harm somebody. At worst, they could cause the inhibition of spiritual advancement which tends to be obstructed by such indulgences. The hardest thing is to accept the terrible things going on in the world without abandoning all thoughts of spirituality.

When this strikes home in the personal life it becomes acute, and many of you will be able to verify this.

Revenge and payback have become traditional in some parts of the world, perpetuating feuds from generation to generation. Breaking this is very hard where family honour is perceived. I sometimes wonder how I would have reacted to the casual slaying of my family. Let us be thankful if we have been spared a situation invoking a need for violent reaction. Teachers of religion who condone and even promote revenge are making a terrible mistake, for which they will have to answer.

On top of all this, there is compassion. It operates through the offices and sacrifice of many who have achieved high status after millions of lives. Some are mentioned in this book, who are able to manipulate the Love Energy of which there is no limit on our behalf. The Universal Force of Love emanates constantly through us all and everything. Our trouble is that we have forgotten how to attune to it.

We are taught to fear God. This is wrong, there is nothing to fear from that which is pure impersonal Love, from that which is the energy behind Creation. It is of a different frequency and intensity, according to the level of existence. This Force cannot be influenced. Any difference in its effect is a reflection of how well, or how little, you accept it and use it.

Here is an example
A man was seeking advice on how to escape damnation from having cursed God in a fit of rage. He went to confession and received absolution and the usual advice on conduct and a number of prayers, as is the normal practice in the Catholic

Church. He came out feeling comforted in the thought that he might only have to serve time suffering in purgatory.

Some years later on his travels he met a Yogi, and took the opportunity to relate his experience. The Yogi laughed, congratulated him on believing in a God, and said, "It is better to have cursed God than to be denying the existence of God. You can be sure it was not even noticed."

He went on to describe the instance of a little child in a fit of pique shouting to its mother, "I Hate You!" in all the childish fury and hatred which a child can express. "What does the mother do? She ignores it, and takes the child in her arms, now weeping in its frustration, and all is forgotten in hugs and tears. Would the Cosmic Mother be any less disposed to your infantile conduct?

"Whatever the concept held as to the nature of God you can be sure that, in the enormity and vast complexity of Creation, human behaviour is of no concern. We are here for experience and mistakes will be made. This may result in discomfort and distress when your higher self deems it necessary to remind you, as demanded by the Laws underlying all existence. You have absolutely nothing to worry about."

This man never went to church again, and became interested in philosophy and the practice of Yoga. It can be said that the truly spiritual never go to church, except perhaps to please their spouse, and for a daughter's nuptials.

Karma can be manipulated. We all have some negative karma, otherwise we would all be saints. Karmic debt can be cancelled out, or modified by unselfish service to the Earth and humanity. This was made quite clear by the teaching of George King and was emphasised by the Master Aetherius. Contributing to Prayer Power is one way. The serious and regular practice of Yoga and meditation will help, because all efforts to know your true Self will also reflect in the rest of humanity, but it is Karma Yoga in unselfish service which is the most powerful for manipulating your karma.

We are all potential antennae for attracting and broadcasting the power of Love. This faculty is built into the energy structure underlying the physical. It is simple and so easy. But the most potent of all is to use The Twelve Blessings.

These days form the transition phase into a higher level of vibration and because of the way things are in the cyclic manner of the Cosmos, you will not have such an equal opportunity for this service for another 287 lives, according to the Master Aetherius.

Metaphysical Law

It soon becomes apparent to the student of metaphysics, that although metaphysics is intended as an intellectual exercise which stretches the imagination and credulity, there is an underlying spirituality. This is because it involves appreciation of, and an attempt to analyse the manifestation which proceeds from the Mind of the Absolute. There is a hierarchical system of celestial agencies in categories of gods, down to the elementals of the three worlds of minerals, plants and animals; all of which, at sometime, and in a certain cycle of creation all Life, have to pass in the first instance.

Every lifestream has to pass through the three kingdoms, then into the human phase as required by all monads from the monadic diaspora at the beginning of time. The human stage is the hub, or pivot, of evolutionary change between the downward arc of Involution into matter, and the upturn into Evolution back to the Original Source as conscious gods.

It is an ever-increasing group consciousness, but never losing the sense of individuality in spite of the sacrifice of freewill, although freewill, on close examination, does not convey freedom at all. The eons of time, and repeated cycles within cycles required for this long journey seem rather forbidding to the human mind, as we consider how each human life is one of many rebirths into different personalities.

In the Alchemical view, Life is The Crucible in the Fires of Karmic Experience. It is all subject to Law, which was determined in the Mind of The Absolute on that level of Abstraction appertaining to The Primary Trinity. This Law can be divided into Three Major and Four Minor laws. Behind all these is the Fundamental Law of Karma, which is a law of Cause and Effect administered by its own hierarchy.

Unfortunately, this humanity has exhibited a recidivistic tendency throughout a very long history, with the serious karmic repercussions responsible for all our present day problems. You may ask why we are allowed to persist in repeated errors? It is because of Freewill, which has to remain sacrosanct. However, there comes a stage which even that has to be limited and cannot be permitted to be the cause of suffering indefinitely.

Herein, lies the prospect of a Karmic Decree, which I make bold to suggest is already in effect in these strange days, in which we are experiencing a vast input of spiritual energies. The transmutation of this humanity and the planet is proceeding. A reflection of this is the increase in turmoil and suffering on a large scale, as some have elected to be here at this time so that some karmic debt can be cleared. Part of this is the population explosion.

If it is any comfort, the time spent in earthly existence is only a small part in comparison with that spent on the more subtle realms between lives. Yet, there are exceptions. These are both the most primitive and some of the most advanced on the path to self-realization, in which rebirths may be occur immediately or very shortly after death.

As Above, So Below

There is an ancient universal maxim, "As Above, So Below," attributed to Hermes Trismegistus, (who also is recognised as synonymous with the Egyptian deity Thoth), there is no word for the superlative in the Egyptian tongue, and so they said "Greatest, Greatest, Greatest Wisest," which the Greeks translated as Trismegistus).

"As Above, So Below" forms one of the tenets of metaphysical philosophy and Law. According to this, there are Demonic hierarchies reflecting in a negative fashion the Devic, and are responsible for resisting all attempts to evolve in their prerogative as agencies of chaos.

This Law allowed the energies released by The Primary Initiation of Earth to be accessed by negative forces, as related in the first chapters. In response to the energy which has been given to the Earth in recent years, the dark forces are very busy indeed. However, their powers are limited on Earth and so they make full use of their ability to inspire vulnerable persons with evil intent. If they manage to get at a particularly charismatic personality with a gift of oratory, they will fill his mind with all sorts of nonsense calculated to sway the emotions and aspirations of thousands, making them devote their money and even their lives to the mission, whatever it is. We have seen extreme examples of this in the last century, when hundreds committed suicide at the behest of their leader, such as when 900 Jones disciples died in South America)

Of Rays and Laws

There are LAWS of Creation, and RAYS of Creation.

There are 3 Major Cosmic Laws and 7 Subsidiary Systemic Laws.

The prevalence of a particular Ray varies according to the stage of evolution of the lifestream, and its passage through a particular sector of space. Monads issue on a certain Ray, and require experience on all seven rays eventually.

There is an interesting correspondence in the relationship between the 3 Major Rays and the 3 Major Laws, in reference to the 3 Supernals of The Sephiroth and The Trinity, together with their symbols:

Symbol	Aspect	Ray	Law	
1. Circle+ Arrow,	Unity	Will	Synthesis	Father
2. Spiral,	Duality	Love	Attraction	Son
3. Vortex,	Trinity	Activity	Economy	Mother

Aspect (1) is symbolised by the Boundless Circle and the Arrow as the impetus of the Will/Intent and the Law promoting ever increasing Group Consciousness and Action in a process of Synthesis.

Aspect (2) is symbolised by a Spiral Motion characteristic of Evolution through Cyclic changes, by way of the Ray of Love/Wisdom and The Law of Attraction.

Aspect (3) is a vortex and the Trinity in Action by The Mother as The Builder and Destroyer of Forms in the evolutionary process.

In addition to the 3 Major Rays, 3 Major Laws; there are 4 Minor Rays and 4 Minor Laws. For further elucidation of this rather complicated subject, reference should made to the Treatise on Cosmic Fire, and The Seven Rays by Alice Bailey.

I rather like the following poem, which is very descriptive of how the Law of Karma affects us all, with some references to the Origin of Life.

The Law Which Is God

From "Poems of Progress"
by Ella Wheeler Wilcox. (1850–1919)

The Sun may be clouded, yet even the Sun – will sweep on its course till the cycle is run.

And when into Chaos the system is hurled – again shall the builder reshape a new world.

Your path may be clouded – uncertain your goal, yet move on into the darkness of night.

The touch of the builder shall give it new light.

You were! You will be! Know this while you ARE – your spirit has travelled both long and afar.

It came from the Source, to the Source it returns, the spark which it lighted eternally, burns.

It slept in a jewel, it leapt in a wave. It roamed in the forest. It rose from the grave.

It took on strange garbs, for aeons of years, and now in the Soul of yourself it appears.

From body to body your Spirit moves on, to seek a new form when the old one has gone,

And the form that it finds – is the fabric you wrought on the loom of your mind, from the fibre of thought.

As the dew is drawn upwards in rain to descend, your thoughts drift away and in destiny blend.

And though you may try, you cannot escape, for evil or noble they fashion your fate.

Somewhere, on some planet, sometime and somehow, your life will reflect the thought of your NOW.

My Law is unending, no blood can atone, the structure you build you will live in alone.

From cycle to cycle, through time and through space, your lives with your longings will ever keep pace.

List to that voice, and all tumult is done - your life is the life – of the Infinite One.

In the hurrying race, you are conscious of pause,

You are your own Devil, you are your own God,

You fashioned the paths – which your footsteps have trod.

And no one can save you, from error and sin – until you have harkened to spirit within.

PART FOUR
Numbers

All is Number (Pythagoras)

Here are some esoteric features of numbers 1 to 10:

Number 1

This is not really a number in the normal sense of the word, because it is the source of all numbers, in that it can be divided into an infinity of parts. It is the same if multiplied by itself, or divided by itself and is its own square root, which, as the root of minus one, became adopted as a useful tool in modern mathematics.

It is emblematic of Oneness, the One Source or The Absolute, which also The Monad, from which derives Duality and Polarity, The Positive and Negative Aspects of Creation, which are Subjectivity and Objectivity, in other words Spirit and Matter.

The Number One, therefore, represents the Point which is everywhere, yet nowhere, between cycles of Creation. It is a great mystery in the concept of The Godhead, and the origin of the monadic diaspora at the beginning of time. It is symbolic of The One Reality. The simple vertical stroke we use as the number One, is also used as the first letter of the Semitic alphabet, which seems appropriate.

Number 2

This number is that of Duality and Polarity, resulting from the First Cause, in which the Absolute initiates the Abstraction of Potential, as already mentioned. Before the Arabic numbers it was two vertical strokes. The Roman system of numbers still persists in manuscripts and is more convenient for incising dates in stone.

This inception of Duality by the positive and negative produced an infinite source of energy, which can be conceived as the tension resulting between the two poles, and is Force in its various aspects behind Creation and Evolution. It is also the origin of evil in the cosmic sense, and an essential element of chaos in opposition to evolution. Bear in mind that nothing can exist without its opposite. It is included in the Yin-Yang sign. The number two is regarded as feminine, and so are all even numbers. It was thought to be unlucky by the Roman soldier. It is interesting that spontaneous parthenogenesis is only possible due to the twin chromosomes in the ovum producing an identical specimen. The odd one of the male is required for differentiation and variety. It is the curious in the way this number makes the modern technology of communication and computers possible. By using the base two, the lines of the ubiquitous twelve digit barcode is on everything you buy.

Number 3

This number is an aspect of the Trinity, in both its Primary and Secondary phases. Proceeding from the 2 and forming the base of a triangle, the other two sides are the positive and negative emanations from the 1. The triangle is the geometric foundation of the universe and is present in all life as Consciousness, Soul, and Mind. This Triplicity forms The Law of Three and is in every lifeform in proportion to the level of evolution, but of the three the monad is the same in everything.

The Primal Triad is a mystery which defies the comprehension of the gods. It is an Abstraction in which the Objectivity of Creation is conceived in its Entirety. It produces a Secondary Aspect which in turn gives rise to those Agencies Who Create and work as The Seven round The One. Thus, originate 7 Laws and 7 Rays.

Number 4

This number can be shown to be a hinge on which The Cosmic Plan revolves. It is symbolic of The Divine Tetraktys of Pythagoras. The Upper Abstract Primary Triad and The Secondary Triad can be shown as two triangles with a common base to form a Square.

The fourth level in the plan of 7, it is in communication by way of resonance with all the other fourth levels of the seven divisions. In this way, the etheric body is the fourth, between the lower three material and the three higher spiritual vehicles, forming a link with the higher consciousness. This is echoed up through the solar and cosmic levels.

In evolutionary terms, humanity on this planet is on the 4th Globe of Seven Globes, and is now passing round these for the 4th time. Of the ten Sephira of the Kabalistic Sephiroth, the 4th Sephira is Chesed (also named Gedulah), and carries the sign of Jupiter, which is a figure 4 with a vertical stroke, like 2 with a line down the centre of the base.

There are 4 Elements in metaphysical lore, deriving from a 5th (ether). They are associated with the 4 directions of the compass, and the Four Archangels Michael, Raphael, Gabriel, and Uriel, and the 4 Apostles of the New Testament.

In the DNA chain, there are 4 amino acid derivatives, distributed along the double spiral in a great variety of spatial configuration. By adding the two columns of the spiral and the central axis with four amino acids we get 7, as an example of the universality of 7. Carbon is a base for the chemical composition of the human body, and a carbon atom has 4 available electrons.

The equal-armed cross is equated with the number 4. Adding bits to the ends forms the Swastika, which is a very ancient symbol for the Tetraktys and the Force of Evolution. The Human Kingdom is the 4th (the lower three kingdoms are the Mineral, Vegetable, and Animal), and is the transition between stages of evolution and a vital link in the whole Cosmic Plan along the Septenary Spiral.

There is another 4 and that is The Fourth Way, a program of Self-Realisation according to Gurdjieff. It is a form of Yoga in Self-Observation and Self-Remembering, as distinct from the idea of self-abnegation of other systems to access the Higher Self.

Number 5

This is the number of the perfected microcosm, when the human unit not only achieves cosmic consciousness, but abandons the physical tie completely, and then the 6 becomes the 5 (symbolically the Hexagram becomes a Pentagram).

This is the stage of Adeptship, concerned only with the ethic of Service. It is a condition of Soul Consciousness on the threshold of Interplanetary Existence.

The Pentagram Ritual forms the basis of Ceremonial Magic. The 5 fingers allowed the development of the Mudras. Each digit has properties related to one of the elements.

5 represents the 5th element Aether, which is the name given to that medium of vibration throughout the numerous divisions and levels of the metaphysical cosmos. In the Cosmic septenate (7) division of existence, the 5th (from above downwards) is that of Manas (Mind). The 5th Law is that of Fixation, relating to the 5th plane (the mental) and ensures development of the Causal Body as a vehicle of the Soul. Its formation requires a great number of lives in the limitation of material existence.

The 5th Sephira, on that which is often referred to as the Tree of Life and the Kabalistic Sephiroth, is Tiphereth. It relates to the psychic centre over the heart and the Sun. It has many names: The Golden City, The Castle Perilous, The Golden Flower, The Golden Lotus, etc.

Number 6

This number is unique by the property of being divisible by all its divisors, 1, 2 and 3. The next one is 28, which is divisible by 1, 2, 4, and 7. As the principle interest, however, it is the number of The Christ Force, L-O-V-E.

It originates on the 6th Cosmic plane (from above downwards), between the cosmic "physical" and the "gaseous," and thus illustrates a correspondence with the esoteric quality of "water" and the association with emotion and the astral planes. The 6th plane of the solar seven is likewise reflected in the earthly "wateriness." The planet Neptune and its Logos is one of the three major planetary schemes influencing this Earth and is symbolised by the three prongs of the trident that is always carried in the portrayal of Neptune as Poseidon, God of The Sea.

The Neptunian emanations affect the deva essence of the 6th sub-plane, matter, through a powerful entity known as the Lord Varuna in the Hindu pantheon. The planet Neptune has a vital relation to the 6th logoic principle in Man, that is the Buddhic (Soul). When this is coordinated, he becomes under the influence of Neptune in some life, and governs one of the Three Paths of Return by the manipulation of the 6th type of energy, associated with mystical devotion and Bhakti Yoga. In this way, the astral centres in man are controlled by the 6th Ray.

The type of astral matter in the human unit decides the quality of the watery substance therein, through the connections of the Law of Correspondences, the 6th solar plane, the 6th planetary plane and the liquid of the body, and the 6th Ray type of energy.

Number 7

This number underlies the whole construction of the metaphysical cosmos, and of course includes the material universe. An attempt has been made to elucidate this concept of The Septenary Divisions of Creation with the appropriate diagram.

The 7 is regarded as derived from the 3, comprising the fundamental triplicity, and the 4 from the totality of the

3 being a 4th. In the same way, the Octave is likewise, the basis of connection between the different levels. It is all very Pythagorean.

The septenary (7) theme runs through the whole gamut of metaphysical cosmogony, in relation to the cycles of the globes, rounds, chains, etc. In addition, there are the 7 Laws under domination of the Law of Karma and the 7 Rays of the Theosophical tradition; and more recently The Seven Supreme Lords of Creation, which work round The One (from The 11th Blessing).

In the material world, we have many examples of the number seven in folklore. In science, the most obvious is The Periodic Table of the Chemical Elements and the Seven Colours of The Rainbow. The literature and folklore of the world contain many references to this number. This idea of the 7, as a basis for appreciating the metaphysical, is not so difficult with reference to simple diagrams of the planes and their subdivisions, and will be an essential concept for a Unified Field Theory which still eludes modern science.

Number 8

The most significant thing about this number is the Principal of the Octave as a basis of connection between the planes of existence. The resonance between particular levels with their respective number above and below, allows an interplay between the Cosmic, Solar and Planetary levels of the same number.

This principle of resonance is best exemplified in the Tonic Solfa musical scale, and on the keys of a piano. Doh resonates with Doh in the adjacent octaves, as in the case of middle C resounding with the C above and below, and indeed so with each numbered key throughout the keyboard.

The cosmogony of Gurdjieff is also based on the octave. For an easy read, I recommend the little book "A Study of Gurdjieff's Teaching," by Dr Kenneth Walker.

The number eight is traditionally regarded as a lucky number in the Orient. A car licence plate with 888 is very much sought after, and changes hands for large sums of money in Hong Kong. It is associated with the planet Jupiter.

Mathematically, 8 has the property so that every odd number above 1, when squared, results in a multiple of 8 + 1. It has always been a convenient number for dividing into smaller amounts in architectural construction. A numerical system based on 16 has, therefore, certain advantages and is preferred on some other planets.

There are 8 points on the Cross of St John. It is the emblem of St. Germain, The Knights of St. John, and used by ambulances and First Aid teams.

Number 9

This is the number of Initiation, and the book "The Nine Freedoms" – that astounding work outlining human destiny and transmutations for the next million years. All serious students of metaphysics should possess a copy.

Note that 9 is 3 times 3. The Triplicity in the makeup of the human unit is just so. The 9-sided figure, The Enneagram, as an integral part of his cosmology has all sorts of implications. The 9-sided figure inscribed in a circle is an Enneagram, and forms part of Gurdjieff's system. It has been a favourite with some writers and seers for use in character analysis. Completing the triangles is an interesting exercise in attempts to establish the significance when applied to the Kabala. The number 7 governs the evolution of substance and form in the solar system and 9 governs the development of consciousness within the psyche.

There are 9 Human Hierarchies. 5 have preceded, which makes this one the 4th from above down. There is much to learn from the Enneagram.

We have Gurdjieff to thank for his disclosing the significance of the Enneagram and correlating it with Kabala and the Platonic Solids.

The Enneagram

It does not look complete without joining 7–4 and 2–5. Imagine the central triangle rotating, or rather the other triangles rotating about the central one for a dynamic representation of the Creation. On the Internet, there is a course of study on the Enneagram. The gap between 4-5 takes some explaining.

Number 10

In the Kabalistic Sephiroth, there are 9 centres reflecting manifestation, the first of the 10 being the One Source, and the summation of the 9. Until the decimal system was introduced into Europe by Fibonacci, the Roman numerals were used. A system of hand and finger signs based on 10 was used by the illiterate, and formed an essential part of trade in the market place. This interesting feature is fully described in the "Evil Eye" by F. Elworthy.

This number is used in the Kabala to depict the Macrocosm, and superimposed on the human frame is the Microcosm. It has 10 Sephira. The uppermost 3 are abstractions. There are different ways of calculating. Have you ever wondered how the ancient Indian mathematicians managed to do quite complicated calculations, without logarithm tables, slide rules or calculators? Well, they had an abacus, but they did it most of it in their heads! They used a method which is based on one-line verses in Sanskrit. The syllables in that language are made to conform to numbers, and each line spells out a particular mathematical formula, in such a way as to facilitate mental calculation.

How this was rediscovered by a Sanskrit scholar named Jain, is described in his book, "Vedic Mathematics Re-discovered." Several books had been written on this system, which vied with the traditional, somewhere around 1960. It can be found on the Internet how this system of calculating was revived. It is of particular interest to mathematicians. It is not unusual for gifted children to use their own system and mentally reach solutions without the proper steps, which can cause embarrassment in exams. This Jain method of teaching calculation has been adopted by some schools in India, and in one or two in England. It has met considerable opposition in India. Perhaps that is why the original books disappeared from their libraries.

The Sumerians and the Egyptians did not use multiplication and division. Instead, they used a sophisticated system based on the number 60, and used tables for successive additions or subtractions. In Europe, they managed for many years using the Roman numerals.

Fibonacci and The Golden Mean

This number 16.180 is of particular interest in Europe in metaphysics. It is present in all manner of forms and life functions. Leonardo Pisano of Pisa (Fibonacci) was a mathematician of the 13th Century. He was the first to introduce the Arabic system of numerals in Europe, but is more renowned for discovering the Golden Mean. It is said to have been taken from a series as proof of a wager, that has been a source of speculation and wonder ever since.

"How many pairs of rabbits can be produced from a single pair in one year. If it is assumed that every month, each pair begets a new pair, which from the second month becomes productive?"

This is represented by the following series:
Months: 1, 2, 3, 4, 5, 6, 7, 8, 9, 10, ...
No. of pairs: 1, 1, 2, 3, 5, 8, 13, 21, 34, 55, ...

The second row represents pairs in terms of the Fibonacci sequence, in which each term (except the first two) is found by adding the two terms preceding.

Starting with n = 3, the formula is always $Xn = (Xn-1) + (Xn-2)$

As the value of n is increased, the result comes closer to the actual Golden Mean Ratio of 1.6180339887...

This is the ratio of artistic proportion, and the ratio of many relationships in nature, such as the ratio between the spirals of a snail shell. It is also the way shoots on a growing stalk are separated in a spiral around the stalk.

(Phi) is the symbol selected for the Golden Mean, in memory of Phideas who was the architect of the famed Greek Parthenon the temple of Athene. There is a considerable literature on this series to be found in mathematical magazines. It has mystical significance after the manner of Pi, the ratio of the diameter of a circle to its circumference, and is also found in the measurements of the Great Pyramid.

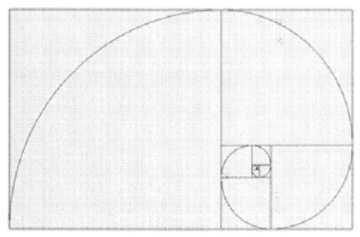

Snail Diagram.

In geometry, a **golden spiral** is a logarithmic spiral. The increase is the golden ratio. The spiral gets wider by a factor of φ for every quarter turn it makes.

The Pentagram

If we draw in all the diagonals in the five-sided figure they each cut each other with the golden ratio (see picture). The resulting pentagram describes a star which forms part of many flags of the world.

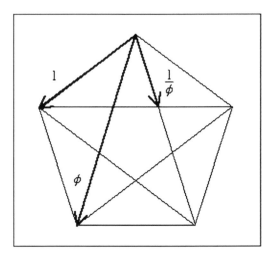

The Pentagram

Phi also occurs surprisingly often in geometry. For example, it is the ratio of the side of a regular pentagon to its diagonal.

Numerology

There is a set system of rules in which numbers can be used for divination. For example, each letter of your name can be paired with the number of its place in the sequence of the alphabet. The addition of these digits tell about the character, your potentialities and destiny, which can be reinforced by applying the principle to the birthdate. In this way, the summation of the digits must come to a number between 1 and 9.

Pythagoras used numerology as a divination tool, and today's professional numerologists have systemised it to a fine degree. Gamblers and others keen to advance themselves consult it. By a knowledge of Numerology you can use this technique in association with the number supplied by a date from the calendar to determine the most auspicious day for an enterprise. I know of one man who managed to do this, and thereby obtained a substantial bank loan on which the bank manager commented some time later, that he did not know how he came to grant it.

It is possible to become completely obsessed in the numbers game, and to see a significant number in every event in life, both personally and generally. I encountered an extreme case as a medical student. As part of the medical course, several visits were made to the local asylum. One inmate had managed to prove to himself, by the manipulation of numerology, that he was the incarnation of a famous person in history.

Time

This is a difficult subject and yet, in the metaphysical mode of thought, some appreciation of its true significance can be seen. First of all, it is necessary to rid the mind of the feeling of life being restricted to any one incarnation.

In metaphysics, it is required to think in terms of Cosmic Time, and to try and imagine the interminable passage of eons and eons in a never-ending process of evolution. In this way, the individual lifespan takes on a trivial aspect and allows the imagination to expand. Time did not exist before manifestation and, in the Mind of The Absolute, is basically a state of abstraction.

It is analogous to the Big Bang, as Creation sprang from in an inconceivable NOW. This was the beginning of Time from the Fiat "Create!" and is only manifest in the linear fashion in this physical world, which is sometimes referred to as the Third Density by New Age writers.

We imagine the monadic diaspora to occur thus as the Primordial Chaos differentiates into matter on the physical plane.

Time, as we know it, cannot BE without motion. There is the notion that there is probably an interweaving of Timelines. In these days there are two main possible Timelines. We are said to exist on the knife edge of choice between a static condition of cybernetic control, and the freedom to evolve. The result depends on the outcome of the Spiritual Crisis which is now approaching its conclusion.

Eternity is the unimaginable interval between the onset of Manifestation and its Dissolution. Attempts are being made to calculate this as part of celestial mechanics, but I feel the figures fall very short of the mark and, anyway, there is no possibility of being able to assess the Times of life on the higher levels of existence. It is deemed possible to live the equivalent of hundreds of years on the other realms and return to the physical plane with hardly any Time having passed.

Time remains a problem for scientists and philosophers alike. The former propose small particles of zero time being responsible for the formation of subatomic units, and have been dubbed gravitons in relation to the String Theory (Stephen Hawking). This is very interesting, if you can follow the latest scientific jargon of quantum mechanics, which is now teetering on the brink of accepting some ideas of the metaphysicist.

The Flashing Universe

It has been proposed that the Universe is created by re-inventing itself repeatedly in an unimaginable scale of infinitesimal intervals representing trillions of zeros behind the decimal point, producing the concept called The Flashing Universe. If this is behind the formation of Time, then the idea of creating a resonance in the makeup of the human with this rhythm during the recitation of a mantra, some realisation of the NOW might be achieved.

There has been some suggestion that rips in space-time were caused by the atomic explosions so that the timeline has been disturbed, causing visits from the future. There are videos of interviews and transcripts from those who were involved, or had access to the secret documents relating to deals with aliens and visitors from the future. These exhibitions of hidden data indeed stretch credulity. The trouble is, there is so much of it and it is corroborated by the various veterans now submitting their experiences.

The Philadelphia Experiment

Recent work on the nature of the subatomic particles, suggests that time is not as immutable as previously thought, sometimes exhibiting passage backwards in time. In a similar, more down-to-earth fashion, was the Philadelphia Experiment in 1943. This was an attempt to make a warship invisible to radar.

The ship was made totally invisible as it disappeared from sight by the watching team. The ship and crew, however, were transported some miles distant inland and 40 years temporarily into the future. The US government tried hard to keep this from the public, but since then some of the people concerned have reached the security of their pensions, and the story has been told in detail.

The results were so disastrous that all such research was abandoned, and never repeated, or so we are led to believe. Some of the crew were killed, some went insane, and bodies are said to have been caught up and embedded in the substance of the ship. The scientist Tesla was involved and, if his advice had been heeded, there would have been no one on board.

In the words of Mars Sector Six, "Fantastic indeed is Truth!"

James Dunne, in his book, "An Experiment in Time," tried to show that the mind advances into the future during sleep. He recorded his dreams meticulously, awaking in the middle of the night to write them down. In this way, he managed to foresee a number of catastrophes which did take place.

The most interesting part of his book postulates an infinite number of Times – a particular time for every succeeding dimension in order for an observer to exist in observing events on a preceding level of time. If this is correct, it specifies a time dimension for every level of existence in the septenary complex of the metaphysical cosmos. As far as I know, his work on dreams has never been corroborated, although there are any number of isolated dream premonitions recorded as being accurate.

To repeat, the Totality of Time is to be imagined as beginning with Creation, and ending in its Dissolution, after an Eternity of Time. The eons and eons implied are beyond comprehension. The calculations of astrophysicists are probably very short of the mark.

What is the smallest possible time unit? Matter is believed to be reducible to the smallest subatomic units, and energy to the ultimate parcel as a photon. It has been calculated and known as Planck's constant and is a well-established part of modern theory.

Is there, then, a similar indivisible unit for time? If so, would it be related to the vibratory activity of an electron, say perhaps the interval for the supposed orbiting around a proton, or again the actual frequency of the electron in its seven-dimensional vibration? Would these units vary according to the particular level on the scale of seven?

The latest theory concerns the graviton, which are dots in zero time, millions of which go to form a subatomic particle. The dimensions of time manifest in space as these tiny dots, but behave as small strings. You can refer to the latest book on the subject by Stephen Hawking, although it is difficult book.

One thing we can sure about is the continued flow of time, or "the river in which it is not possible to step in the same place twice." In the mathematical treatment of time, it is the 4th dimension, after the three measures of length, breadth and height. The human phase of life is securely imprisoned in the grip of Time. We are essentially four-dimensional creatures. The totality of a human life from beginning to end is to be imagined as a complete entity as viewed from the 5th dimension. Any instant of time in the life of an individual is then a cross-section of the 4th-dimensional aspect.

In the terminology of Theosophy, as borrowed from the Hindu tradition by Helena Blavatsky, eternity is a Mahavantara and consists of a whole cycle of Creation/Dissolution. The ancient Brahmin priests calculated a lesser Mahavantara to be 308,448,000 years, and was part of a Kalpa (4,320,000,000 years). This in turn comprised 4 Yugas, the present being the Kali Yuga (esoterically the Iron Age), so often mentioned in literature, and is 432,000 years.

The previous yugas are recorded as much longer, in order of occurrence: The Golden Age 4 times as long, the Silver Age 3 times, and the Bronze Age 2 times as long.

Regarding the individual lifestream, an isolated incarnation is only a very small part of that which goes to become Soul Conscious. The life experiences of each embodiment are connected, as it were, like a string of pearls called the Sutratma. The sum total of these in a transmuted state constitutes the Buddhic Unit of an individual lifestream, and is the same as the Self realised as a Soul.

Some Thoughts On The Subject Of Time

We are informed that it is possible to raise the base frequencies of this world up to those corresponding with the higher levels of existence. This is made possible by the principle of resonance, as used by those of the Third Blessing who transmute the forces of Nature into those of LOVE.

In that case, it should be possible to do this in reverse of that process, and thereby tune in the vibrations of the human mind to synchronise with the infinitely fine ones in which the universe repeats itself in its continuous creation, and so engage the NOW MOMENT between creations, of which there are some millions present in one nanosecond as phases dividing reality.

The strobe lighting effect allows the human eye to see a continuous picture on the screen of what is really a rapid succession of images. In the same way one, can one postulate the possibility of the human mind viewing the repeated creation of the universe in the process of change as perceived in Comic Consciousness?

There is some perception in the population that time is speeding up. Can it be merely a subjective experience? It is related to the increase in the natural Schumann Resonance waves which pass through the Earth, from about 8 to 11 cycles per second.

Schumann Resonance Waves

Schumann Resonance waves echo between the earth surface and the Ionosphere layer and form standing waves. Some pass through the earth resonating in different frequencies. They are intensified during electrical storms, and commonly in the summer months. In 1952, Professor W.O. Schumann, a German scientist, found that these waves have similar frequency which is almost the same as brain waves, and follow a similar daily pattern.

It has been suggested that these waves help regulate the body's internal clock, thus affecting sleep patterns, hormonal secretions, menstrual cycle in women, etc. The American space agency NASA became interested in this phenomenon when the early astronauts returned to Earth after only a short time in space feeling distressed and disorientated. Subsequently NASA installed equipment to generate Schumann waves artificially in their spacecraft with a positive effect.

Because there is a close association with the human brain, it is contended that there is a possibility of using this to affect human attitudes and the response to stress. It can be further stated that there is some evidence that experiments have already been performed to test this theory and to influence the weather.

Measurements of the brain waves of humans show that the brain produces electromagnetic waves which lie in the range between 1 and 40 Hz. This spectrum, as previously mentioned, is divided into four ranges that accompany different conditions of consciousness:

1. Delta waves (1–3 Hz) are characteristic for dreamless deep sleep and coma conditions.
2. Theta waves (4–7 Hz) are characteristic for the dream sleep.
3. Alpha waves (8–12 Hz) arise in the relaxed awake condition, e. g. in a meditation or briefly before falling asleep and/or immediately after awaking.
4. Beta waves (13–40 Hz) are dominant in the normal awake condition.

The accurate value of the basic Schumann frequency is 7.83 Hz.

It is generally agreed that the human brain frequency is not coincidental, because this value corresponds accurately to the fundamental brain frequency of most mammals. Through the Schumann waves all humans are in resonance to the earth, conforming with the earth resonance frequencies. The Schumann frequency spectrum is remarkably similar to that of the human brain.

With the help of technically manipulated Schumann waves, which are inaudible and invisible it is possible to manipulate the emotional conditions or the state of health of whole populations or to feed suggestions directly into the brain. Such a technology is not based on science fiction, but already exists in the form of the HAARP project (High Frequency Auroral Research Programme) in Alaska, which has been blamed for sudden and unpredictable storms and outbursts of psychotic behaviour in young people.

An American patent specification from the year 1987 became the basis of the HAARP antennas, by which the possibility of weather manipulation is expressly mentioned. It is well known to science that in thunderstorms, apart from the elementary Schumann frequency of 7.83 Hz, further resonant vibrations are actually produced.

At least eight such frequencies were identified. The rounded-off frequencies are 8, 14, 21, 27, 34, 40, 46, 53 and 60 Hz. Not only does the first Schumann frequency lie in a range to which the human brain is sensitive, but so do the next five.

The frequency of the basic Schumann wave is said to be increasing and could reach values of 13 Hz. If this is so, then it might affect human consciousness. The Schumann phenomenon produces a grid pattern in a form corresponding to the platonic solids, resulting in nodes of force which have been mapped out.

Power Grids

Ivan P. Sanderson was the first to make a case for the structure of the icosahedron (20 faces) at work in the Earth. There are areas of the Earth where mysterious disappearances, mechanical failures and time-space distortions have occurred.

Explorers have simply disappeared in these areas, correlating with points on the grid. Sanderson's work promoted a group of three Russian scientists: Nikolai Goncharov, a Muscovite historian, Vyacheslav Morozov, a construction engineer, and Valery Makarov to further his research by the superimposition of the platonic solids on a grid formation in almost the exact same location, adding 50 more points with the dodecahedron added to the Grid.

Bruce Cathie describes the grid in his book "Harmonic 33," superimposed over a map of the Earth. He used to supply copies drawn on a ball.

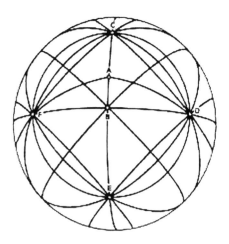

The Disclosure

For the world to be exposed to the prospect of realising that we are on a much lower level of evolution than the visitors from other worlds, leaves little doubt as to the furor and panic which might have ensued, had it been suddenly released. Now that we have been to the moon and all the secrets are coming out in the testimonies of the aging personnel involved, this excuse is no longer acceptable. The time has arrived when the ultimate disclosure of all that is known has to be made public.

One of the most noteworthy testimonies is the appearance on the Internet of Robert Dean being interviewed. He does this in three parts, each lasting nearly an hour. Having high security clearance, he had access to the records of many meetings with aliens. He makes a strong point of stating that the civilisations of the extraterrestrial visitors are many thousands of years ahead in evolution, possessing sophisticated ways of travelling between stars, and in the remote past were responsible for our present DNA composition. He relates how the historical researches by a team of specialists employed by NATO showed that visits of Aliens and interaction with some communities have happened over 5,000 years. "This sounds as though we are on the level of something like a slave community, or a zoo," was the expression of dismay by a general after reading the report.

The wife of Bob Dean has had meetings with aliens since childhood, and has written a book entitled, "My experiences as an intergalactic anthropologist." From their combined account you will be impressed by the sincerity of this remarkable pair. This sort of thing is getting to be quite common. There are other cases of retired technicians, scientists and politicians with the similar experiences. They are appearing on TV shows and lectures around the country. Some of them had been silenced by various means involving threats, extortion and ruined careers.

One of these is Don Burisch who was associated in the creation of international treaties with a group of Aliens. Apparently, he was the only one able to communicate telepathically with the survivor of an alien vessel. The most astounding feature being that some came from the future, consisting of groups from 24,000 years, 45,000 years, and 52,000 years in the future.

The website (www.ProjectCamelot.org) shows a list of individuals who, in spite of threats and intimidation, continue to provide accounts of their experiences with UFO's and aliens in both transcript and on videos.

One of the most startling things to come out of these revelations is the assertion that there is already an operable form of spacecraft that has been used for secret expeditions to colonies on Mars and the Moon. This was made possible by the back-engineering of downed UFO's, which if true makes the money spent on the rocket ships to the moon inexcusable.

There have been lies and cover-ups ever since the crash of a UFO (1947) in Roswell, New Mexico, which was attributed due to interference caused by radar. Intimidation and threats of imprisonment have been effective in discouraging disclosure until recently. Now, after the expiry of the twenty years demanded by the Official Secrets laws, many are coming forward to tell their story.

It becomes apparent that there have been dealings with different types of aliens all along, even to the point of turning a blind eye to abductions of adults for experiments and the theft of human fetuses for the creation of hybrids, which is being created by another race as their genome is declining badly.

The crew of the Roswell ship came from 24,000 years in the future and, on their timeline, are our descendants. Their mission was peaceful and concerned the welfare of this humanity, and changes occurring in the timeline. Rather than dismantling the nuclear weapons in return for assistance by the more benevolent species, governments have traded with other types. This has resulted in technological advances, but there has been friction and occasional armed conflicts.

Just how it is all covered up is tribute to the security clampdown and its ruthless efficiency. How long this can be kept up? As the use of the Internet increases and public conventions more frequent, this information will become universal and the Truth will be demanded. All the governments of the world are aware of the interplanetary visitors. They were freely recognised in the US in 1947. It was in all their newspapers, but was soon reversed and the press was persuaded to deny it all in the cause of National Security.

The 1938 radio broadcast of a supposed Martian invasion by Orson Welles, and the widespread panic and casualties which resulted, may have had something to do with it. This embargo persists, but has become ridiculous now as many important people have openly described their contacts with aliens in the course of their work for the governments. Those of Mexico,

Brazil and Russia, and certain authorities in the US have freely admitted the true nature of UFO's.

There is an energetic team of lobbyists trying hard to get at the Truth, and they are making progress. Check www. ExopoliticsInstitute.org, their radio broadcasts and journal.

For enthusiastic researchers about Aliens there is another website, www.Alienshift.com. It has a huge menu which would take weeks to browse through.

Symbols

Some abstract ideas are best considered in the form of symbols. The subconscious mind is more amenable to this way of communicating. Primitive man and ancient cultures used this intuitively in their religious motifs and imagery. Modern man has lost this faculty, and finds the interpretation of symbols difficult. We are in debt to Carl Jung for his work in this connection, relating the symbols in dreams to the subconscious, and to Joseph Campbell in his researches into the world myths.

I will present a few symbols which I think are of interest. Some are related to The Creation, and are to found in the Grecian Myths, hidden in allegorical tales of incest and violence. In the connection of The Creation with symbols, Pythagoras used geometric shapes. The Basis of All is so regarded, and founded on the Triangle and the Circle, seen frequently in the old frescoes and antiquity as the Unbounded and Infinite Universe. The One produces Duality by its bisection, and from thence the Triangle incorporating the Force in the Tension between the Polarities. Thus, the Triangle is The Trinity pointing upwards in its primary abstract mode, inverted as the Manifest Creation in Objectivity.

Concentric circles, usually seven in number, and simple labyrinthine drawings are also to be found, especially in the art of the Australian aborigines. The multiple spoked wheel and the spider's web can also be cited. The Labyrinth is well known in the story of Theseus and the Minotaur, and taken to mean the convoluted multidimensional spiral of the manifest universes, and hidden pathway back to The One Source. The Web and the Spoked Wheel indicate the connection of all things to a Common Source, an essential feature of metaphysical thought.

In the Middle East, there is a mosaic floor showing a picture of the zodiacal forms, not twelve in number but including a thirteenth, displayed as Arachnida, the Spider. There is a myth which goes something like this: Having competed and beaten the Goddess Athena at weaving, the goddess changed the maiden into a spider in a fit of pique.

There is a book entitled Arachnida, dealing with this version of the Zodiac, and also a website showing the star map. Is a true sun sign and relates to the period 30th November to 17th December. It qualifies for its position as much as the other signs of the Zodiac. It has been ignored ever since Claudius Ptolemy (120–170 AD), father of astrology, decided to follow the traditional Twelve signs of the Zodiac. Arachnida is associated with the area of space named Ophiuchus (serpent bearer), and exists between the star map areas of Scorpio and Libra.

The Theme of Blackness intrigued the ancients, who associated certain blackbirds with the primordial state preceding manifest objectivity, in which there was light but nothing to shine on and therefore only darkness. The Raven in the northern regions, and the Black Swan in the south were so regarded as symbolic. Animals earned the reputation of being sacred, and were worshipped in ancient Egypt. Thousands of mummified cats, cows and bulls have been unearthed to prove it.

The different epochs favoured a particular animal. The Jackal, Crocodile, Ibis and the Scarab beetle were all held in the greatest reverence. A frog effigy was invariably left on the sarcophagus, the amphibian nature of which seemed to the Egyptians as connecting the two worlds, being at home in the two mediums of both earth and water. The Jaguar in South America and the Leopard in Africa have been worshipped and identified with because they convey impressions of power. The Eagle, soaring above the earth and keen of vision, is suggestive of the soaring aspirations of the human soul. In the Hermetic tradition, it is a symbol of Fire. Have you seen the Brass Eagle with outstretched wings supporting the heavy Bible in many churches, commonly mounted on a brass-ornamented stand?

I wonder how this symbol came to be adopted by the Christian Church. There are many symbolic gestures to be found in Christianity which were copied from much older systems, and are evident in the priestly costumes and headgear. The Dove was sacred to Venus, and is often shown on effigies and paintings of The Virgin Mary. It became symbolic of the Soul and Holy Spirit as the carrier of Peace.

About the Serpent, there is a wealth of literature as to its symbolic significance. It is frequently shown coiled around a tree, a cross or pillar, and derives from the Kabalistic Sephiroth. It is symbolic of the Serpent Power, Kundalini, and also of Wisdom. There is a saying in the Bible, "Be Ye Wise As Serpents!" As used in the scientific symbol for the sine wave, it expresses the universality of Energy as the basis underlying all manifestation.

The Twelve Signs of the Zodiac are divided into four sets of three, each of which contains one of the four elements:

FIRE	Aries, Leo, Sagittarius
EARTH	Taurus, Virgo, Capricorn
AIR	Gemini, Libra, Aquarius
WATER	Cancer, Scorpio, Pisces

It is usual to find the Four Gospels displayed in churches in symbolic form of the Four Elements as a Lion, an Ox, an Eagle and a Face. The Eagle is often used as an alternative to the Scorpion as a symbol for Water. The Human Face representing AIR, which is essentially SPIRIT in the mystical sense is meant to be the Sepharim, high in of the Devic Kingdom.

Ouroboros

Drawing by Theodoros Pelecanos, in alchemical tract titled Synosius (Wikipedia).

The Ouroboros is the name given to the Serpent forming a circle with its tail in its mouth, indicating the End of things as it eats its tail and consumes Itself, and conversely the Creation issuing from its mouth. The manner in which the snake casts its skin during growth impressed the ancient people as a renewal of life. In the East, it is The Dragon as a friendly emblem of wisdom when fiery red or golden; but green or black in its negative. It has also been made to represent the power of Evil and the Lower Self, as depicted in St George and the Dragon motifs.

In the story of Andromeda, the Sea Monster is so foiled when the Warrior as the Power and Discrimination of the Mind rescues her. In Fairy Tales, the Dragon has a hoard of treasure, sleeping but alert to attempts to steal it, and is a symbol of Soul-Realisation protected and imprisoned by the constraints of the conscious mind.

In an Indonesian tradition, there is a story of a large winged creature which was friendly and would fly carrying a man on its back. It is said to have been intelligent and was able to speak. Its name was Garuda and is the emblem of Indonesian Air. Finally, the arc of the crescent moon connected to its inverted reflection is a serpentine emblem. It is the sine of trigonometry, and is emblematic of vibration generally. Together with the Circle and the Cross, the Crescent satisfies all the requirements for various astrological signs. Dr Dee, of Elizabethan fame, wrote a Treatise on a composite of these elements to depict the Universe.

The Cross is very special to Christianity as a result of the Crucifixion, and unfortunately, is widely exhibited as such in gory detail in Catholic churches, schools and homes. The Early Christians regarded the Cross with horror. Their emblem was the Fish coinciding with the Piscean Age.

The essential meaning of the Cross, in the most profound esoteric sense is, "A Symbol of Man's Resurrection Through Karmic Experience," as announced after The Twelfths Blessing. Its usage by the churches depicting the crucifixion demeans its high symbolism.

A most important form of symbolism is to be found in the I Ching. This is based on the concept of two lines, one being broken into two and the other unbroken, representing the positive and the negative. This was developed into an ingenious method of explaining the Creation and developed into a system of divination, by creating the 64 hexagrams from the two basic lines.

The I Ching and Three Coins

This is one of the five classics which escaped the book burning of the Chinese emperor, Ch'in Shih Huang Ti, in 215 BC. It is a profound philosophical work, as well as a source of divination based on the 64 hexagrams. The interpretation of the divination relies on the concept of the Yin and Yang, although this was formalized much later.

The Yin/Yang is the principal of Polarity in a dynamic balance. The Yang is positive and represented by an unbroken line, and the Yin negative and as a broken line, and so we have: _____ and ___ ___. Combining the broken and unbroken lines in groups of three forms the basis of the I Ching.

Placing one vertically through the other forms The Cross.

Adding the third line   _____   ___ ___

                             _____ or ___ ___

                             _____   ___ ___

completes the symbology of The Trinity, and this Trigram presented in eight different forms is suggestive of the Divine Tetraktys in its both positive and negative aspects.

The importance of this in the Orient is demonstrated by the portrayal of four trigrams on the national flag of South Korea:

The Four Trigrams illustrate the Four Elements in the different aspects of Positive and Negative proportions fulfilling the maxim of Balanced Duality.

The 8 trigrams are combined in 64 Hexagrams, being the total possible variations. Of the 8 trigrams, 6 are selected in a random fashion. The traditional method involves the use of 64 yarrow stalks being thrown into a pile, the upper ones are removed until only six are left. The use of three coins has largely replaced this method, which are thrown six times and the appearances of the upper surfaces recorded. Heads count as even, Tails as odd. In this way a series of numbers are formed 6 (or 8), 7 (or 9) in the variations from 6 throws. Even numbers are represented by broken lines and odd numbers unbroken lines. The hexagrams so formed are then referred to the table of 64 hexagrams, each of which has a text relating to the significance in terms of good or bad, suggesting the trends of the situation.

The text is in the idiom of ancient Chinese society depicting different social and political scenarios in a poetic and colourful fashion. This can make interpretation difficult.

The emphasis is always on the dynamic balance in Life, leaving a choice for action or inaction according to the hexagram, which is why it is also called The Book of Changes. It also presents a philosophical system.

Correspondences between the I Ching, The Kabala, and The Tarot can be shown and books on this have been written. There are several English translations of The I Ching.

The Four Elements

The Medicine of the Middle Ages rested on The Principle of The Four Elements, known as the Four Humours: Blood, Bile, Phlegm and Air, derived from a 5th, Aether (or Ether). It was handed down from Greek and Roman times and long before that. It remains the foundation of Traditional Chinese Medicine as Wood, Metal, Water, and Earth. The Chinese call the 5th one Fire. And so, terminology has varied but is essentially the same.

We will examine the four elements as Water, Earth, Fire, Air, and Aether.

Water

Water is symbolic of the Watery Chaos, and is thought to have preceded the formation of matter. The Ancient Egyptians went a bit further and suggested it was milky, and in the process of creation became curdled as particles precipitated to form substance. In Indian philosophy, this was first held in a state of potential called Mulaprakriti and in the objective Prakriti. The idea of a milky medium was more appealing and gave rise to the material source of this liquid to be held sacred. The cow is still allowed this distinction, and has the privilege of wandering free and to forage in India to this day.

The chemical composition of water is H_2O – two hydrogen atoms and one oxygen atom per molecule – and can be regarded as a reflection of the Universal Triplicity inherent in all things. It is unique in some of its physical properties, expanding instead of contracting when frozen, and so floats on the surface. It is sometimes called The Universal Solvent, and forms an essential part of Homeopathy in this way.

The importance of water in life cannot be over-emphasised. It began in the ocean, and blood serum still maintains its salinity. The human body is made up of a vast number of cells which act in concert in a very complex ecology of subordinate ecosystems. There is a relationship with the number 6, in the cosmogony of interchange between watery planes.

It is interesting to note that snowflakes are never found to be duplicated, and are made in the form of a hexagon, so that all the arms of a snowflake radiate from a centre at an angle of 60 degrees. Different ice crystals are to be found after the water has been subjected to a magnetic field, and may be of octagons or dodecahedrons. In religious symbology, Water is the same as Wine representing Spirit. When visualised as a descending triangle it forms the six-pointed star with ascending triangle of Fire, forming the sign of Solomon and the Star of David. The Hexagram is symbolic of the culmination of an evolutionary phase.

The role of the watery influence from Neptune is of significance, as energy flows from there and concentrates in three psychic centres, linking the head centres, the heart centre, and the solar plexus centre.

The Astral Plane is watery in the esoteric sense, reflecting the emotions, and may be correspondingly calm or turbulent. In the future, when stability and calmness has been achieved in the minds of the race as a whole, the condition described in The Bible, "And There Shall Be No Sea." This will mean that Mind has become dominant and complete control of the emotions established in the subjugation and transmutation of the personality or lower self into Soul Consciousness. It is then on the threshold of Adeptship and the Astral will cease to be an integrated component. Some seers assert that the Astral plane will gradually reduce in significance and finally not exist when all have been raised up into the Mental Plane.

The Devic Agencies in control of Water nourish all organic life. In folklore, they are water sprites called Undines. In their highest echelons, they are the builders of manifestation. Their path of evolution is one of the least resistance over eons of time, during which they evolve into the next higher devic realm of the gaseous and the fiery devas through the septenary spiral up to the Cosmic Gaseous level of Manas.

Water is one of the four most important of the Devic Agencies in relation to the four elements. Its Archangel is Gabriel, who in the Hermetic tradition controls the various aspects of the Element Water, and is associated with the cardinal compass point of The West.

In the Pentagram Ritual, Gabriel is visualised as filling the western sky in a shimmering blue robe, shot with orange, and holding aloft a Cup overflowing with water. There are references to this particular name, in both the Christian and Islamic religions in the role of messenger.

Earth

Earth is symbolised as Salt. A salt crystal has the shape of a perfect cube. (Who said it's a square world?) At one time it was a common medium of exchange, and in great demand to flavour and preserve food. It is still carried in camel trains from Timbuktu to the Sudan.

The ritual consumption of bread and salt occurs in some mystery schools and the old Crusaders soon learned that to be captured and then contrive to eat salt if passed around in their presence, conveyed acceptance as a guest instead of a prisoner.

The elementals of the Earth are the Gnomes, and there is a wealth of folklore about them. Their function is to control the currents of energy and magma in the body of the planet. The symbol for Earth is a Triangle pointing down with a line drawn across.

Fire

Fire is symbolised as a Triangle, point uppermost in opposition to that of water.

In the most fundamental terms, everything in creation is fiery, as the origin lies in that energy which results from the opposing polarities in the Primal Trinity, but it can be divided into classifications according to function and planes of action. However, some ancient texts prefer call the primordial energy Water, in reference to watery nature of Chaos, which precedes all.

I think it is sufficient to bear in mind that Mind is Fire as a part of that total energy we call Manas, and all matter is illusory by definition of its atomic and subatomic structure and is mostly space. In these terms, matter is a form of energy and fire. This has been brought home to us in a most frightening manner in the way it can escape as hard radiation from the inefficient control of atomic power.

Another view of the metaphysical and higher function of Fire is its Transmuting Effect, and forms an important role in the evolution of humanity, on both a personal and a racial level, and is therefore an instrument of Evolution.

At the lowest and more familiar level, it is the fire of the hearth, and the flames of the terrible bush fires. In this sense we are witnessing the action of the fire elementals, the Salamanders, which are bound to take advantage of such conditions.

In England, I read the biography of a self-initiated Magician. He could utilise his talents to persuade a salamander to assist in healing. To do this, he was able to take it into himself and project it into the sufferer. It was not always successful, because a scream of fear in witnessing the release of a ball of fire approaching would be liable to cause the operation to abort. This man was a self-styled Witch. He borrowed books from the restricted part of the London Museum of the original text of The Ritual of Abramelin The Mage and followed through the complete course, alone in his apartment. In the determination to provide the mandatory elements of rural scenery, he used models. Unfortunately when his unauthorised loan of the rare book was discovered, he lost his job.

In the Hindu Pantheon, Agni is the Lord of Fire and of Mind, the 5th plane and Kundalini.

Air

It is to be expected that, having said something about Water and Fire as belonging to the four elements of antiquity, to mention the most elusive of all, Air. It is representative of Spirit, and so in metaphysical thought is emblematic of Consciousness. It is most mysterious, and is aptly associated with air in that it moves and "goeth where it listeth" (a Bible quote). The astrological symbol is Aquarius, shown as the bearer of Water which is self-evident if you look up and see the hundreds of tons of water floating by in clouds. In the language of mysticism, it carries that which is the Water of Life. The symbol of Air is a triangle pointed upwards with a line across it, opposite to that of Fire.

Aether

The 5th Element Aether is elusive and has been abandoned by science. This was not always so. Before the Einstein theory, this was axiomatic to scientific theory, in that there has to be a medium for electromagnetic waves to exist. Without the inclusion of this mysterious medium in research, there will be no free energy or a workable space drive. Nothing exists without it. It exhibits features akin to a fluid in its role as the vehicle of energies, for this it preserves a quality peculiar to each level of existence. It is elusive and resists identification by science. It can be said to be integral to space-time, and is sometimes confused with the Space-Time Continuum.

The Metaphysical Cosmos

This dissertation is fundamental to understanding the Metaphysical Universe. The ancient system of Metaphysics, its Cosmology and interpretation of humanity and its place in the universe is an attempt to express Truth, as far as we can imagine It.

It may have been preferable to have put this section at the beginning, as it forms the basis of the Metaphysical System. Some seem to be afraid of it, especially Roman Catholics in the face of the prohibition and adverse authority of the Vatican, as with all literature which questions the Catholic dogma.

There is nothing to fear in the exercise of that which makes man above the animals, which is the ability to think. The greater the use, the less it is prone to atrophy in old age, regardless of the number of neurons said to be decreasing, as the function is actually not impaired due to the wonderful adaptability of the human brain. There have been many books asserting a mechanistic view of the universe, and that everything has developed by chance through a process of natural selection, or due to control by a particular gene. However scholarly and plausible, there still remains the question of how things were wound up in the beginning, and how the gene became to be so designed.

The postulation of design and pre-calculation inherent in the Philosophy of Metaphysics is an alternative approach and more credible in accepting the Septenate (7) and Triune (3) aspects of Creation as taught by of Pythagoras and Plato.

Knowledge which was hidden and suppressed for 2,000 years is now available in books, starting with Helena Blavatsky's in the 19th Century and others since then, including various writers belonging to the mystery schools. The present time is one of scientific discovery, and an urge to know the secrets behind existence. It is hoped this work will encourage such enquiry, and exercise the imagination and curiosity in what, hitherto, has been regarded as occult and dangerous by the Church.

There is no danger in indulging the spirit of enquiry, but a word of caution there is one mode of investigation which should not be used, and that is the Ouija Board, which has been known to provide access to mischievous entities.

New knowledge is not to be feared, however strange, although some things are expected to strain the imagination and credulity in minds conditioned by materialism or religion. The common view asserts that there is only one life span, and that all is finished when it is over. It could not be more wrong!

Metaphysical ideas are very ancient, and only became available in written form comparatively recently. They were always preserved in a language understood by only a few people, privileged by their long service to humanity and their high status in that mystical fraternity, The Great White Brotherhood. Hidden in places inaccessible and known only to the few, the symbols in which the ancient language are inscribed can be read on at least three levels of meaning in The Stanzas of Dzyan (Blavatsky's "Secret Doctrine.") It is curious how the name Zion (which is phonetically the same as Dzyan) has been preserved in The Bible.

This work is only a brief outline of the mass of information which is available. The book references and websites should be noted for serious study.

The Hidden Worlds

The most intriguing and mysterious feature of the metaphysical system involves parallel universes. Existence is based on the number 3 and all forms and all levels are connected by the number 7. This is according to the most ancient doctrine as verified by those human intelligences in the vanguard of evolution, the Cosmic Masters.

There is no proof, as such, which would satisfy the scientific mind of the positivist attitude. There are analogies which can be drawn with our physical world, as anyone with the psychic ability to access the Akashic Records can personally verify. All is recorded in meticulous detail on a certain etheric level. However, demonstrative proof still eludes us for the time being. There are myths and legends about different worlds and there is an element of truth in all myths, which are universal, differing only in the names of gods, personalities and elements of folklore.

To begin with, the world of physics is essentially that of the five senses, aided by the use of instruments and scientific observation. Very fine work it is to be sure, and we are rightly proud of its achievements. Nevertheless, it is a serious error to assume that because we have no scientific proof from our science, which is only a few generations old, that different levels of existence are not possible.

The Octave represents the resonance between individual levels with the corresponding note in the octaves above and below, and forms the basis for connection between the different worlds. Each level is in a state of resonance with its corresponding level of both the higher and the lower octaves, even as the resonance between individual notes in the octaves of the piano keyboard and the Tonic Solfa scale of music. It should be apparent to the discerning mind that it might be possible for advanced technology to devise a method of travelling between the different levels and experience those worlds by exploiting the resonance principle.

Diagrams of The Septenary Divisions and Subdivisions of The Metaphysical Cosmos attempt to illustrate this, which is really a Spiral of many dimensions emanating from a centre and returning to it. The upper, more subtle realms precede the lower in the Creative Cycle, a factor which is difficult to reconcile with The Big Bang Theory. Dissolution occurs in reverse, like a ladder being rolled up (cf. Jacob's Ladder in the Old Testament).

The concept of the metaphysical cosmos, based on the number seven and the octaves, is one of the more difficult propositions in the face of scientific scepticism. Nevertheless, it is real and potent in its influence on the physical in a most profound manner.

Let us take, for an example, a crude analogy of the metaphysical realms of a planet. Consider an onion, the thin, outer skin is like the material world and all the different layers of the onion encountered, as they are peeled off carefully, are the hidden worlds beneath the physical. It's not quite like that because, in actuality, all the worlds are co-existent in the same volume of space but effectively separated by virtue of their substance being out of vibratory phase with each other.

There is an ever-increasing frequency of vibration from the gross to the more rarefied and subtle. In this way, the Earth has 49 different levels, all in the same volume of space. These are called cloaks, or globes, in Theosophy and Metaphysics. There are 49 globes made up of seven chains. Each chain has seven globes. Our physical Earth is the 4th globe and is the lowest of the seven globes comprising the 4th chain.

This idea of 7 is extant throughout the Cosmos in all the different realms, from the grosser material to the most rarefied and abstract levels at the root of manifest Creation. There are indeed many, many worlds of these in the multiple universes. For instance, in our Sun alone there are nine million, four hundred and fifty-six thousand and nine hundred and twenty-one cloaks, on the word of Jesus in the 8th of The Twelve Blessings.

Manifestation is based on the 3 and the 4 in the idea of the whole being a result of the Dual Polarity formed from the ONE, producing a Third, which is the Infinite Power from the opposing polarities +ve and -ve, or Spirit and Matter. The 3 is then considered to make 4 with the original ONE SOURCE, giving rise to what may appear, in a somewhat inadequate fashion, the 7 from the 3 and the 4.

Do not devote too much time on this, dear friends. The concept of The Trinity has been a source of confusion and frustration to seers and philosophers throughout the ages. A degree of humility and acceptance of the limitations of the human mind is desirable when it is faced with the more abstract notions encountered in metaphysics. Pythagoras tried to illustrate the idea of the Trinity by the use of symbols, showing a circle arising from a point and dividing the circle into 2, then 3, and then 4. So, by using the Triangle as the geometric principle underlying all things, the 4 is the source of ever-changing manifestation. This is The Divine Tetraktys (i.e. 4).

Now, let us revert again to the Cosmos and its foundation on the number seven. This can be dealt with in three sections, in accordance with the Triplicity prevalent throughout its operation and substance. In every plane and in every lifestream there is a reflection of The Primordial Trinity, and is mentioned frequently in the text.

And so, there are the three divisions, Cosmic, Solar, and Planetary, each of which divides into Seven Subdivisions in terms of Planes of Existence, each characterised by an ether and its frequency of vibration. The three divisions are in a descending order of involution, the lowest of the Cosmic Seven planes subdividing to form the Seven Solar and the lowest Solar likewise branches into the Seven Planetary.

This is a very brief summary of the septenary nature of the metaphysical. Actually, it is exceedingly complex, in that every subdivision divides and subdivides again and again in a bewildering hierarchy of planes of existence, realms or mansions.

Furthermore, the multiple frequencies of the Earth's substance has allowed some very ancient civilisations to exist within it in complete isolation. One of these is of reptilian origin, peaceful and highly advanced in technology. It developed slowly over thousands of years, and seemingly predates our known civilisations. There are Portals of access to the surface but are rarely used.

Globes and Chains

This section forms a necessary part of the Cosmogony and its Foundation on number 7 and for an understanding of the Earth in this respect. It relates to what is essentially the Esoteric Anatomy of a Planet.

After a number of rounds and cycles (see diagrams) on the evolutionary spiral of existence, life ascends to other levels. This has already happened on the other planets, where transferring between the planes of existences is now a common occurrence.

There are 49 Earths, called globes in the Theosophical Literature, to which we are indebted for recovery of the Ancient Wisdom suppressed for almost two thousand years by the early Church Fathers and the Catholic Church. Our globe is the most dense of seven, occupying the fourth place on the circle of Plotinus. Involution is increasing in density following a downward path through the first three globes, culminating in the fourth, which is our own Earth at the bottom of the circle, and is one of forty nine of such globes, as there are seven of these chains altogether. All exist in the same volume of space.

The chain in which our globe is situated, is the fourth of seven chains. Humanity has completed the passage through the previous three chains. All life proceeds round the circle of seven globes before going to the next seven globes of the chain.

It is stressed that we are now passed the critical and lowest point of our circle of Plotinus and engaged in the upward arc of endless evolution.

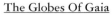

The Globes Of Gaia

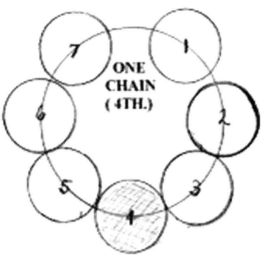

Life has to pass through Globes 1, 2 and 3 before our present one, which is the 4th. There are 7 Chains of Globes (or Earths) existing in the same volume of space, separated by the disparity in the vibration of the material.

The Moon Chains are in the same configuration. The Moon has completed its "rounds" and is in its obscuration phase. Venus is in its 7th Round.

Because of the complexity of this aspect of cosmology, I suggest reading the original texts of Blavatsky, or refer to the Internet and read the little book by Gertrude W van Pelt, which is an excellent and more readable version.

The Sun and The Moon

The ancient tradition of Theosophy gives the Moon as the origin of the early Prehistoric Man, a concept completely foreign to modern thought. There is, of course, a Moon Chain as with all the planets, and having reached the end of a 7th Round, the higher life forms transferred to the Earth. They had completed an evolutionary phase, but were lacking in the ability achieve the capacity for the Manas Factor (mind), which was finally introduced to Earth by a group from Venus. (For biblical ref. see Genesis ch.6 v.4)

When organic life leaves a planet, that physical part of its complex becomes a desert. Such is our Moon, which is said to having completed its 7th round and became totally bereft of Life, but leaving psychic emanations inherent in its substance. Presumably, so will the Earth be when it reaches that stage. It is possible, therefore, that the moon is much older than the Earth and is foreign to the solar system.

There is quite a mass of literature on the moon and the various occult properties ascribed to it. In some folklore, planting crops at the appearance of the new moon is said to be the best prospect for a good harvest. The waxing phase is said to beneficial for metaphysical and occult operations, and the waning more negative.

The full moon has a peculiar effect on the inhabitants of asylums for the insane. I have this on good authority from psychiatric nurses, that distress is so common and predictable during the full moon, that double sedation is indicated for some patients on those nights. Police have also observed that there tends to be more trouble when the moon is full, and the same applies to hospital emergencies. The moon controls the movements of the tides by its gravitational action, and that it has a physiological effect is all too apparent in women.

On the Internet, there is information regarding Angels for each day of the Moon cycle, and their particular uplifting energies, together with associated musical notes, colours and names and sigils for invocation of their specific properties. Our Sun is closely connected to Sirius in opposite polarity which in some way is regarded as its senior, much as the planet Saturn is to Venus. A third star in the region of the Great Bear is said to form the Triplicity, which is a universal characteristic in all Life.

This Sun is the 2nd in this Scheme of things. The 1st was concerned with the evolution of Matter. This one, the 2nd, is concerned with the development of Mind. The 3rd to be, is regarded for developing Will.

The radiation from the Sun changes its character and frequency every 32 minutes. Face the Sun and send your Love. If you like, you can take certain energy in sunlight deep into your Third Eye area in the centre of the forehead. This a profound mystical and cleansing exercise and refers to the 8th Blessing. I advise to do it only for a few seconds and without looking directly to the Sun, which could damage the retina.

The centre of the Sun is said to be cool, and that there are planets inside it. This is contrary to science which says there is a nuclear reaction going on in the centre.

In this solar system, all manas comes from the Sun. In turn this arrives from Sirius, the Sun being in a negative polarity to Sirius. The star Sirius was very important in ancient Egypt, its rising being coincident with the flooding of the Nile. There are some very interesting things to be learned from the Dogon tribe in Mali. They seem to have always known about Sirius and its small dark partner which orbits it, which was only recently discovered by astronomers.

The Dogon maintain that there is a planet also, but this has not been confirmed. The tradition of this people is that they originate from a part of Greece, and wandered as far as that particular part of Africa a long time ago, and mingled with the Africans. Their story is, that about 3,400 years ago they were visited by an amphibian race in a large disc-shaped spacecraft, and learned that they were from the Sirius system.

The size of the moon is atypically large in relation to its parent. The way it neatly obscures the disc of the sun in an eclipse is quite remarkable, and always presents one face to the Earth. The dark side was only revealed on photographs by the recent moon probes. Large structures on the dark side of the moon have been photographed, and carefully smudged out from public viewing. These are displayed on the Internet and clearly show attempts were made to hide large installations, the outlines of which are visible when magnified. It is conjectured that the moon may be foreign to the solar system and, at some stage became caught up in the Earth's gravity from another solar system passing by. In which case, if life was transferred to the Earth in the remote history of humanity it originated outside the solar system.

There is no satisfactory theory for explaining the origin of the moon. It is an enigma. It is bigger and older than it should be, and much lighter than it should be. It is maintained that the inclination of the axis of the Earth depends on the presence of the gravitational action of the moon, and without this angle of inclination to the ecliptic there would be no seasons, and the development of life on Earth would have been compromised. It is almost as though it had been put there.

Geological moon specimens – 842 pounds of various sizes of rocks, pebbles and sand – were collected between 1969 and 1972 from six different sites. Some specimens have been found to contain elements which are unknown on Earth. The ages of some moon rocks are estimated to be of the order of two billion years older than the oldest of the Earth, which suggests that at least some of it is foreign to this solar system.

The moon may be hollow. It rocked as it resounded for 40 minutes like a bell when the third stage of the Apollo Saturn vehicle, weighing 15 tons, crashed on the moon 85 miles northwest of the where the seismic recorder was placed. A mathematical treatment indicates that the "hollowness" is supported by the volume being greater than it should be for its mass.

Endnote. "Who Built The Moon?" (C. Knight and A.B. Butler)

Life On The Planets

On the basis of what has been written, you will want to know about life on other planets. The septenary foundation of the cosmos allows existence on the different levels, each of which has its peculiar etheric medium and corresponding type of substance. The higher you go up the ladder of evolution, the more there is rarity of substance. Where there is life, it is correspondingly raised to greater heights, reaching godlike powers and opportunities for service.

The barren and forbidding nature of the planetary surfaces of the planets, as revealed in recent years suggests that that organic life cannot existing there. There is reason to suspect that colonies on the Moon and Mars are possible.

The whole principle of the existence of intelligent life on the planets, therefore, is that it exists on a higher dimension. To presuppose the development of technology by a race which has reached that stage, and to be able to translate themselves between the various levels and planes of existence, is quite in keeping with ancient tradition and metaphysical theory. Their visits into realms which are in a lower state of evolution than their own are seen as investigations and monitoring, to record and help where permitted in the development of lower forms. They are capable of interfering in a helpful manner only as far as the Law of Karmic Limitation will permit. It is because of such restrictions that we are virtually in a state of quarantine.

The evidence, which is surely to be demanded, is to be found in our night skies and strange tales of encounters, and the testimony of those, who in spite of the threats and discrimination have come out to relate their experiences with alien civilisations.

Most convincing is the testimony of workers from the secret research centres, who are now coming forward and establishing themselves on the Internet, notably on www.ProjectCamelot.org, on which there are videos and transcripts of their interviews

The only reliable information about life on the planets comes through The Aetherius Society, direct from those who reside there.

Saturn

Saturn is the centre of control in the solar system. The energy manas arrive to the planets from Saturn after it receives them from the Sun.

The inhabitants of Saturn are the most advanced in this solar system. They have spent eons on the various planets, and in other parts of the galaxy. They have reached that point of evolution to be described as perfect, and in their next stage presumed destined to qualify for integration with The Logos of The Sun, in accordance with the Law of Synthesis.

Their lives have required millions of years to reach an acme of spiritual evolution beyond our imagination. A Saturnian is able to split the consciousness into 1,860 different parts, creating different embodiments according to the particular environment, in different parts of the galaxy. Each unit is fully conscious of and with every other member. The Masters of

Saturn can even double this feat and are called the "Perfects of Saturn." The Star of Bethlehem was one of these.

Jupiter

Jupiter is a centre of learning for the planets and visitors from other solar systems. Here again, the bogey of the alleged impossibility of interstellar travel comes to the mind of the reader, and as long as we restrict ourselves to the notion that the speed of light is the limit.

Visitors from the galaxy without the ability to teleport themselves are provided with a form of transport. This vehicle is produced by the mind power of an inhabitant of Jupiter from within itself, and, when no longer needed, it is reabsorbed. In one transmission from Jupiter we were invited to tune into its continuous broadcasting of symphonies of music, colour and perfumes.

The great mass of Jupiter enables it to be a sort of vacuum cleaner, sweeping up many drifting bodies of interstellar debris which would devastate a smaller planet. This was seen in the pictures taken by the Hubble telescope in July 1994, when a comet broke up in the gravitational field of Jupiter and landed on its surface. There is speculation that the great size of Jupiter suggests that eventually it may be destined to break away from the Sun and become a sun itself. From what we know of the gaseous nature of the planet and the conditions inimical to organic life, existence is confined to another level of vibration; and is likely to be true of other planets.

Venus

Venus is nearing the end of its 7th round, while we, in our profound limitation of that stage between involution and evolution, are still only half-way in our 4th round. The connection between the Earth and Venus is an ancient and well-established one, being in opposite polarity. There is a Biblical reference to this in esoteric interpretation, and in their symbols, which are inverse in reflection.

There have already been details about the connection between Jesus and Venus, and the tradition of it being a source of manas in early man. A triune relationship exists between the Earth, Venus and one other planet. Likewise, with our Sun and Sirius, and a star in the region of the Great Bear sector.

The Lord Buddha was also from Venus, in a 4th Aspect manifestation, as was Krishna from Saturn.

Mars

This planet harbours an advanced civilisation which passed through a similar phase to which we are going through, but they managed to avoid the pitfalls which have beset us on Earth. On that etheric level above our familiar existence, and mostly below the surface of the planet, they make it their business to provide spacecraft for the other planets, the most familiar of which are frequently observed and occasionally reported.

The Martians make very large vessels capable of intergalactic probes. Some are 5000 miles long, with whole cities and all the infrastructure and appurtenances for long voyages. A smaller one (2,000 metres long) has orbited the Earth regularly at certain times of the year for precise periods since 1955, but it is screened against photon and radar particles to avoid interference. The particular role of this vessel in earthly affairs requires separate treatment. (Ref. chapter on the 3rd Satellite).

The mature inhabitants of Mars and Venus live on seven different levels, each being in full communication with the other six.

Neptune

As mentioned earlier, emanations from Neptune resonate with the higher watery aspects of the Astral body. This energy comes via the 6th level of the Cosmic planes and is Love, and is in harmony with the Buddhic plane which is the 6th in the human unit. It is greatly concerned with the watery element in man, which is the Astral body. Neptune is one of the more occult planets, and is one of three planetary systems. This is symbolised by the three triangles at the tips of the trident carried by Poseidon. There is much more about the emanations of Neptune in "A Treatise on Cosmic Fire," by Alice Bailey.

Mercury

Mercury is concerned with communication. How did the ancients know that?

Uranus

I can say nothing of interest about Uranus except for one thing, which came from an unknown source, and really should be about the Moon. It says that at one time the Moon was a satellite of Uranus.

Life

Through evolution, existence becomes ever more advanced, mobile and richer in experience. The goal is, "Life in Greater Abundance," as expressed by Jesus in the New Testament, as the purpose for His presence on Earth.

What is Life? It is a Facet of Consciousness. Anything which exists derives from Consciousness. In this sense there is nothing which is not alive. The perception of LIFE as being essentially related to movement is wrong. Even the stones and the ultra-microscopic subatomic units have a rudimentary conscious, inconceivable to us though it may be.

This principal of Everything in Nature being Alive is a basic tenet of metaphysical philosophy called Hylozoism, and is secondary to the Monadic principle. Attempts to create life are fruitless. However, it does not mean that it cannot be trapped and exploited, as attempted in black magic. Efforts to imbue consciousness and life into computers may come into that category. Artificial intelligence seems to present this prospect, having no soul or resident monad.

The Golems of old in the biblical myths, if they ever existed, must have been of this ilk. This is a theme dear to the writers of Science Fiction, illustrating the fearful slavery and impotence of mankind in the face of a power capable of running an industrial complex, dictating policies, controlling the judiciary and education and indeed, the whole of a civilisation. When, or if it should produce mobile units of itself to monitor and police the world, the prime directives of its creators had better not be flawed. In an extrapolation of present day trends, this does not seem to be so fanciful. The incident of the Alien Android showed the great power an artificial intelligence can have.

Death? There is no such thing as Death, only transition to a different environment, followed eventually by rebirth. "You will never be more dead than you are now." (St. Germain). This seems to be a difficult thing for the rationalist mindset to envisage, although the fear of death is a built-in and necessary part of the survival instinct. In the Western world, death is something not readily spoken of; it used to be sex which was the taboo subject. Some tribes used to leave their aged members in a cold and desolate place in the depths of winter, to quietly succumb to the elements and literally freeze to death; or they would often decide to quietly slip away to die themselves, when they felt they were becoming a burden to the tribal family.

Are we more civilised by preserving suffering to deny death, when it is obviously due? The whole Western world is full of the fear of death and dying, in contrast to the more ancient and pagan view of the Orient, where the demise of the departed is celebrated as a release from the limitations and privations of material existence.

The identification of the self with the physical body is apparent in the morbid fascination with graves and their contents. This reverence to the memory is not to be decried. However, it often involves a reluctance to accept that the life that was, still lives in another dimension. And so, let us mourn our losses for a little while, but never be too sorry for those who are free at last from the hard school of earthly experience. Many preserve the anguish of bereavement all their lives. It is unnecessary, and a source of unease in the minds of the departed.

In order to prolong life, it is fairly common for anyone suffering from a terminal heart condition, to have a heart transplant from a donor who has died a violent death. This has produces an interesting phenomenon. The recipient tends to adopt the mannerisms and some personality traits of the donor. When the donor has been of the opposite sex, it has led to some embarrassing experiences. There are now a sufficient number of recorded cases for it to be studied systematically. The identity of the donor is not normally divulged, but in these instances the secrecy has been waived for research purposes, and often for the satisfaction of the recipients' relatives.

Infants who have had a heart donated manifest a type of dual personality by referring to the presence of the deceased child as an invisible companion and always by the correct name. This has also been observed in the transfer of other organs, leading to the theory of a possible cell memory by Dr G.E. Schwarz of Arizona University.

The idea of the self being essentially the physical body and the last resort of a consciousness only arose with the perverted doctrine of the Christian Church, denying and forbidding teaching the principle of reincarnation. It was replaced with the bizarre notion of resurrection of the body, in a remote future of a paradisiacal existence, or the opposite according to merit or demerit. Why the old founders of the Church found this necessary is open to speculation. It was not due to ignorance, because some of them were initiates of a high order in the mystical schools of the time. To ignore the warnings against teaching anything contrary to the established orthodoxy was met by speedy reaction, often with violent and fatal results. The Lady Hypatia was one of the first to so meet her end at the hands of enraged monks, due to her teaching the ancient truths of Plato and Pythagoras.

On the one hand, we have the conviction that all ends with death of the body, as held by The Humanists (The Sadducees were the early Humanists, Mark 12 v18), and, on the other hand, the belief in its resurrection and eternal paradise or damnation of Orthodox Christianity. Proof, unfortunately, is difficult to come by, but in the records of the Psychical Research Society in London there is documented evidence for life after death sufficient to fill many bookshelves.

The only really satisfactory conviction comes via the Faculty of Intuition, which, unfortunately, is rarely accessible to those educated and conditioned in the rationalist philosophy of our time. There are some interesting accounts of individuals being brought back to life after dying, but, of course, it is easy to explain this in terms relevant to neurology and brain activity. There are scores of people who are convinced of having received an apparition of the deceased, occasionally leaving tangible proof of their continued existence.

A pseudo-immortality is being attempted by transplanting parts of the body, and some progress is being made to prolong life in this way, but, even if perfected, is likely to be limited, if only because of the shortage of spare parts. The marketing of these is rife with illegal and criminal aspects. Research is still in its infancy, but in regard to mechanical replacements, progress for mechanical limb prostheses is showing promise.

Some wealthy individuals have had their bodies put into deep freeze, with the intention of being resuscitated at such time so that they can be healed of their terminal disease and live again. In some instances, the head alone is preserved in the hope that, in the future, a suitable body may become available and attached. The Cryonics Institute is only one of such organisations which contract to speedily freeze the body in liquid nitrogen. In addition to the fee for this service, there has be enough funds for the servicing of the equipment for an indefinite period. Pets are also served in this way if requested. The Lifestream is a repository of each life's experience on a particular etheric level, and preserved faithfully in that part of mind which is the subconscious.

The actual repository of experience is held in The Three Permanent "Atoms." These are centres of energy in the lifestream throughout the totality of its existence, and are integral to the human unit. When the string is complete, it means that the final initiation has been gained in the earthly phase of existence, producing a higher state of consciousness beyond our imagining. It is all under THE LAW, which is built into the metaphysical cosmos in the great variety and possibilities of a complex septenate configuration, as conceived arising from the Primordial Polarity. The core of individual consciousness is forever, as conceived in the Monadic Principle.

Existence continues after death. The life's experience is examined and then gravitation to a level of commonality and to such institutions of education and leisure, as indicated by preference. The desire for earthly experience and to serve will eventually return, and rebirth will inevitably follow either shortly after death or many years later. It will always produce a different personality, in a new environment calculated most suitable for evolutionary experience.

The Cosmic Plan

There is a Plan behind all that is manifest in the Creation of worlds and galaxies. The whole astronomical picture is one of awesome grandeur, and appalling magnitude. To accept the notion that All arose from a Mechanical and Random sequence of events is too simplistic for the discerning mind, and should be so for the rational and pragmatic with a bit of imagination. In this planet, we are privileged by being able to observe the workings of the material cosmos and marvel. Other planets may not be so lucky due to a persistent cloud layer and therefore never seeing anything of the heavens in the night sky.

In essence, The Plan is thought to be one of Ceaseless Creation followed by Dissolution at the end, and repeating the cycle over and over again without beginning and without end. The idea does not appeal to the rational mind, but it is a conceit to presume that all can be understood and interpreted by our limited intellects and short lives. The Force behind the Plan is Impersonal Love, guaranteed to propel every lifestream through the three kingdoms, and then via the human phase into higher realms of the gods, as gods.

The human phase is the extremity of individualisation possessing Freewill, but which is to be transmuted into a condition of unselfishness and higher consciousness in the formation of integrated groups.

The beauty and grandeur of the minutiae and complexity of The Plan are not possible without the design and forethought of a Mind. This originates in The Mind of The Absolute in an Eternal NOW. IT issues the Fiat Create, and sends forth the monadic diaspora, taking every lifestream on its incredibly long journey back to its Source, enriched through Karmic experience.

And all this without any mention of Religion… and so it should be.

The New Age

Before dealing with the more practical aspects of this topic, which constitutes part of the Title of this work, we should consider what It is, and what does It mean? It is much discussed in the various magazines on Astrology and related subjects, and involves the idea of the Next Phase in Human Evolution, the metaphysical factors of which I have tried to describe.

The rate of vibration in all earthly substance is being speeded up on all levels, and that is the crux of the matter. It is affecting our minds and the very fabric of which our bodies are made. Society as a whole is suffering stress and rapid changes, as evident in the rapid development of communications and localised wars of unprecedented savagery and mass murder. In this way, the negative aspect of things is only too familiar in the world as portrayed on television. The positive is not so obvious.

This planet is being subjected to a great influx of energies from a higher octave, stimulating its very substance and every lifestream. In other words, everything is being speeded up, but the phrase is totally inadequate. You hear that Time is going so much faster, which sounds ridiculous, but the assertion that the subjective side of life is so affected is not. The process of evolution is accelerating, and for the most part we are not well-prepared for it. The New Age, so-called, is regarded as a phase during which the world will be transformed.

The days of tribulation are a precursor of better things to come. The date 2012 is a favourite, based on the Mayan calendar. This may well be true, but is not going to happen overnight, and I suspect it may take a long time.

The idea is rife in metaphysical circles, that there is a quantum jump of evolution in the offing, and speculation as to when. There are some who speak with authority on the proposed date, but, rest assured, that date is not known, even in the highest echelons of the Hierarchy. The new conditions will be for those who can stand the course, and may necessitate a further series of embodiments. Ultimately, we will be endowed with greatly enhanced mental powers together with subjection of all the passions and frailties which plague us today.

Behind all the blather about what The New Age is, it really boils down the fact that we are labouring under an enormous Karmic Debt, and that the Spiritual Crisis of many centuries is now a Crisis of Crises. Without the certain measures described earlier in this book, we would have been eliminated from the surface of the Earth.

The Entity which is physically manifest as the planet Earth has long delayed its own evolutionary progress until life could withstand the increase in the solar and cosmic radiation. A good part of humanity has already proved to be incompatible and will have to move on. Another Earth-like planet is prepared. It is a more primitive planet and may be on a different level of vibration undetectable to us.

These are the deciding factors in the first steps on the journey into the New Age. Things are being controlled to the extent that energy is being released gradually by The Logos of the Earth, so we are still here. Metaphysical Operations are an essential part for ushering in the New Age.

The New Age Metaphysics

This Title implies knowledge appertaining to the metaphysical aspects and operations ushering in this new phase of existence and is of singular interest and importance. It has been said by a Cosmic Master who has provided this material that, "To reject the offer of this knowledge and study these events is an error of the greatest magnitude!"

All this material is available in print from its source via The Aetherius Society and from their website in lectures and podcasts. It was widely disseminated in lectures throughout the UK, US, NZ and Australia in 1961. There were also numerous broadcasts on radio and television.

It is deeply etched in my mind as I was involved in one of the most important metaphysical operations leading up to the release of this information. The intention is to reinforce the view that all is not as it seems to be in this most superficial of worlds. There is an undercurrent of events in the hidden worlds that are of vital importance to us. It has been my intention to let you know of this.

At certain periods during the year, the Spiritual Push periods (see Satellite Number Three chapter), all spiritual efforts are magnified many times and assist evolution. It happens, not only on a personal level but also on a global level, and in this way karma is manipulated. Being privy to such knowledge, it is fitting for me to include it in this work for others to peruse, and if inclined to use it. This narrative will have seemed fantastic to some, and the old adage that "Truth Is Stranger Than Fiction," is well borne out. We are living in very strange times, at the crossroads of an important phase in the history of the Earth and humanity.

Metaphysics tallies with the ancient wisdom of the Gnostics and Theosophy, but it is a further development of this line of thought with essentially practical features. I have described how there are metaphysical operations on a vast scale. Intervention was required for the prevention of our destruction several times, all in the space of a few years.

The Aetherius Society

There has been frequent references to The Aetherius Society throughout this work. I will now say something about this organisation, in which I have the honour to belong as a full member.

It was founded in 1955 at the suggestion of Saint Goo Ling, the Adept who is the keeper of the Seal of The Great White Brotherhood. In those days, the Earth faced several crises which threatened mankind. In anticipation, it was decided by the gods responsible for our protection to arrange for a certain entity to be born here on Earth who would be able to organise a few people to be trained as agents of the Cosmic Masters. Although they can do all that and much more, by the Laws of the Cosmos, their action is strictly limited by our karmic debt. Thus, it was necessary for human agencies to be enlisted.

It is often asked why one of the existing organisations was not allowed to perform this service. Actually, I don't know, but I am aware that there was a profusion of Mystery Schools keen to serve, but for one reason or another were rejected. One problem was the prospect getting all parties to accept the leadership of an outsider who was to be in full control. The Theosophical Society was a likely candidate, but had already grown into a multi-faceted complex of different Lodges. The new instrument was to be led by George King, who had already a reputation, elsewhere in the galaxy, of feats beyond the capacity of earthly Adepts.

There is no doubt in my mind that George King was here in his 4th Aspect as part of a much larger Intelligence, and that is also the opinion of The Aetherius Society. As numbers go, it is a small organisation, but spread into different countries. For the present, these are mostly countries with an English-speaking background. Translation of books and tapes into Spanish is in the process, with a view to add other languages when possible.

All funds from the sale of books and lectures go back into the support of the Society. There is only a small nucleus of full-time, salaried officers who have devoted their lives in service to the ethic and aims of the Aetherius Society. It will remain a relatively small body, and is unlikely to develop into a monolithic structure. In this way, it will preserve the aims of The Masters without the schisms and sectarian splits which have plagued other Spiritual Brotherhoods. This is important for it to be able to perform the duties which allow it to be an integral part of the metaphysical machinery which is holding the developing New Age in balance.

The Aetherius Society is the only reliable source of information regarding the nearby planets and extraterrestrial involvement, and that includes the nature and function of UFO's. The UK and US authorities have sought the advice of the Aetherius Society from time to time during the life of George King, who was viewed in high standing by the establishments of both countries.

There are three types of membership: sympathiser, associate member, and full member. The latter requires the demonstration of a firm spiritual commitment. This type of structure is an ancient tradition, and was insisted upon by Pythagoras. There have always been one inner and two outer circles in esoteric societies.

We are fortunate in having such a dedicated group at the head of The Aetherius Society. They are well-trained in the intricacies of constructing and managing radionic equipment for the distribution of spiritual power. The elite group called "The Operation Sunbeam Task Force" have taken a lifetime oath to the Spiritual Hierarchy of Earth to maintain secrecy as to the nature of the special equipment.

Much has depended on The Aetherius Society. So far, we are doing well, with 26 centres in different parts of the globe. After a time, it was decreed by the Cosmic Masters that the Aetherius Society should create a Church with ordained priests and bishops (including women). I have never been comfortable with it forming a Church, which I suppose makes me something of a maverick. That can't be so bad; after all, it was the mavericks of Gotha who saved their planets.

Because there have been frequent references George King and his work. I have taken the following extract from the Aetherius Society website (www.aetherius.org).

Dr George King, DSc, ThD, DD.

Early History

Dr George King was born in Shropshire, England on January 23, 1919. Early in life, his deep spiritual interests found expression in traditional Christianity, but he soon learned there was more to life than the orthodox could show him.

First turning to psychic phenomena, he quickly became an adept of this research, delving beneath the superficial nature of things to their causes. Still looking for more, he began to study yoga. For the next 10 years, he practiced this ancient science for 8–12 hours a day until his mastery of terrestrial phenomena and of his mind made him a "Knower."

He was still in his early thirties.

The Command

Determined to help humanity raise itself from universal suffering and ignorance, his life's mission became apparent on May 8th, 1954. Alone in his London apartment, a loud physical voice delivered the following Command, "Prepare yourself! You are to become the voice of Interplanetary Parliament."

He was initially shocked by the implications of this statement. It came out of the blue without warning or explanation. All he knew, with his mastery over terrestrial phenomena, was that was what he had heard.

A few days later, he was visited by a world-renowned Yoga Master, whom he knew to be alive and active in India at that time. This Master, in every way physical, entered and left through a locked door that he did not open.

During the meeting, Dr King was given a series of highly specialized exercises enabling him to bring about a state of consciousness necessary for the establishment of mental rapport with the Cosmic Masters who inhabit the higher planes of other planets.

In the previous ten years, Dr King had become a Master of Raja, Gnani, and Kundalini Yoga, and was able to attain the elevated state of consciousness known as Samadhi. It was for this reason that the Cosmic Masters of the Solar System began to use him as their "Primary Terrestrial Mental Channel" in order to give their message to Earth. His Mission had begun.

1955–1959, England

From the moment of the Command, all Dr King's personal business ambitions were abandoned as the information from the Space Intelligences grew in importance and urgency.

On their direction, he founded The Aetherius Society and began publishing the journal, Cosmic Voice. He lectured throughout Britain, serving as the channel for numerous Transmissions from Cosmic Intelligences.

On May 21st, 1959, under the glaring lights of the British Broadcasting Corporation, he demonstrated yogic Samadhi over live television so that a Cosmic Master from another planet could speak to Britain. This unique event was broadcast to an estimated viewing audience of several million.

1959–1997, America

In June 1959, guided by Cosmic Authority, Dr King came to the United States of America, where the Aetherius Society was incorporated as a non-profit organization in November 1960.

Over the next two decades, he continued to act as Primary Terrestrial Mental Channel, recording over 600 Cosmic Transmissions from the Space Masters.

This collection of transmissions constitutes the most priceless metaphysical library in the world, with a range and depth of teachings without equal in the annals of occult Truth.

During his life, Dr King also performed and designed several Cosmic Missions. These metaphysical operations were in cooperation with the Cosmic Masters, providing global healing and a greater karmic balance for humanity as a whole.

On July 12th, 1997, Dr King passed away in Santa Barbara, California.

The Cosmic Teachings and Spiritual Missions that he left behind provide the foundation stones of the New Age and are the heritage of us all.

Recognition For His Work

Despite being ahead of his time and a virtual revolutionary to traditional orthodox doctrine, Dr King received considerable recognition for his life's work from many different sources. In 1981, he was crowned as an Archbishop and later as a Prince.

He also received numerous awards and titles for his charitable and tireless work for humanity, including:

The Prize of Peace and Justice from The International Union of Christian Chivalry. Previous recipients of this prize include Albert Einstein, Mother Teresa, Henry Kissinger and Albert Schweitzer.

A Grant of Arms by Her Majesty's College of Arms in London, England.

Chaplain of The American Federation of Police.

EPILOGUE

Some of the metaphysical operations have been described which were vital to our survival on this planet, and others to assist the evolution of both Humanity and that of The Earth Herself. Not all of them are listed, but sufficient for the purpose of this work, which is essentially to be a Guide to The New Age Conditions, based on metaphysical principles and information released to us through The Aetherius Society.

It is hoped it will stir the minds of the pragmatic who will not accept anything without proof, which at present is not possible, and until the governments of the world release what they already know it is not likely to change. The acceptance of occult metaphysical truths depends on a degree of intuitive perception. There is the basis of Metaphysical Philosophy described in this work, and some personal details about how the author came to be involved in the practical aspects of metaphysics.

The revelations about UFO's and the life on the planets are to be found in no other work apart from the books of George King, from which they are taken.

Ways of how to assist the World in these difficult times are described in his books.

BIBLIOGRAPHY

Chrissie Blaze, "Mercury Retrograde"

Chrissie Blaze, "Workout for the Soul"

Chrissie Blaze, "Superstar Signs: Sun Signs of Heroes and Superstars"

Helena Blavatsky, "The Secret Doctrine"

Helena Blavatsky, "Isis Unveiled"

Alice Bailey, "The Treatise on Cosmic Fire"

Alice Bailey, "White Magic"

Alice Bailey, "The Soul" (a Compilation of her writings)

Richard M. Bucke, "Cosmic Consciousness"

Mr E. Butler, "Ritual Magic"

Chevalier, "The Sacred Magician"

Alexandra David-Neel, "With Mystics and Magicians in Tibet"

Frederick Elworthy, "The Evil Eye"

Sir J.G. Frazer, "The Golden Bough"

Gopi Krishna, "Kundalini for The New Age"

Stephen Hawking, "A Brief History of Time"

Christmas Humphries, "A Western Approach to Zen"

C.G. Jung, "Collected Works"

Charles Johnston, "The Yoga Sutras of Patanjali"

Eliphas Levi, "Transcendental Magic"

Michio Kaku, "Hyperspace"

F. King and S. Skinner, "Techniques of High Magic"

Dr George King, "You Are Responsible"

Dr George King, "The Twelve Blessings"

Dr George King, "The Nine Freedoms"

Dr George King, "Contacts with The Gods From Space"

Dr George King, "The Holy Mountains of The World"

Dr George King, "Visit to The Logos of The Earth"

Dr George King, "Operation Earth Magic"

Dr George King with Richard Lawrence, "Realize Your Inner Potential"

A.R. Hope Moncrieff, "Romance and Legend of Chivalry"

Christopher Knight and Alan Butler, "Who Built The Moon?"

James Legge, "I Ching"

Bruce Moen, "Adventures into The Afterlife"

Gertrude van Pelt, "Rounds and Races"

Ramacharaka, "Raja Yoga" and "Gnani Yoga"

Israel Regardie, "The Middle Pillar"

Israel Regardie, "The Golden Dawn"

Israel Regardie, "The Tree of Life"

Peter Russell, "The White Holes In Time"

Mouni Sadhu, "Concentration"

Anne Marie Schimmel, "The Mystery of Numbers"

Rudolf Steiner, "Spiritual Science and Medicine"

Kenneth Walker, "A Study of Gurdjieff's Teaching"

J. Richard Wilhelm, "The Secret of The Golden Flower"

James Wasserman, "The Templars and the Assassins"

Owen Waters, "The Shift: The Revolution in Human Consciousness"

Alan Wolf, "Parallel Universes"

Yogananda, "Autobiography of A Yogi"

Aetherius Society Centres

NEW ZEALAND
New Zealand Branch
269 Hinemoa Street
Birkenhead
Auckland
Tel: (09) 418-1170
Fax: (09) 418-1180
e-mail: aetherius@xtra.co.nz
web: www.innerpotential.co.nz

AUSTRALIA
Brisbane Group
Rod & Megan Middleton
P.O. Box 6140
Fairfield Gardens
QLD 4103
Australia
Tel: 07 3892 5253
Email: aetherius@bigpond.com

AMERICAN HEADQUARTERS
6202 Afton Place
Los Angeles, CA 90028
USA. Tel. (323) 465-9652
Email: info@aetherius.org

EUROPEAN HEADQUARTERS
757 Fulham Road
London SW6 5UU U.K. Tel. 020 736 4187
Email: info@aetherius.co.uk

Made in the USA
San Bernardino, CA
20 February 2015